Migration to South Carolina: Movement from the New England and Mid-Atlantic States, 1850 Census

Abstracted by
Margaret Peckham Motes

CLEARFIELD

Other books by the author:

Laurens & Newberry Counties, S.C.: Saluda and Little River Settlements 1749-1775, co-authored with Jesse H. Motes, III Winner of the National Genealogical Society 1995 Award for Excellence (Methods and Sources)

South Carolina Memorials: Abstracts of Land Titled - Vol. 1, 1774-1776, co-authored with Jesse H. Motes, III.

Free Blacks and Mulattos in South Carolina - 1850 Census

Blacks Found in the Deeds of Laurens and Newberry Counties, SC: 1785 to 1827: Listed in Deeds of Gift, Deeds of Sale, Mortgages, Born Free and Freed

Butcher, Baker, Candlestick Maker and Other Occupations in Newburyport, Massachusetts - 1850 Census

Irish in South Carolina - 1850 Census

Copyright © 2004 by Margaret P. Motes
All Rights Reserved.

Printed for
Clearfield Company, Inc. by
Genealogical Publishing Co., Inc.
Baltimore, Maryland
2004

Reprinted for
Clearfield Company, Inc. by
Genealogical Publishing Co., Inc.
Baltimore, Maryland
2006

International Standard Book Number: 0-8063-5223-X

Made in the United States of America

CONTENTS

Introduction	iv
Microcopy Records	vi
Abstract Format	vi
County Codes	vii

Surnames (Alphabetical)

Section One New England States	1
Section Two Mid-Atlantic States	37

Index

Name	111
Place	119
Occupation	122

INTRODUCTION

This is the third book in a series that deals with migration into South Carolina by 1850. The first book of this series dealt with *Free Black and Mulattoes, South Carolina – 1850 census*, followed by *Irish In South Carolina -- 1850 census*. This book covers people found in the 1850 South Carolina census who were born in New England and the Mid-Atlantic states.

The New England states consist of Connecticut, Massachusetts, New Hampshire, Vermont, Maine and Rhode Island. The Mid-Atlantic area is made up of New York, New Jersey, Pennsylvania, Delaware, Maryland and Washington, DC.

The first migration into South Carolina began during its colonization under the Crown of George II of England and continued to grow with the opening of new lands for farmers and others who brought with them their various trades, religious beliefs and values to the new frontier.

The 1850 census is an important research tool for researchers since it is the first census which sheds light on the family, family groupings, place of birth, and occupations in the household.

Of the two areas covered in this book, the largest movement came from the Mid-Atlantic. However, many of those born in these two areas of the country were often found in households of persons who were born in other states in the United States; were found in households of parents or siblings or were servants born in England, Holland, Ireland, Italy, France, Germany, Poland, Prussia, Scotland, St. Domingo, Sweden, Switzerland, and the West Indies.

There are over 2,600 names listed, with approximately 900 from the New England and about 1,800 from the Mid-Atlantic area. The largest number from New England were from Massachusetts (415), followed by Connecticut (237). The largest number from the Mid-Atlantic were from New York (892), followed closely by Pennsylvania (358) and Maryland (230).

People moved for varies reasons: job opportunities, land, weather, economic growth, education and/or religious movements. They brought with them new cultural ideas, foods, religious ideals, and trades which brought continued change and growth into each community.

Many of the same occupations which were found in *Irish Found in South Carolina – 1850 Census* were also found among those from the New England and Mid-Atlantic. Many of these people came with a trade: blacksmiths, bricklayers, brick masons, carpenters, coach makers, farmers, laborers, mechanics, plasters, peddlers, saddlers, saw mill operators, servants, stone cutters and tinners.

Other occupations were professionals: attorneys, editors, bankers, clergymen, commercial merchants, jewelers, confectioners, engineers, grocers, hotel keepers, judges, manufacturers, master mariners, merchants, teachers and professors, policemen, postmen, tavern keepers and U.S. Army personnel.

New occupations which began to appear were artists, dauguerretype artists, engravers, book binders, book sellers, bookkeepers, dentists, editors, race horse trainers, ice house keepers, ship masters, writing teachers, professors of music, professors of theology, college students and students of theology.

Thirteen reels of microcopy were read covering the twenty-nine counties in the 1850 South Carolina Federal Census. The information was abstracted and sorted by place of birth, then by name and age. If an individual is listed in another household, then the head of household is stated below, even if that individual was born in South Carolina.

Every effort has been made to keep the spelling of first and last names as they appear in the census record. The spelling of names is always difficult and variations appear for the same surname.

Margaret P. Motes
Newburyport, Massachusetts
July 2003

MICROCOPY RECORDS:

The 1850 South Carolina Census Reels

M432-848	Abbeville and Anderson Counties
M432-849	Barnwell and Beauford Counties
M432-850	Charleston County
M432-851	Chester, Chesterfield, Colleton and Darlington Counties
M432-852	Edgefield and Fairfield Counties
M432-853	Georgetown and Greenville Counties
M432-854	Horry, Kershaw and Lancaster Counties
M432-855	Laurens and Lexington Counties
M432-856	Marion, Marlboro and Newberry Counties
M432-857	Orangeburg and Pickens Counties
M432-858	Richland and Spartanburg Counties
M432-859	Sumter and Union Counties
M432-860	Williamsburg and York Counties

The Microcopy used was purchased from American Genealogical Lending Library, Bountiful, Utah.

ABSTRACT FORMAT:

Last name, first name, age, sex, occupation (if indicated), color, (-) all are white unless listed as m for mulatto, birthplace, dwelling #, family #, county. Notes if any apply. See examples below.

Example: Raymond, Charles A., 28, M, Baptist Clergyman, -, CT, 1792, 1792, ABB. In HH of William P. Hill, M 46, Baptist Clergyman born in SC.

COUNTY CODES:

Abbreviation, county and the date the census was taken.. Two census were recorded in January 1851.

ABB:	Abbeville. 20 July to 14 December 1850.
AND:	Anderson. Western Division.17 July to 12 Octtober 1850.
AND*:	Anderson. Easter Division. 22 July to 19 October 1850.
BARN:	Barnwell. 16 July to 22 November 1850.
BEAU:	Beaufort, St. Helena Parish: 3 October to 10 December 1850. (Note: last page out of order)
BEAU*:	Beaufort, Prince Williams Parish (Whites). 6 September to 16 December 1850.
BEAU#:	Beafort, Prince Williams Parish (Free Black). 6 September to 16 December 1850. Pages 35-36)
BEAU+:	Beaufort, St. Lukes Parish. 16 September to 16 November 1850.
BEAU-:	Beaufort, St. Peters Parish. 12 July to 12 September 1850.
CHAS:	Charleston. City of Charleston, Ward 1, Parishes of St. Philips & St. Michael's. 1 August to 16 August 1850.
CHAS*:	Charleston. City of Charlteston, Ward 2. The Parish of St. Philips & St. Michael's. 20 August to 18 Auuust 1850.
CHAS-:	Charleston. City of Charleston, Parishes of St. Philips and St. Michael's, Ward 4. 10 October to 12 November 1850.
CHAS%:	Charleston. Charleston Neck, Parish of St. Philips & St. Michael's. 9 November to 22 December 1850.
CHAS#:	Charleston, Parish of St. James Santee. 23 July to 18 August 1850.
CHAS!:	Charleston, St. Andrews Parish. 26 August to 18 October 1850.
CHAS$:	Charleston. Christ Church Parish. 1 August to 20 September 1850. CHAS & Charleston, Parish of St.

	Thomas and St. Dennis. November to 16 November 1850.
CHAS^:	Charleston, Parish of St. Johns, Colleton. 13 August to 23 October 1850.
CHAS-:	Charleston, St. Johns Berkley. 2 September to 12 October 1850.
CHAS2:	Charleston, St. Stephens Parish. 21 August to 19 November 1850.
CHAS3:	Charleston, St. James Goosecreek. 25 July to 26 November 1850.
CHES:	Chester. 22 July and 16 November 1850.
CHFD:	Chesterfield. 30 July to 13 January 1851.
COLL:	Colleton, St. Bartholomew's Parish. 14 August and 25 December 1850.
COLL*:	Colleton, St. George's Parish. 28 October to 16 November 1850.
COLL+:	Colleton, St. Paul's Parish. 21 October to 24 December 1850.
DARL:	Darlington, First Division. 26 July to January 1851.
EDGE:	Edgefield. 11 July to 19 December 1850.
EDGE*:	Edgefield. 23 October to 19 December 1850.
FAIR:	Fairfield. 13 July and 23 November 1850.
GEOR:	Georgetown, City of George Town. 19 August 1850.
GEOR*:	Georgetown, Prince George, Winyaw. 20 August to 22 August 1850.
GEOR+:	Georgetown, Lower All Saints. 23 August to 23 August 1850.
GREE:	Greeville. 22 July to 13 December 1850.
HORR:	Horry. 24 July and 4 November 1850.
KERS:	Kershaw. 19 July and 16 December 1850.

LANC:	Lancaster. 11 November to 16 November 1850.
LAU:	Laurens. 23 July to 13 December 1850.
LEX:	Lexington. 27 July to 13 October 1850.
MAR:	Marion. 19 July to 26 November 1850.
MARL:	Marlboro. 29 July and 15 October 1850.
NEWB:	Newberry. 18 July to 16 November 1850.
ORNG:	Orangeburg, between the River Road from Orangeburgh CH to Branchville and Four Hole Swamp. 13 December to 18 January 1851.
ORNG*:	Orangeburg, between Santee and Edisto North of Bellville Road. 12 November to 26 December 1850.
ORAN+:	Orangeburg, Orangeburg District. 29 July to 25 Dec. 1850.
PICK:	Pickens, Western Division. 26 July to 25 December 1850.
PICK+:	Pickens, Eastern Division. 19 July to 12 October 1850.
RICH:	Richland, Town of Columbia. 3 October to 28 October 1850.
RICH+:	Richland. 20 July to 1 October 1850.
SPART:	Spartanburg. 15 July to 18 December 1850.
SUMT:	Sumter. 19 July to 22 November 1850.
UNION:	Union. 17 July to 23 November 1850.
UNN+:	Union: 29 October to 21 November 1850.
WILL:	Williamsburg. 22 July to 22 November 1850.
YORK:	York. 29 July to 22 October 1850.
YORK*:	York. 22 July to 10 December 1850.

Section I

Migration to South Carolina: New England States, 1850 Census

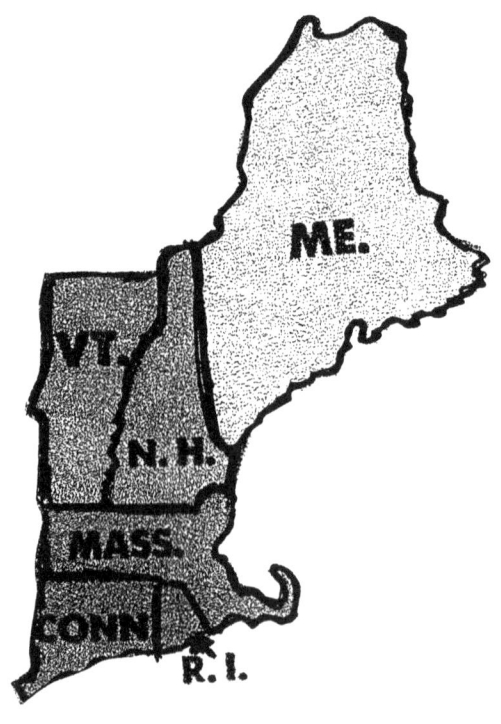

New England States

Abbreviation	State	Population in SC
CT:	Connecticut	237
MA:	Massachusetts	415
ME:	Maine	70
NH:	New Hampshire	42
RI:	Rhode Island	99
VT:	Vermont	<u>39</u>
		Total 902

A

ABBOT, GEORGE, 30, M, one listed, -, MA, 836, 816, CHAS- . In Boarding House.
ABBOT, MARTHA, 25, F, None listed, -, MA, 836, 816, HAS- . In Boarding House.
ADAMS, ANDREW, 25, M, Printer, -, CT, 303, 287, CHAS-. In HH of Austides Bristol m 32 born CT.
ADAMS, JAMES, 60, M, Butcher, -, NH, 887, 887, CHES. In HH of Biggers Mobley m 42 born SC.
ADAMS, LYDIA, 34, F, None listed, -, NH, 434, 434, EDGE. In HH of Hiram Adams m 45 planter born SC.
ADAMS, R.P., 46, M, Teacher, -, CT, 53, 53, ORNG*. In HH of Mrs. N.E. Darby f 63, born SC.
ADKINS, MARY, 35, F, None listed, -, MA, 2023, 2026, EDGE. In HH of Thomas Adkins m 45, slave trader, born SC. Mary born Boston, MA.
ALDEN, GEORGE, 35, M, Merchant,-, MA, 263, 263, KERS.
ALDRICH, ROBERT, 70, M, Wharfinger, -, MA, 18, 21, CHAS.
ALLEN, ALDEN S., 50, M, Shoemaker, -, MA,72,72, BEAU.
ALLEN, THOMAS P.,47, M, Bookseller, -, MA, 581, 539, CHAS+.
ALRED, IRA, 63, M, Schoolmaster, -, NH, 9, 9, GEOR*.
ANDREWS, A., 44, M, Gin maker, -, CT, 714, 714, LANC*.
ANDREWS, DAVID, 45, M, Overseer,-, CT, 1776, 1776, SUMT.
ANDREWS, J. M., 38, M, Mariner, -, MA, 160, 151, CHAS+. In HH of Henry Stams 20 born Germany.
ANDREWS, LOUISA, 28, F, None listed, -, MA, 160, 151, CHAS+. In HH of Henry Stams 20 born Germany.
ANDREWS, M. M., 36, M, Mechanic,-, RI, 158, 158,GEOR.
ARAIL, JOHN, 46, M, Farmer, -, CT, 653, 653, PICK+.
ARNOLD, CHS., 25, M, Clerk, -, RI, 836, 816, CHAS-. In Boarding House.
ARNOLD, LYMAN, 30, M, Merchant,-, RI, 1723, 1724, EDGE. In HH of Hiram Jordan m 36, landlord, born SC.
ARNOLD, S.W., 51, M, Attorney,-, RI, 895, 895, DARL. In HH of James Osley m 55 born NC.
ARNOLER, GEORGE, 19, M, Clerk, -, RI, 822, 780, CHAS+. In HH of J.H. Taylor m 40 born MA.
ASHTON, JACOB F.,40, M, Farmer, -, MA, 421, 421, COLL.
ATHERTON, ALICE, 21, F, None listed, -, NH, 1628, 1628, EDGE. In HH of Thomas Atherton m 24 born England.
ATWOOD, C.B., 67, M, Farmer, -, CT, 2319, 2319, GREE.
ATWOOD, J.B., 47, M, Laborer, -, MA, 465, 422, CHAS. In HH of Leslie O'Wen m 47 born Ireland.

B

BACON, U.V., 37, M, Machinist, -, MA, 147, 147, LEX.
BAFSET, SARAH, 64, F, None listed, -, CT, 105, 98, CHAS-. In

HH of Mary R. Hayden f 70 born VA. Sarah Bafset {Basset?}, born New Haven, {CT}.
BAILEY, CHAS., 50, M, Farmer, -, CT, 232, 232, KERS.
BAILEY, SAMUEL P., 52, M, None,-, CT, 399, 409, RICH.
BAKER, GEORGE, 26, M, Clerk, -, CT, 65, 66, ORNG+. In HH of James Harley at Hotel.
BALLARD, JOSEPH, 49, M, Clerk, -, MA, 219, 196, CHAS*.
BALLOU, JAMES, 37, M, Stonecutter, -, RI, 346, 346, YORK.
BALLOU, STEPHEN, 29, M, Stonecutter, -, RI, 346, 346, YORK. In HH of James Ballou m 37 born RI.
BANCROFT, JAMES, 48, M, Merchant,-, MA, 580, 563, CHAS-.
BANCROFT, JAMES K., 24, M, Clerk, -,VT, 721, 701, CHAS-. In HH of Edwin Bates m 23 born Canada.
BANCROFT, WM. G.,27, M, Clerk, -,VT, 721, 701, CHAS-. In HH of Edwin Bates m 23 born Canada.
BARBER, JOHN, 32, M, Mariner, -, MA, 237, 222, CHAS-. Poor House.
BARKER, GEORGE M, 25, M, Clerk, -, CT, 65, 66, ORNG+. In HH of James Harley - Hotel.
BARNET, MARY P., 36, F, None listed, -, MA, 759, 739, CHAS-. In HH of Harriet E. Miller f 29 born MA.
BARNEY, HENRY, 50, M, Painter, -, CT, 688, 689, And*. In HH of Aaron Vandiver m 55 born SC.
BARR, GEORGE, 30, M, Seaman, -, ME, 326, 301, CHAS. On Steam Ship Southerner.
BARR, SAMUEL, 34, M, 2nd Mate,-, ME, 326, 301, CHAS. On Steam Ship Southerner.
BARTLETT, ALEXR., 60, M, Shoe dealer, -, MA, 167, 149, CHAS. In Boarding house.
BARTLETT, EARL, 27, F, None listed, -, RI, 949, 926, CHAS%. In HH of William Bartlett m 56 born MA.
BARTLETT, H., 39, M, Shoe dealer, -, MA, 107, 107, CHAS%.
BARTLETT, MARY, 32, F, None listed, -, MA, 107, 107, CHAS%. In HH of H. Bartlett m 39 born MA.
BARTLETT, WILLIAM, 56, M, None listed, -, MA, 949, 926, CHAS%.
BASS, HENRY., 64, M, Methodist Clergyman, -, CT, 2132, 2132, ABB. Living in Institute Boarding house.
BASSETT, CYRUS, 39, M, Farmer, -, MA, 122, 123, MAR.
BATES, AGNES, 22, F, Teacher, -,VT, 422, 380, CHAS. In HH of Jane Bates f 25 born VT.
BATES, CLARK, 52, M, Farmer, -, MA, 114, 114, COLL.
BATES, JANE, 25, F, School mistress, -,VT, 422, 380, CHAS
BATES, WILLIAM, 50, M, Machinist, -, RI, 2203, 2203, GREE.
BATTLES, BENJ. P., 29, M, Oversee factory, -, MA, 1735, 1738, EDGE.

BATTLES, ELLEN, 3, F, None listed, -, MA, 1735, 1738, EDGE. In HH of Benj. P. Battles m 29 born MA.
BATTLES, JOHN D., 24, M, Card repairer, -, NH, 1735, 1738, EDGE. In HH of Benj. P. Battles m 29 born MA.
BATTLES, LUCRETIA, 25, F, None listed, -,VT, 1735, 1738, EDGE. In HH of Benj. P. Battles m 29 born MA.
BATTLES, WILLIS P., 2, M, None listed, -, NH, 1735, 1738, EDGE. In HH of Benj. P. Battles m 29 born MA.
BEACH, ADDISON, 28, M, Merchant,-, CT, 77, 78, ORNG+.
BEACH, ADDISON, 28, M, Merchant,-, CT, 77, 78, ORNG+.
BEACH, DIANNA, 48, F, None listed, -, CT, 78, 79, ORNG+. In HH of Sylvester Beach m 54 born CT.
BEACH, DIANNO, 48, F, None listed, -, CT, 78, 79, ORNG+. In HH of Sylvister Beach m 54 born CT.
BEACH, E.M., 40, M, Grain merchant, -, MA, 511, 477, CHAS*.
BEACH, NORMAN, 25, M, Clerk, -,VT, 78, 79, ORNG+. In HH of Sylvester Beach m 54 born CT.
BEACH, SYLVESTER, 54, M, Merchant,-, CT, 78, 79, ORNG+.
BECK, CHARLES, 58, M, Sash/Door manufacturer, -, MA, 547, 562, RICH.
BELCHER, MANNING, 62, M, Farmer, -, RI, 718, 722, AND.
BELCHER, SUSAN, 50, F, None listed, -, RI, 718, 722, AND. In HH of Manning Belcher m 62 born RI.
BELS, C.H., 28, M, Priv. U.S.A., -, ME, 47, 43, CHAS$. In HH of John Ewing m 50 born MA.
BENDEN, THOMAS, 37, M, Physician, -, MA, 664, 656, CHAS%. Born: Boston {MA}. In HH of Henry Scholtz m 27 born SC.
BENHAM, WILLIAM, 56, M, Farmer, -, CT, 1267, 1267, LAU.
BENIDICT, J.H., 54, M, Watch maker, -, CT, 2250, 2250, GREE.
BENSON, A.T., 45, M, Wheelwright, -, MA, 270, 270, COLL. In HH of Stephen Crosby m 40 born SC.
BENSON, WM., 45, M, Merchant,-, MA, 102, 94, CHAS+.
BENSON, ZELPAH, 40, F, None listed, -, MA, 102, 94, CHAS+. In HH of Wm. Benson m 45 born MA.
BERRY, MARY, 30, F, None listed, -, NH, 198, 186, CHAS-. In HH of Emily Timbrook f 49 born PA.
BETTS, E.C., 29, M, Clerk, -, CT, 308, 284, CHAS+. In HH of Eliza Selleman f 69 born SC.
BIGELOW, F. J., 22, F, None listed, -, MA, 1105, 1105, CHES. In HH of James D. Crawford m 52 born SC.
BILBO, HARRIET, 45, F, None listed, -, MA, 929, 930, FAIR. In HH of Theodore L. Dubose m 41 born SC.
BISSELL, M., 46, M, Dentist, -, CT, 691, 671, CHAS-.

BLACK, ALEXANDER W., 45, M, Shipping master, -, MA, 457, 424, CHAS*.
BLACK, F.O., 53, M, Tuner ?, -, CT, 265, 265, BARN.
BLACK, HARRIETT, 40, F, None listed, -, MA, 457, 424, CHAS*. In HH of Alexander W. Black m 45 born MA.
BLACK, REBECCA, 35, F, None listed, -, MA, 457, 424, CHAS*. In HH of Alexander W. Black m 45 born MA.
BLACK, THOMAS, 41, M, Carpenter, -, ME, 50, 50, CHAS^.
BLACK, WILLIAM P., 54, M, Baker, -, ME, 684, 664, CHAS-.
BLANCHARD, ELIZA, 45, F, None listed, -, MA, 869, 846, CHAS%. In HH of John Blanchard m 21 born MA.
BLANCHARD, JOHN, 21, M, None listed, -, MA, 869, 846, CHAS%.
BLANDING, MARY A., 54, F, None listed, -, MA, 532, 568, RICH. In HH of Shubel Blanding m 55 born MA.
BLANDING, SHUBEL, 55, M, Surgeon Dentist, -, MA, 532, 568, RICH.
BLISS, T.W., 34, M, Tinplate worker, -, MA, 278, 262, CHAS-. In HH of A.H. Moodie m 29 born VT.
BOLLES, S.A., 64, M, None,-, CT, 736, 716, CHAS-.
BONETHEAU, N. STRONG, 28, M, Professor of Music, -, MA, 770, 750, CHAS-. In HH of W.B. Beasely m 36 born SC.
BONNEY, E.W., 40, M, Merchant,-, MA, 717, 717, KERS.
BOOTH, WILLIAM, 73, M, None listed, -, MA, 97, 90, CHAS-. In HH of Mary Perry f 53 born SC.
BOSTWICK, AMOS, 31, M, Merchant,-, CT, 202, 206, RICH.
BOSTWICK, MARY J., 24, F, None listed, -, CT, 202, 206, RICH. In HH of Amos Bostwick m 31 born CT.
BOSWORTH, HEZEKIAH, 59, M, Cloth drippier, -, CT, 237, 222, CHAS-. Poor House.
BOYD, EDWARD, 23, M, Clerk, -, MA, 482, 439, CHAS. In Planters Hotel.
BRADFORD, JESSE, 60, M, Landlord, -, MA, 17, 17, COLL.
BRADLEY, EDWARD, 29, M, Mariner, -, ME, 58, 52, CHAS+. In HH of Fetz Hallenback m 28 born Germany.
BRAYMAN, L.H., 28, M, Cigar manufacture, -, RI, 454, 451, CHAS%. In HH of W.H. Boring m 28 born VA.
BRERWER, JOHN, 28, M, Taylor, -, CT, 275, 275, Edge*.
BREWSTER, CHARLES R., 42, M, Attorney at Law, -, ME, 11, 11, CHAS%.
BRIGGS, J.H., 28, M, Bricklayer, -, MA, 73, 73, BARN.
BRISTOL, AUSTIDES, 32, M, Tailor, -, CT, 303, 287, CHAS-.
BRISTOL, C.E., 16, M, Clerk, -, CT, 838, 818, CHAS-. In HH of T.M. Bristol m 30 born CT.
BRISTOL, T.M., 30, M, Shoe merchant, -, CT, 838, 818, CHAS-.
BRONSON, E.M., 58, M, Tin plate maker, -, CT, 18, 18, KERS.
BRONSON, HIRAM C., 38, M,

Merchant,-, CT, 345, 351, RICH.
BROOKMAN, MARY, 22, F, None listed, -, ME, 424, 424, HORR. In HH of Henry Buck m 45 born Maine.
BROOKS, HENRY C., 30, M, Superintendent driping room, -, ME, 1623, 1623, EDGE.
BROOKS, JAMES, 58, M, Mechanic,-, MA, 78, 78, BEAU-.
BROOKS, LAURA, 31, F, None listed, -,VT, 1623, 1623, EDGE. In HH of Henry C. Brooks m 30 born ME.
BROOKS, LAURA, 31, F, None listed, -,VT, 1623, 1623, EDGE. In HH of Henry C. Brooks m 30 born ME.
BROOKS, SAMUEL, 50, M, Planter, -, CT, 13, 13, EDGE. Samuel Brooks m 50 born Middlesex, CT.
BROWN, CORNELIA W., 13, F, None listed, -, RI, 756, 736, CHAS-. In HH of Isaac T. Brown m 35 born SC.
BROWN, E.G., 41, M, Store keeper, -, CT, 692, 672, CHAS-.
BROWN, E.W., 35, M, Merchant,-, MA, 526, 509, CHAS-.
BROWN, FRANCES, 12, F, None listed, -, MA, 526, 509, CHAS-. In HH of E.W. Brown m 35 born MA.
BROWN, FRANCES M., 9, F, None listed, -, MA, 490, 473, CHAS-. In HH of Scott K. Brown m 45 born ME.
BROWN, HENRIETTA, 34, F, None listed, -, MA, 526, 509, CHAS-. In HH of E.W. Brown m 35 born MA.
BROWN, J.W., 34, M, Commission merchant,-, MA, 127, 118, CHAS+. In Boarding House.
BROWN, JAMES WM., 37, M, Grocer, -, RI, 834, 792, CHAS+.
BROWN, JOSEPHINE, 13, F, None listed, -, MA, 490, 473, CHAS-. In HH of Scott K. Brown m 45 born ME.
BROWN, MARIA, 16, F, None listed, -, MA, 490, 473, CHAS-. In HH of Scott K. Brown m 45 born ME.
BROWN, MARTHA A., 35, F, None listed, -, CT, 959, 959, DARL. In HH of Jas. M. Brown m 35 born SC.
BROWN, MARY, 35, F, None listed, -, MA, 490, 473, CHAS-. In HH of Scott K. Brown m 45 born ME.
BROWN, SCOTT K., 45, M, Carpenter, -, ME, 490, 473, CHAS-.
BRUCE, EMILY, 34, F, None listed, -, RI, 280, 282, AND. In HH of Charles Bruce m 59 born GA.
BRUNSON, NORMAN, 25, M, Clerk, -,VT, 78, 79, ORNG+. In HH of Sylvister Beach m 54 born CT.
BRUSE, CORENLIA, 38, F, None listed, -,VT, 756, 714, CHAS+. In HH of Wm. C. Bruse m 44 born NY {Breese}.
BRYAN, JANE L., 30, F, None listed, -, CT, 757, 737, CHAS-. In HH of J.M. Bryan m 30 born GA.
BRYAN, LEWIS H., 39, M, Merchant, -, MA, 482, 482, WILL.
BUCK, HENRY, 45, M, Merchant,-, ME, 424, 424, HORR.

BUCK, MARY J., 17, F, None listed, -, ME, 424, 424, HORR. In HH of Henry Buck m 45 born Maine.
BUCK, WM. H., 24, M, Merchant,-, ME, 6, 6, HORR. In HH of Jane Normon f 59 born SC.
BUCKINGHAM, ESTHER, 27, F, None listed, -, CT, 26, 26, BARN. In HH of J.C. Buckingham m 32 born CT.
BUCKINGHAM, J.C., 32, M, Merchant tailor, -, CT, 26, 26, BARN.
BULL, A.V., 26, M, Merchant,-, CT, 80, 81, ORNG+. In HH of J.N. Bull m 32 born CT.
BULL, ELIZA S., 36, F, None listed, -, MA, 391, 401, RICH. In HH of Henry D. Bull m 38 born MA.
BULL, HENRY D., 38, M, Merchant,-, MA, 391, 401, RICH.
BULL, J.N., 32, M, Merchant,-, CT, 80, 81, ORNG+.
BULL, L., 27, F, None listed, -, CT, 80, 81, ORNG+. In HH of J.N. Bull m 32 born CT.
BURBRIDGE, JNO. W., 40, M, Merchant,-, CT, 11, 11, COLL.
BURNHAM, RICHARD, 57, M, Painter, -, CT, 2306, 2306, GREE.
BURNHAN, WILLIAM, 40, M, School master, -, MA, 2245, 2245, GREE. In HH of J.L. Hemming m 27, landlord, born in SC.
BUSH, CAROLINE A., 34, F, None listed, -, RI, 24, 24, GEOR. In HH of R.O. Bush m 35 born RI.
BUSH, R.O., 35, M, Merchant,-, RI, 24, 24, GEOR.
BUSH, R.O., 6, M, None listed, -, RI, 24, 24, GEOR. In HH of R.O. Bush m 35 born RI.
BUSHNEL, ABNER, 37, M, Coach maker, -, CT, 16, 16, EDGE. Abner Bushnel born Hutford, (Hartford) CT
BUTLER, AMELIA, 49, F, None listed, -, MA, 949, 929, CHAS-. In HH of P. Newman m 40 born SC.
BUTLER, GEORGE, 14, M, None listed, -, ME, 377, 386, RICH. In HH of Zebulon Butler m 42 born ME.
BUTLER, JOHN F., 19, M, Carpenter, -, MA, 949, 929, CHAS-. In HH of P. Newman m 40 born SC.
BUTLER, SOPHRONA, 45, F, None listed, -, ME, 377, 386, RICH. In HH of Zebulon Butler m 42 born ME.
BUTLER, THOMAS, 51, M, Carpenter, -, MA, 949, 929, CHAS-. In HH of P. Newman m 40 born SC.
BUTLER, ZEBULON, 42, M, Mechanic,-, ME, 377, 386, RICH.
BUTTERFIELD, A., 24, M, Clerk, -, NH, 438, 421, CHAS-. In HH of H.L. Butterfield m 35 born VT.
BUTTERFIELD, H.L., 35, M, Hotel Keeper, -,VT, 438, 421, CHAS-.

C

CALLOCK, O.H., 60, M, Farmer, -, MA, 857, 857, MARL.
CALVERT, ANN E., 40, F, None listed, -, RI, 12, 11, CHAS$. In HH of Thos. H. Calbert m 40 born

CAMPBELL, ELIJAH, 40, M, Trimmer, -, MA, 501, 505, AND. In HH of James Cochran m 30 born SC (Innkeeper).
CAMPBELL, JAMES, 28, M, Physician, -,VT, 101, 93, CHAS+. In Boarding House.
CANDLER, EDWARD, 50, M, Nautical store, -, MA, 153, 136, CHAS.
CAPRON, NEWTON, 30, M, Weaver, -, RI, 1333, 1333, BARN. In HH of Benj. Kimball m 25 born RI.
CARPENTER, WILLIAM, 40, M, Bricklayer, -, RI, 105, 102, CHAS*.
CARRINGTON, CHARLES V., 35, M, Clerk, -,VT, 636, 654, RICH.
CARRINGTON, ISABELLA, 62, F, None listed, -, MA, 636, 654, RICH. In HH of Charles V. Carrington m 35 born VT.
CARR?, S.R., 25, M, Merchant, -, RI, 175, 175, GEOR. Name could be Can
CARTWRIGHT, WILLIAM, 55, M, Millwright, -, CT, 542, 557, RICH. Date 1847 by name. In Lunatic Asylum.
CHAFFE, OTES J., 35, M, Merchant,-, RI, 856, 836, CHAS-.
CHALKEN, W., 55, M, Farmer, -, CT, 725, 725, HORR.
CHAMBERLAIN, E.H., 42, M, Farmer, -, MA, 2308, 2315, EDGE.
CHANNCEY, STEPHEN, 28, M, None listed, -, CT, 20, 21, AND.
CHAPIN, LEONARD, 26, M, Carriage dealer, -, MA, 842, 822, CHAS-.
CHASE, P.S., 44, M, Clerk, -, MA, 63, 57, CHAS-.
CHENEY, E. JR., 60, M, Merchant,-, MA, 167, 149, CHAS.
CLARK, ALFRED, 33, M, Tanner, -, CT, 743, 744, FAIR.
CLARK, B.D., 29, M, Blacksmith, -, ME, 377, 378, ORNG+.
CLARK, GAD, 51, M, Saddler, -, CT, 558, 558, UNION.
CLARK, JNO. A., 26, M, Stonecutter, -, ME, 346, 346, YORK. In HH of James Ballou m 37 born RI.
CLARK, JOHN, 66, M, Farmer, -, RI, 682, 682, LAU.
CLARK, MARY, 54, F, None listed, -, RI, 685, 685, LAU. In HH of John Clark, m 66 born RI.
CLARK, W.O., 48, M, Farmer, -, NH, 437, 437, HORR.
CLARKE, ELIZABETH A., 48, F, None listed, -, CT, 1765, 1769, EDGE. In HH of Joseph Clarke m 51 born Scotland.
CLARKE, H.B., 30, M, Store keeper, -, MA, 688, 668,CHAS-
CLARKE, MARTHA B., 22, F, None listed, -, MA, 688, 668, CHAS-. In HH of H.B. Clarke m 30 born MA.
CLARKE, S.S., 34, M, Merchant,-, CT, 373, 356, CHAS-. In HH of G.E. Clarke m 25 born Cuba.
CLARKE, SAMUEL, 35, M, Blacksmith, -, ME, 59, 60, ORNG+.
CLARKE, SOLOMON, 60, M, Merchant,-, CT, 1711, 1712, EDGE.

CLEVELAND, J.A., 50, M, Dentist, -, CT, 689, 669, CHAS-.
COALEY, MARK, 36, M, Miller, -,VT, 570, 570, LAU.
COBB, EDWARD, 24, M, Merchant, -, MA, 304, 288, CHAS-. In HH of C.T. Dunham m 29 born MA.
COFFIN ABRAHAM, 65, M, Farmer, -, MA, 346, 348, AND.
COFFIN, LYDIA, 60, F, None listed, -, MA, 346, 348, AND. In HH of Abraham Coffin born MA.
COLBURN, B.P., 35, M, Planter, -, MA, 211, 211, CHAS%. Birthplace listed as Boston {MA}.
COLBURN, J.S., 45, M, Merchant,-, MA, 252, 226, CHAS*.
COLEMAN, EMERSON, 33, M, Clerk, -, MA, 417, 428, RICH.
COLEMAN, FRANCES A., 28, F, None listed, -, MA, 417, 428, RICH. In HH of Emerson Coleman m 33 born MA.
COLEMAN, GEORGE J., 25, M, Clerk, -, MA, 139, 129, CHAS-. In HH of Hugh Stoop m 60 born Ireland.
COLEMAN, HENRY W., 30, M, Merchant,-, MA, 139, 129, CHAS-. In HH of Hugh Stoop m 60 born Ireland.
COLEMAN, JOHN HY, 14, M, None listed, -, MA, 139, 129, CHAS-. In HH of Hugh Stoop m 60 born Ireland.
COLLINS, MERIAH, 22, F, None listed, -, MA, 542, 557, RICH. Date 1850 by name. In Lunatic Asylum.
CONGDEN, W.P., 40, M, Merchant,-, RI, 21, 21, GEOR.

CONNELLY, WILLIAM, 45, M, Trimmer, -, MA, 501, 505, AND. In HH of James Cochran m 30 born SC (Innkeeper).
CONVERSE, AUGUSTUS L., 51, M, E.P. Clergyman, -, CT, 1211, 1211, SUMT.
COOPER, J., 47, M, Laborer,-, MA, 213, 190, CHAS*.
CORNISH, A.H., 36, M, Protestant Episcopal Clergyman, -, MA, 265, 267, AND.
COURTNEY, E.C., 75, F, None listed, -, MA, 533, 499, CHAS*. In HH of W.C. Courtney m 33 born SC.
COWAN, JOHN, 55, M, Cabinet maker, -, MA, 192, 180, CHAS+.
COY, F.M., 28, M, Priv. U.S.A., -, MA, 47, 43, CHAS$. In HH of John Ewing m 50 born MA.
CRANE, CATHERINE, 52, F, None listed, -, CT, 486, 501, RICH.
CRANE, R., 47, F, None listed, -, MA, 220, 198, CHAS. In HH of Taba. Scott f 45 born MA.
CRAW, ALONZO, 23, M, Overseer/Mill, -, RI, 1723, 1724, EDGE. In HH of Hiram Jordan m 36, landlord, born SC.
CREWS, ANN,94, F, None listed, -, RI, 345, 319, CHAS. In HH of Martin E. Monroe m 45 born RI.
CREWS, ANN M., 40, F, None listed, -, MA, 773, 731, CHAS+.
CREWS, ELIZABETH, 16, F, None listed, -, MA, 773, 731, CHAS+. In HH of Ann M. Crews f 40 born MA.
CREWS, LECRETIA, 15, F, None listed, -, MA, 773, 731, CHAS+. In HH of Ann M. Crews

f 40 born MA.
CRITTENDEN, C., 30, F, None listed, -, MA, 2364, 2364, SPART. At Limestone High School.
CROCKER, GENO, 54, M, Carpenter, -, MA, 170, 170, BEAU.
CROPLAND, ANN, 28, F, None listed, -,VT, 78, 78, MARL. In HH of W.M Cropland m 50 planter born SC.
CUMPSTY, WILLIAM, 14, M, None listed, -, MA, 1642, 1642, EDGE. In HH of William Cumpsty m 51 born England.
CUNNINGHAM, SARAH, 28, F, None listed, -, MA, 549, 515, CHAS*. In HH of Saml. H. Patterson m 46 born SC.
CURRANS, ABIGAIL, 23, F, None listed, -, MA, 302, 286, CHAS-. In HH of Shephard Daggett m 54 born MA.
CURTIS, FRANKLIN, 33, M, Druggist,-, CT, 365, 374, RICH.
CURTIS, MARTHA, 3, F, None listed, -, MA, 178, 161, CHAS. In HH of William Curtis m 35 born MA.
CURTIS, MARTHA P., 35, F, None listed, -, MA, 178, 161, CHAS. In HH of William Curtis m 35 born MA.
CURTIS, WILLIAM, 35, M, Store keeper, -, MA, 178, 161, CHAS.
CUTTINE, E.G., 47, F, None listed, -, RI, 31, 31, GEOR. In HH of Benson Cuttine m 52 born SC.

D

DAGGETT, JOHN W.,13, M, Clerk, -, MA, 302, 286, CHAS-. In HH of Shephard Daggett m 54 born MA.
DAGGETT, L.W., 28, M, Machinist, -, MA, 302, 286, CHAS-. In HH of Shephard Daggett m 54 born MA.
DAGGETT, SHEPHARD, 54, M, Carpenter, -, MA, 302, 286, CHAS-.
DAGGETT, SHEPHARD, 17, M, Carpenter, -, CT, 302, 286, CHAS-. In HH of Shephard Daggett m 54 born MA.
DAGGETT, THO. W.,21, M, Engineer,-, MA, 302, 286, CHAS-. In HH of Shephard Daggett m 54 born MA.
DALOZIER, HANNAH, 60, F, None listed, -, MA, 92, 93, RICH+.
DANE, W.C., THE REV., 40, M, Priest, DD, -, MA, 614, 572, CHAS+. In HH of Elizabeth Mathieson f 59 born SC.
DANIELS, JAMES, 55, M, Farmer, -, CT, 419, 422, MAR.
DANIELS, MARY E., 30, F, None listed, -, ME, 492, 496, AND. In HH of Ann Morris f 36 born SC.
DARBY, M.C., 32, M, None listed, -, RI, 52, 52, ORNG*. In HH of Artemas F. Darby m 44, planter, born SC.
DARBY, M.C., 32, M, None listed, -, RI, 52, 52, ORNG*. In HH of Artemas F. Darby m 44 born SC.
DAVENPORT, CHARLES A., 4, M, None listed, -, MA, 52, 52, COLL. In HH of Mrs. Mary Gilling 40, teacher, born SC.

DAVIS, CORNELIUS, 30, M, RR Conductor, -, CT, 694, 713, RICH.
DAVIS, H., 23, M, Clerk, -, MA, 74, 74, BEAU+.
DAVIS, J.B., 43, M, None listed, -, MA, 587, 569, CHAS-.
DAVIS, WILLIAM, 92, M, Farmer, -, MA, 1234, 1235, AND*.
DAY, FISHER, 56, M, Boarding House, -, MA, 829, 809, CHAS-.
DEAN, BENIAH, 62, M, Carpenter, -, MA, 932, 932, SUMT.
DELAND, CHARLES, 30, M, Merchant,-, MA, 467, 450, CHAS-. In HH of Martha Mitchell f 30 born SC.
DELEAUMONT, MARGARET, 65, F, Printer, -, MA, 727, 685, CHAS+.
DERDIN, ISASH, 38, M, Painter, -, MA, 190, 173, CHAS.
DESSER, CAROLINE, 26, F, None listed, -, ME, 760, 760, SUMT. In HH of W.K. Stewart m 33 born Ireland.
DEVING, J.C., 34, M, Merchant,-, MA, 882, 840, CHAS+. In Charleston Hotel.
DEVING, R.V., 29, F, None listed, -, MA, 882, 840, CHAS+. In Charleston Hotel.
DEWIN, JAMES, 43, M, Carpenter, -, MA, 665, 657, CHAS%. Born: Boston {MA}.
DIBBLE, P.V., 41, M, Hatter, -, CT, 231, 209, CHAS.
DICKEY, REUBEN, 31, M, Farmer, -, MA, 976, 953, CHAS%.
DICKMAN, LEWIS, 24, M, Blacksmith, -, CT, 172, 162, CHAS+. In HH of John Haley m 40 born Ireland.
DILLINGHAM, THO., 30, M, Carpenter, -, ME, 119, 134, CHAS. Birth place listed as Freeport, M. {most likely Freeport, Maine}.
DONNEHO, ARNOLD, 54, M, Laborer,-, MA, 353, 353, BEAU-.
DORAN, WILLIAM, 36, M, Grocer, -, MA, 405, 369, CHAS.
DORIS, DRUCILLA, 34, F, None listed, -, MA, 2321, 2321, GREE. In HH of J.T. Doris m 34 born MA.
DORIS, J.T., 34, M, School master, -, MA, 2321, 2321, GREE.
DORR, GEORGI, 50, M, Farmer, -, NH, 1152, 1153, AND*.
DOUGAL, CHARLES, 15, M, None listed, -, CT, 230, 235, RICH. In HH of Henry P. Dougal m 43 born CT.
DOUGAL, DOTHA, 42, F, None listed, -, CT, 230, 235, RICH. In HH of Henry P. Dougal m 43 born CT.
DOUGAL, HENRY P.,43, M, Shoemaker, -, CT, 230, 235, RICH.
DOUGAL, MARY J., 18, F, None listed, -, CT, 230, 235, RICH. In HH of Henry P. Dougal m 43 born CT.
DOWD, A.W., 17, M, None listed, -, CT, 47, 47, EDGE. In HH of E.M. Ward f 45 milliner & mantria maker born CT.
DOWD, E.A., 22, F, Tutosek?, -, CT, 47, 47, EDGE. In HH of E.M. Ward f 45 milliner & mantria maker born CT.

DOWD, JANE L., 20, F, Tutosek?, -, CT, 47, 47, EDGE. In HH of E.M. Ward f 45 mill-iner & mantria maker born CT.
DOWNEY, E.H., 32, M, Tinner, -, MA, 35, 35, EDGE. In HH of Charles J. Glover m 41 born SC.
DRAKE, F.C., 30, M, Merchant, -, RI, 176, 176, GEOR. In HH of A. Seward m 64 born RI.
DRAKE, F.S., 4, M, None listed, -, RI, 176, 176, GEOR. In HH of A. Seward m 64 born RI.
DRAKE, MARY, 25, F, None listed, -, RI, 176, 176, GEOR. In HH of A. Seward m 64 born RI.
DUNAHM, ESDRA, 27, M, Clerk, -, MA, 304, 288, CHAS-. In HH of C.T. Dunham m 29 born MA.
DUNCAN, L.C., 38, M, Clerk, -, RI, 753, 733, CHAS-. In HH of John McAllister m 37 born Ireland. In America Hotel.
DUNHAM, BENJAMIN, 65, M, None listed, -, MA, 1189, 1189, GREE. In HH of Roger Lowland m 57 born MA.
DUNHAM, C.T., 29, M, Merchant,-, MA, 304, 288, CHAS-.
DUNKIN, B.F., 58, M, Chancellor, -, RI, 8, 8, GEOR+.

E

EARLE, BENJAMIN, 40, M, Builder, -, MA, 848, 806, CHAS+. In HH of James P. Earle m 34 born MA.
EARLE, JAMES P., 34, M, Builder, -, MA, 848, 806, CHAS+.
EASTON, GEO. L., 41, M, Master Mariner, -, RI, 314, 288, CHAS*.
EBIES, THOMAS, 16, M, Clerk, -, MA, 274, 248, CHAS*. In HH of J.C. Jervey m 30 born SC.
EDGERTON, E.W., 45, M, Merchant tailor, -, CT, 300, 274, CHAS*.
EDGERTON, S.F., 22, M, Merchant,-, CT, 300, 274, CHAS*. In HH of E.W. Edgerton m 45 born CT.
EDWARDS, ELIZABETH B., 27, F, None listed, -, ME, 613, 630, RICH. In HH of Josiah H. Edwards m 30 born Maine.
EDWARDS, JOSIAH H., 30, M, Telegraph operator, -, ME, 613, 630, RICH. Telegrpah Operator
EHNEY, CAROLINE, 25, F, None listed, -, CT, 75, 76, ORNG+. In HH of W.H. Ehney m 35 born SC.
EHNEY, W.H., 35, M, Merchant,-, CT, 74, 75, ORNG+.
EMORY, WILLIAM, 25, M, Stonecutter, -, ME, 346, 346, YORK. In HH of James Ballou m 37 born RI.
ENNUOUS, FRANKLIN, 38, M, Coach maker, -, CT, 32, 32, LANC.
ERETENDEN, JOHN, 67, M, Merchant,-, CT, 2310, 2310, GREE.
ERNEROUS, E., 38, F, None listed, -, CT, 13, 13, LANC. In HH of L.B. Ernerous m 50 born CT.
ERNEROUS, L.B., 50, M, Merchant,-, CT, 13, 13, LANC. In Jail.

ESTERBROKE, ELLEN, 25, F, None listed, -, MA, 2114, 2114, ABB. In HH of Charles Smith m 42 born SC.
EUDE, T., 35, M, Painter, -, MA, 357, 329, CHAS. In HH of E. Groves f 50, runns boarding house, born SC.
EVANS, CHARLES, 7, M, None listed, -, MA, 834, 835, AND*. In HH of Caward Evans m 50 born PA.
EWING, ANNA, 7, F, None listed, -, MA, 47, 43, CHAS$. In HH of John Ewing m 50 born MA.
EWING, ELISA, 35, F, None listed, -, MA, 47, 43, CHAS$. In HH of John Ewing m 50 born MA.
EWING, ELISA, 13, F, None listed, -, MA, 47, 43, CHAS$. In HH of John Ewing m 50 born MA.
EWING, JOHN, 50, M, Col. U.S.A., -, MA, 47, 43, CHAS$.
EWING, WILLIAM, 17, M, None listed, -, MA, 47, 43, CHAS$. In HH of John Ewing m 50 born MA.

F

FARRAR, EDITH, 26, F, None listed, -, NH, 134, 134, LEX. In HH of Jno. Farrar m 35 Mich. Spinner born England.
FARRAR, SAMUEL, 1, M, None listed, -, MA, 134, 134, LEX. In HH of Jno. Farrar m 35 Mich. Spinner born England.
FARRAR, THOMAS, 29, M, None listed, -, MA, 134, 134, LEX. In HH of Jno. Farrar m 35 Mich. Spinner born England.
FELSH, DANIEL, 21, M, Machinist, -, NH, 113, 113, LEX.
FIELD, STEPHEN, 36, M, Baker, -, MA, 1727, 1730, EDGE. Stephen Field born Boston, MA.
FIELDS, THOMAS, 30, M, Clerk, -, CT, 65, 66, ORNG+. In HH of James Harley at Hotel.
FISHER, WM., 48, M, Merchant,-, MA, 769, 769, KERS.
FISK, GEORGE, 26, M, Merchant,-, ME, 1, 1, HORR. In HH of James Beaty m 46 born SC.
FITCH, AUGUSTUS, 55, M, Druggist,-, CT, 397, 407, RICH.
FITCH, SOPHIA M.,48, F, None listed, -, MA, 397, 407, RICH. In HH of Augustus Fitch m 55 born CT.
FLINT, HENRY E., 26, M, Clerk, -, MA, 723, 703, CHAS-. In HH of A.L. Hazletons m 40 born MA.
FOLGER, EDWARD, 50, M, Packer, -, MA, 745, 703, CHAS+. Born Nantucket, {MA}
FOLLEY, D., 38, M, Mariner, -, MA, 322, 297, CHAS. In Boarding house.
FORBS, JOHN, 25, M, None listed, -, CT, 3, 3, GEOR. In HH of D.A. Sperry m 31 born CT.
FORD, WILLIAM, 27, M, Stonecutter, -, RI, 346, 346, YORK. In HH of James Ballou m 37 born RI.
FORREST, THOMAS, 20, M, Clerk, -, CT, 692, 672, CHAS-. In HH of E.G. Brown m 41 born CT.
FOSTER, CHARLES, 34, M, Planter, -, NH, 6, 6, CHAS~. In HH of James Poyas, Jr. m 35 born SC.

FOSTER, JOHN, 37, M, Bricklayer, -, MA, 530, 530, CHES. In HH of Absalom Housar m 37 born NC.
FOSTER, JOHN, 37, M, Brickmason, -, MA, 255, 255, UNN+. In HH of Elizabeth Page f 58 born SC.
FOSTER, JOSEPH, 45, M, Merchant,-, NH, 44, 44, SPART.
FOWLER, ANDREW, 90, M, Clergy, Episcopal, -, CT, 539, 505, CHAS*.
FRANKLIN, BENJAMIN, 24, M, Mariner, -, MA, 40, 37, CHAS-. Listed as prisoner.
FRAZER, HANNAH P., 42, F, None listed, -, CT, 477, 443, CHAS*. In HH of Charles P. Frazer m 45 born SC.
FULEY, HENRY, 33, M, Tinner, -, MA, 124, 115, CHAS+. In Boarding House.
FULLER, ALLEN, 53, M, Preacher,-, MA, 158, 158, PICK+.

G

GAGE, ROB., 28, M, Mariner, -, MA, 334, 308, CHAS. In HH of William Bennett m 40 born NY.
GAILLARD, FRANCES MRS., 43, F, None listed, -, ME, 2, 2, CHAS~. Born: Belfast, ME. In HH of Dr. Theodore S. Gaillard m 54 born SC.
GAY, L.B., 30, M, Teacher, -, MA, 304, 288, CHAS-. In HH of C.T. Dunham m 29 born MA.
GAYLORD, T.W., 45, M, Tanner, -, CT, 1473, 1473, GREE.
GEIRGER, SARAH E., 23, F, None listed, -, MA, 1230, 1230, EDGE. In HH of W.W. Geiger m 42 born SC.
GERARD, P.G., 60, M, Tailor, -, MA, 72, 66, CHAS-.
GIBBON, CAROLINE, 50, F, None listed, -, MA, 338, 312, CHAS*. In HH of George Gibbon m 57 born MA.
GIBBON, GEORGE, 57, M, Merchant,-, MA, 338, 312, CHAS*.
GIBBON, GEORGE E., 27, M, None listed, -, MA, 338, 312, CHAS*. In HH of George Gibbon m 57 born MA.
GIBBON, JOHN, 35, M, Merchant,-, MA, 296, 273, CHAS. In HH of Jane Muir f 60 born SC.
GIBSON, ABIGAIL, 35, F, None listed, -, MA, 374, 347, CHAS*. In HH of Harriot Gray f 45 born SC.
GIFFORD, EBENEZAR, 62, M, Planter, -, MA, 166, 166, BEAU-.
GIFFORD, EBENEZAR, JR., 21, M, Planter, -, MA, 166, 166, BEAU-. In HH of Ebenezar Gifford m 62 born MA.
GIFFORD, ELLEN, 23, F, None listed, -, MA, 166, 166, BEAU-. In HH of Ebenezar Gifford m 62 born MA.
GIFFORD, LOVEY, 24, F, None listed, -, MA, 166, 166, BEAU-. In HH of Ebenezar Gifford m 62 born MA.
GIFFORD, ROBERT, 20, M, Planter, -, MA, 166, 166, BEAU-. In HH of Ebenezar Gifford m 62 born MA.
GILBERT, A., 40, M, Fisherman, -, MA, 276, 256, CHAS+.

GILLMAN, J. J., 33, M, Teacher, -, NH, 5, 5, AND. In HH of William Hubbard m 51, Innkeeper, born SC.
GILMAN, CAROLINE, 56, F, None listed, -, MA, 299, 273, CHAS*. In HH of Samuel Gilman m 60 born MA.
GILMAN, SAMUEL, 60, M, D.D. Unitarian minister,-, MA, 299, 273, CHAS*.
GILMAN, SARAH, 64, F, None listed, -, RI, 345, 319, CHAS. In HH of Martin E. Monroe m 45 born RI.
GLINES, THOMAS A., 30, M, Painter, -, NH, 4, 4, AND*.
GODDARD, R.W., 33, M, Carriage maker, -, CT, 2248, 2248, GREE.
GOFF, SAMUEL, 65, M, Artist, -, MA, 1003, 1003, EDGE. In HH of Robt. Anderson m 35, merchant, born SC. David Goff, Daguersian Artist.
GOODMAN, W.W., 28, M, Landlord,-, MA, 26, 26, EDGE.
GORDON, CATHERINE, 28, F, None listed, -, MA, 154, 144, CHAS-.
GOWER, E.M., 36, M, Black smith, -, ME, 2312, 2312, GREE.
GOWER, THOMAS C.,28, M, Coach maker, -, ME, 2313, 2313, GREE.
GOWING, CHARLES, 54, M, Shoemaker, -,VT, 559, 559, UNION.
GOWING, RECKTY, 42, F, None listed, -,VT, 559, 559, UNION. In HH of Charles Gowing m 54 born VT.

GRAVES, ELDRIDGE Y., 14, M, None listed, -, NH, 124, 124, LEX. In HH of Jacob Graves m 42 born NH.
GRAVES, JACOB, 42, M, Civil Engineer, -, NH, 124, 124, LEX.
GRAVES, MARY E., 8, F, None listed, -, MA, 124, 124, LEX. In HH of Jacob Graves m 42 born NH.
GRAVES, ORVILLE, 10, M, None listed, -, MA, 124, 124, LEX. In HH of Jacob Graves m 42 born NH.
GRAVES, SUSAN, 5, F, None listed, -, MA, 124, 124, LEX. In HH of Jacob Graves m 42 born NH.
GRAVES, SUSAN L.,42, F, None listed, -, NH, 124, 124, LEX. In HH of Jacob Graves m 42 born NH.
GRAY, ANN E., 36, F, None listed, -, MA, 437, 420, CHAS-. In HH of James W. Gray m 55 born SC.
GRAY, JAS., 40, M, Clerk, -, MA, 836, 816, CHAS-. In Boarding House.
GREATON, JOHN, 58, M, Ship Master, -, MA, 3, 3, CHAS.
GREATON, LYDIA P., 54, F, None listed, -, MA, 3, 3, CHAS. In HH of John Greaton m 58, ship master, born MA.
GREEN, FREDERICK W., 50, M, Mechanic,-, MA, 615, 633, RICH.
GREEN, WM. R., 32, M, Stevedore, -, CT, 383, 345, CHAS+.
GREENLEAF, ABRIM., 25, M, Clock Maker, -, CT, 474, 474,

LAU. In HH of Thomas Darnal m 41 Farmer born SC.
GREGG, CORNELIA M., 55, F, None listed, -, RI, 494, 509, RICH. In HH of James Gregg m 60 born SC.
GREGORIO, J.H., 31, M, Planter, -, CT, 164, 164, BEAU+.
GREGORY, F.M., 32, M, None listed, -, CT, 121, 127, CHAS.
GREGORY, SARAH ANN, 30, F, None listed, -, RI, 121, 127, CHAS. In HH of F.M. Gregory m 32 born CT.
GRIDLEY, EDWARD, 55, M, Stone masonman, -, MA, 1249, 1249, GREE.
GRIFFIN, ANDREW, 35, M, None, -, RI, 542, 557, RICH. Date 1842 by name. In Lunatic Asylum.
GUNNISON, JAMES, 40, M, Merchant,-, MA, 836, 816, CHAS-. In Boarding House.
GUNNISON, NANCY, 20, F, None listed, -, MA, 836, 816, CHAS-. In Boarding House.

H

HAMILTON, ARTHUR ST. C., 1, M, None listed, -, RI, 185, 185, BEAU+. In HH of Dr. D.H. Hamilton m 35 born SC.
HAMILTON, JAMES, 9, M, None listed, -, RI, 185, 185, BEAU+. In HH of Dr. D.H. Hamilton m 35 born SC.
HAMILTON, LUCY, 33, F, None listed, -, MA, 848, 848, EDGE. In HH of Thos. Hamilton m 35 born SC.
HANSON, THOS. B.,22, M, School teacher, -, ME, 2263, 2277, EDGE. In HH of John M. Clarke m 37 born NJ.
HARDING, WILLIAM, 48, M, Store keeper, -, MA, 341, 305, CHAS+. In HH of Jane Hamilton f 49 born England.
HARLOWE, BENJAMIN F., 26, M, Plasterer, -, MA, 517, 521, AND.
HARPY, CATHERINE, 50, F, None listed, -, RI, 220, 198, CHAS. In HH of Taba. Scott f 45 born MA.
HARRIS, CHARLES, 25, M, Clerk, -, RI, 836, 816, CHAS-. In Boarding House.
HARRIS, ELIJAH, 50, M, Schoolmaster, -, NH, 562, 562, BARN.
HARRIS, MARY, 42, F, None listed, -,VT, 68, 69, RICH. In HH of Edward Harris m 66 born VA.
HARRISON, J.W., 35, M, Painter/Glazier, -, MA, 5, 5, CHAS+.
HARRISON, JOHN, 65, M, None listed, -, MA, 5, 5, CHAS+. In HH of J.W. Harrison m 35 born MA.
HARRISON, LUCRETIA, 90, F, None listed, -, MA, 821, 779, CHAS+. In HH of John B. Gray m 50 born SC.
HARROW, REBECCA, 54, F, None listed, -, RI, 345, 319, CHAS. In HH of Martin E. Monroe m 45 born RI.
HASELL, GEORGIANA, 11, F, None listed, -, CT, 33, 33, GEOR. In HH of Andrew Hasell m 47 born Scotland.

HASSELTINE, J.A., 28, M, Merchant,-, NH, 28, 28, LANC.
HASY, SUSAN, 25, F, None listed, -, MA, 1974, 1980, EDGE. In HH of William Hasy ?, m 26 born MA.
HASY?, WILLIAM, 26, M, Carpenter, -, MA, 1974, 1980, EDGE.
HATCH, LEWIS, 40, M, Merchant,-, MA, 585, 543, CHAS+.
HAWLEY, ANTOINETTE, 10, F, None listed, -, CT, 297, 303, RICH. In HH of Levi Hawley m 45 born CT.
HAWLEY, JANE E., 35, F, None listed, -, CT, 297, 303, RICH. In HH of Levi Hawley m 45 born CT.
HAWLEY, JANE E., 14, F, None listed, -, CT, 297, 303, RICH. In HH of Levi Hawley m 45 born CT.
HAWLEY, LEVI, 45, M, Saddler, -, CT, 297, 303, RICH.
HAWLEY, MARY F., 12, F, None listed, -, CT, 297, 303, RICH. In HH of Levi Hawley m 45 born CT.
HAWS, D., 24, M, Coach Painter, -, MA, 379, 344, CHAS. In HH of N.R. Schineder m 32 born Germany.
HAYDEN, A.H., 33, M, Jeweler, -, CT, 1014, 991, CHAS%.
HAYDEN, ABBEY, 34, F, None listed, -, CT, 1088, 1065, CHAS-. In HH of H.S. Hayden m 35 born CT.
HAYDEN, AMELIA, 32, F, None listed, -, CT, 49, 49, BEAU. In HH of John S. Tyler m 36 born SC.
HAYDEN, H.S., 35, M, Merchant, -, CT, 1088, 1065, CHAS-.
HAZLELTONS, A.L., 40, M, Merchant,-, MA, 723, 703, CHAS-.
HEAD, AMOS, 40, M, Bookseller, -, NH, 9, 9, CHAS$.
HEAD, LAURETTA, 40, F, None listed, -, MA, 9, 9, CHAS$. In HH of Amos Head m 40 born NH.
HEDDSTON, H.M., 22, M, Merchant, -, CT, 70, 70, GEOR.
HENDRICK, ALVINA, 35, F, None listed, -, MA, 393, 366, CHAS*. In HH of James J.B. Heyward m 35 born SC.
HENDRICK, J., 40, M, Minister,-, MA, 393, 366, CHAS*. In HH of James J.B. Heyward m 35 born SC. J.Hendrick, D.D. Baptist.
HENRICK, HANNAH, 30, F, None listed, -, MA, 1969, 1975, EDGE. In HH of W.F. Henrick m 30 born MA.
HENRICK, W.F., 30, M, Merchant,-, MA, 1969, 1975, EDGE.
HENRICK, WARREN W., 8, M, None listed, -, MA, 1969, 1975, EDGE. In HH of W.F. Henrick m 30 born MA.
HERFORD, MOSSES, 67, M, Laborer, -, MA, 134, 134, WILL.
HERNDON, JOHN J., 5, M, None listed, -,VT, 347, 347, MARL. In HH of John J. Herndon m 27 born VA.
HERNDON, JULINA M., 34, F, None listed, -,VT, 347, 347, MARL. In HH of John J. Herndon m 27 born VA.

HIGGINS, MARY ANN, 15, F, None listed, -, MA, 550, 509, CHAS+. In HH of Michael Higgins m 35 born Ireland.
HILLS, CHARLES E., 25, M, Clerk, -, CT, 830, 810, CHAS-. In HH of John W. Storr m 40 born GA.
HILLYARD, F.P., 28, M, Harness maker, -, RI, 11, 11, EDGE. In HH of J.L. Doby m 32, landlord, born SC.
HINCKLEY, CHARLES, 20, M, Merchant,-, RI, 836, 816, CHAS-. In Boarding House.
HIX, WILLIAM, 50, M, None,-, MA, 123, 123, LEX.
HOBSON, JAMES, 49, M, Shoemaker, -, MA, 955, 935, CHAS-.
HOBSON, MARY, 46, F, None listed, -, MA, 955, 935, CHAS-. In HH of James Hobson m 49 born MA.
HODGES, SARAH J.,7, F, None listed, -, ME, 3, 3, UNION. In HH of Jane Jones f 48 born SC.
HOLLISTER, HOWEL W., 48, M, Saddler, -, CT, 293, 299, RICH.
HONEYWEEN, JAS., 30, M, Clerk, -, CT, 677, 657, CHAS-. In HH of Elizabeth Fell f 40 born SC.
HOOD, B., 55, M, Merchant,-, CT, 1216, 1216, SUMT.
HOREY, W.H., 28, M, Merchant,-, MA, 2302, 2302, GREE. In Hotel.
HORSEY, FLORANTHO, 56, F, Boarding house, -, MA, 101, 93, CHAS+.
HORTON, B.F., 60, M, Brick layer, -, MA, 2257, 2257, GREE.
HORTON, REBECCA, 75, F, None listed, -, CT, 1555, 1555, YORK. In HH of William Horton m 31 born York Dist., SC.
HOTCHKISS, L., 45, M, Coach maker, -, CT, 22, 22, LANC.
HOTCHKISS, WM., 50, M, Mechanic,-, CT, 287, 287, KERS.
HOWE, GEORGE, 48, M, O.S.P. Clergyman, -, MA, 527, 542, RICH.
HOWE, PHILIP, 50, M, Clerk, -, MA, 96, 94, CHAS*.
HOWLAND, WILLIAM, 53, M, Merchant,-, MA, 649, 629, CHAS-.
HOYT, F., 45, M, Watch-maker and Jewler, -, NH, 1828, 1828, SUMT.
HOYT, J.C., 60, M, School master, -, MA, 1220, 1220, GREE. In HH of R.P. Goodlite m 40 born SC.
HOYT, W.S., 32, M, Carpenter, -, NH, 1830, 1830, SUMT.
HUGGINS, GEORGE, 31, M, Merchant,-, CT, 377, 387, RICH.
HUMPHREY, WILLIAM, 46, M, Machinist, -, RI, 2204, 2204, GREE.
HUMPHRIES, ALEXR., 55, M, Stationer, -, MA, 473, 456, CHAS-. In HH of Margaret M. McKenzie f 35 born SC.
HUNNEWELL, F., 21, M, Clerk, -, MA, 837, 817, CHAS-. In HH of George Oates m 55 born England.
HUNT, BENJAMIN F., 56, M, Attorney at Law, -, MA, 1104, 1081, CHAS-.
HUNT, JOHN A., 24, M, Stonecutter, -, MA, 346, 346,

YORK. In HH of James Ballou m 37 born RI.
HUNT, NATHANIEL, 41, M, Com. Merchant, -, MA, 508, 466, CHAS+.
HUNTER, H.E., 32, F, None listed, -, CT, 1263, 1263, DARL. In HH of Wm. R. Hunter m 34 born SC.
HUNTER, H.E., 9, M, None listed, -, CT, 1263, 1263, DARL. In HH of Wm. R. Hunter m 34 born SC.
HUNTER, WM. G., 4, M, None listed, -, CT, 1263, 1263, DARL. In HH of Wm. R. Hunter m 34 born SC.
HUNTING, WILLIAM, 26, M, Merchant,-, RI, 697, 677, CHAS-. In HH of Susan Wood f 45 born GA.
HURD, CAROLINE, 12, F, None listed, -, CT, 28, 28, NEWB. In HH of Stiles Hurd 36 m born CT.
HURD, EMILY, 14, F, None listed, -, CT, 28, 28, NEWB. In HH of Stiles Hurd 36 m born CT.
HURD, H.A., 33, F, None listed, -, CT, 28, 28, NEWB. In HH of Stiles Hurd 36 m born CT.
HURD, MARY, 8, F, None listed, -, CT, 28, 28, NEWB. In HH of Stiles Hurd 36 m born CT.
HURD, STILES, 36, M, Saddle, -, CT, 28, 28, NEWB.
HURLBUT, O.C., 35, M, Brickmason, -, MA, 1886, 1886, SUMT.
HUSKINS, DANIEL J., 25, M, Machinist, -, NH, 113, 113, LEX. In HH of Daniel Felsh m 21 Machinist born NH.

HUSKINS, ELIZA, 19, F, None listed, -, NH, 113, 113, LEX. In HH of Daniel Felsh m 21 Machinist born NH.
HUTCHINGS, WM. S., 37, M, Machinist, -, MA, 2216, 2216, GREE.
HUTCHISON, TEMOS, 50, M, Clockmaker, -,VT, 24, 24, YORK+. In Hotel.
HYDE, SIMEON, 40, M, Merchant,-, CT, 897, 877, CHAS-.

J

JACOBS, ANNE R., 28, F, None listed, -, ME, 297, 297, CHAS%. In HH of Ferdind Jacobs m 40 born VA.
JAMESON, CAROLINE, 2, F, None listed, -, MA, 395, 377, CHAS-. In Boarding House.
JAMESON, JOHN, 26, M, Clerk, -, MA, 395, 377, CHAS-. In Boarding House.
JAMESON, LYDIA, 19, F, None listed, -, MA, 395, 377, CHAS-. In Boarding House.
JAQUITT, ARLIMAS, 39, M, Stonecutter, -, ME, 346, 346, YORK. In HH of James Ballou m 37 born RI.
JEROME, HENRY, 28, M, None listed, -, CT, 573, 573, YORK.
JESSUP, GERTRUDE, 22, F, None listed, -, CT, 982, 961, CHAS-. In HH of Z.R. Jessup m 46 born CT.
JESSUP, Z.R., 46, M, Shoe dealer, -, CT, 982, 961, CHAS-.
JINKS, G.S., 30, M, Farmer, -, RI, 145, 145, KERS.

JOHNSON, ADNA, 53, M, Planter/merchant, -, CT, 63, 63, FAIR.
JOHNSON, CHARLES P., 8, M, None listed, -, CT, 227, 232, RICH. {Page out of order}, follow HH 177/181. In HH of Giles M. Johnson m 38born NJ.
JOHNSON, HOLLIS, 53, M, Shoe dealer, -, NH, 835, 815, CHAS-.
JOHNSON, LEWIS, 74, M, Saddler, -, MA, 1893, 1893, SUMT.
JOHNSON, TIMOTHY, 50, M, Tavern keeper, -, CT, 504, 497, CHAS%.
JOHNSTON, ELIZA, 35, F, None listed, -, MA, 75, 75, GEOR. In HH of H. Johnston m 56 born MA.
JOHNSTON, H., 56, M, Shop keeper, -, MA, 75, 75, GEOR.
JOHNSTON, NICHOLAS, 67, M, Carpenter, -, CT, 237, 222, CHAS-. Poor House.
JONES, C.H., 27, M, Silversmith, -, CT, 7, 7, GEOR. In HH of Saml. Wilmot m 55 born CT.
JONES, ELIZABETH C.F., 35, F, None listed, -, MA, 799, 782, CHAS%. In HH of Thomas S. Jones m 45 born SC.
JONES, HARTFORD, 40, M, Farmer, -, CT, 230, 230, HORR.
JONES, THOMAS, 34, M, Rigger, -, MA, 192, 175, CHAS.
JUDD, CAROLINE F., 35, F, None listed, -, NH, 45, 45, SPART. In HH of D.C. Judd m 50 born MA.
JUDD, D.C., 40, M, Merchant,-, MA, 45, 45, SPART.

JUDD, ELIZA, 20, F, None listed, -, MA, 1241, 1241, UNION. In HH of Nancy McBride f 43 born SC.

K

KENNEDY, AMARINTHA, 13, F, None listed, -, MA, 524, 507, CHAS-. In HH of Thomas Kennedy m 43 born MA.
KENNEDY, EUDORA, 8, F, None listed, -, MA, 524, 507, CHAS-. In HH of Thomas Kennedy m 43 born MA.
KENNEDY, JULIA, 38, F, None listed, -, MA, 524, 507, CHAS-. In HH of Thomas Kennedy m 43 born MA.
KENNEDY, JULIA, 16, F, None listed, -, MA, 524, 507, CHAS-. In HH of Thomas Kennedy m 43 born MA.
KENNEDY, MADISON, 10, M, None listed, -, MA, 524, 507, CHAS-. In HH of Thomas Kennedy m 43 born MA.
KENNEDY, THOMAS, 43, M, Clerk, -, MA, 524, 507, CHAS-.
KENRICK, H.A., 33, M, Merchant,-, MA, 52, 52, EDGE.
KENRICK, W.F., 30, M, None listed, -, MA, 52, 52, EDGE. In HH of H.A. Kenrick m 33 born MA.
KERR, DANIEL H., 13, M, None listed, -, CT, 450, 450, FAIR. In HH of Daniel H. Kerr m 65 born PA.
KERR, ELIZABETH J., 49, F, None listed, -, CT, 450, 450, FAIR. In HH of Daniel H. Kerr m 65 born PA.

KERR, WILLIAM H.,10, M, None listed, -, CT, 450, 450, FAIR. In HH of Daniel H. Kerr m 65 born PA.
KETCHAM, JANE A., 30, F, None listed, -, CT, 1987, 1990, EDGE. In HH of William Kitcham m 38 born NJ.
KETCHAM, MARGARET E., 10, F, None listed, -, CT, 1987, 1990, EDGE. In HH of William Kitcham m 38 born NJ.
KETTIER, CHARLES, 22, M, Clerk, -, CT, 368, 351, CHAS-. In HH of John Jeffords m 49 born SC.
KIMBALL, BENJ., 25, M, Mill Wright, -, RI, 1333, 1333, BARN.
KING, F.M., 22, F, None listed, -, RI, 753, 733, CHAS-. In HH of John McAllister m 37 born Ireland. In American Hotel.
KING, G.W., 34, M, Farmer, -, CT, 1068, 1068, GREE.
KING, G.W., 33, M, None listed, -, RI, 753, 733, CHAS-. In HH of John McAllister m 37 born Ireland. In American Hotel.
KING, PETER, 53, M, Farmer, -, MA, 410, 411, AND*.
KING, W.S., COL.,48, M, Editor, -, CT, 355, 327, CHAS.
KINSMAN, H.W., 26, M, Window shade maker, -,VT, 13, 13, CHAS+.
KNAPP, PETER W., 36, M, Merchant,-, CT, 457, 440, CHAS-.

L

LADD, GEORGE W., 48, M, Teacher, -, NH, 475, 475, FAIR.

LAWTON, BASMATH ?, 42, F, None listed, -, MA, 317, 317, ABB. In HH of Hague Lawton m 62 born England.
LAWTON, MARY, 40, F, None listed, -, CT, 317, 317, ABB. In HH of Hague Lawton m 62 born England.
LAWTON, PHOEBE A., 49, F, None listed, -, RI, 74, 68, CHAS-. In HH of Roger B. Lawton m 56 born RI.
LAWTON, ROGER B., 56, M, Clerk, -, RI, 74, 68, CHAS-.
LEARY, JACOB B., 34, M, Engineer,-, NH, 157, 161, RICH. HH out of order, follows 185/189.
LELAND, AARON W., 63, M, Professor of Theology, -, MA, 589, 606, RICH.
LELAND, DEXTER, 49, M, Teacher, -, MA, 70, 68, CHAS*. In HH of Peter Rottereau m 50 born SC.
LEMUED?, ADALINE, 29, F, None listed, -, MA, 1969, 1975, EDGE. In HH of W.F. Henrick m 30 born MA.
LEMUED?, LUCY, 25, F, None listed, -, MA, 1969, 1975, EDGE. In HH of W.F. Henrick m 30 born MA.
LEWIS, JAMES, 34, M, Tinner, -, MA, 85, 85, YORK+.
LEWIS, LUTHER, 44, M, Cabinet maker, -, CT, 25, 25, SPART.
LIEBER, OSCAR, 20, M, Miner, -, MA, 688, 697, RICH. In HH of Francis Lieber m 50 born Prussia. Oscar Lieber born Boston, MA
LINDESAY, ROSE W.G., 27, F, None listed, -, MA, 73, 73,

YORK+. In HH of John T. Lindesay m 25 born York Dist., SC.
LITTLEFIELD, T.G., 35, M, Carpenter, -, ME, 426, 426, HORR.
LIZERL(?), B., 50, M, Farmer, -, CT, 54, 54, LANC*.
LLOYD, WILLIAM, 52, M, Carpenter, -, MA, 282, 256, CHAS*.
LOCKE, GEO. A., 33, M, Merchant,-, MA, 825, 783, CHAS+.
LOCKE, GEORGE B., 52, M, Merchant,-, MA, 839, 797, CHAS+.
LOCKE, LUCRETIA A., 30, F, None listed, -, MA, 825, 783, CHAS+. In HH of Geo. A. Locke m 33 born MA.
LONG, DAVID, 65, M, Land lord, -, MA, 2302, 2302, GREE.
LONG, JOSEPH H., 35, M, Mechanic,-, MA, 656, 675, RICH.
LONG, JOSEPH W., 29, M, Merchant,-, MA, 2262, 2262, GREE. In HH of Samuel Mauldin m 40 born SC.
LONG, RODOLPHUS, 48, M, Merchant,-, MA, 2252, 2252, GREE.
LORD, SAML., 54, M, Merchant,-, MA, 820, 778, CHAS+.
LOWLAND, ROGER, 57, M, Farmer, -, MA, 1189, 1189, GREE.
LUGRIM, AUGUSTINE, 35, M, Book keeper, -, ME, 1784, 1790, EDGE. In HH of John Marsh m 60 born SC.
LUTHER, HARRY, 25, M, Overseer/Mill, -, RI, 1723, 1724, EDGE. In HH of Hiram Jordan m 36, landlord, born SC.
LUTHER, STEPHEN, 24, M, Overseer/Mill, -, RI, 1723, 1724, EDGE. In HH of Hiram Jordan m 36, landlord, born SC.
LYMAN, SARAH, 23, F, None listed, -, ME, 1622, 1622, EDGE. In HH of Levi Lyman m 24 born NY.
LYMAN, ST. J., 32, M, Clerk, -,VT, 101, 93, CHAS+. In Boarding House.
LYON, ABBOT?, 25, M, None listed, -, MA, 1038, 1038, DARL. In HH of John Hart m 25 born SC.

M

MAGELL, W.P., 27, M, Clerk, -, MA, 127, 118, CHAS+. In Boarding House.
MALLERY, SARAH, 40, F, None listed, -, CT, 314, 298, CHAS-.
MALLETTE, DANIEL, 32, M, Saddler, -, CT, 293, 299, RICH. In HH of Howel W. Hollister m 48 born CT.
MALLOREY, FREELOVE, 28, F, None listed, -, RI, 335, 309, CHAS. In HH of Eliza-beth Thomas f 28 born NY.
MANGA, M.L., 38, M, Farmer, -,VT, 35, 35, EDGE. In HH of Charles J. Glover m 41 born SC.
MARCCEY, VIRGIL, 40, M, Clerk, -, MA, 9, 9, CHAS*.
MARION, MARIA MRS., 61, F, None listed, -, RI, 14, 14, CHAS2. In HH of Robert W. Mazyck m 60 born SC.

MARKS, JULIA P., 56, F, None listed, -,VT, 858, 868, RICH+. In HH of Elias Marks m 60 born SC.
MARQUIS, LAVIRA, 22, F, None listed, -, ME, 328, 328, CHAS%. In HH of James Marquir m 35 born PA.
MARSH, LOUISA, 42, F, None listed, -, MA, 8, 8, CHAS$.
MARSHALL, JOHN ? P., 22, M, Merchant,-, CT, 1686, 1686, EDGE. In HH of Thomas H. Marshall m 51 born CT.
MARSHALL, NANCY P., 48, F, None listed, -, MA, 1686, 1686, EDGE. In HH of Thomas H. Marshall m 51 born CT.
MARSHALL, THOMAS H., 51, M, Merchant,-, CT, 1686, 1686, EDGE.
MASON, CHARLES B., 24, M, Stonecutter, -, ME, 346, 346, YORK. In HH of James Ballou m 37 born RI.
MAXCY, SUSANNA, 82, F, None listed, -, RI, 881, 891, RICH+. In HH of Hart Maxcy m 43 born SC.
MAY, JOHN, 60, M, Cabinet maker, -, RI, 142, 133, CHAS+.
MCCARKS, J.J., 54, M, Book seller, -, MA, 527, 486, CHAS+.
MCCAUDLES, F.A., 27, F, None listed, -,VT, 854, 854, KERS. In HH of L. McCaudles m 30 born NJ.
MCCLELLIN, ALFRED, 37, M, Peddler, -, MA, 1147, 1147, GREE.
MCDONALD JOHN E., 60, M, Corn merchant, -, CT, 2394, 2398, EDGE.

MCGINLEY, GEORGE, 34, M, Merchant,-, MA, 882, 840, CHAS+. In Charleston Hotel.
MCKAGAN, J.W.P, 38, M, None listed, -, MA, 868, 868, DARL.
MCLOVELANA, MALLA, 30, M, Farmer, -, MA, 792, 793, AND*.
MCMAN, EDWARD, 22, M, None listed, -, CT, 3, 3, GEOR. In HH of D.A. Sperry m 31 born CT.
MCNEAL, GEORGE, 30, M, Blacksmith, -, CT, 28, 28, EDGE.
MCNEAL, H.E., 25, F, None listed, -, CT, 28, 28, EDGE. In HH of George McNeal m 30 born CT.
MCNEAL, JOSEPH H., 2, M, None listed, -, CT, 28, 28, EDGE. In HH of George McNeal m 30 born CT.
MERVIN, ANDREW, 35, M, Bricklayer, -, CT, 65, 66, ORNG+. In HH of James Harley at Hotel.
MIDDLETON, M.M., 35, F, None listed, -, RI, 52, 52, CHAS!. In HH of N.R. Middleton m 40 born SC.
MILLER, HARRIET E., 29, F, None listed, -, MA, 759, 739, CHAS-.
MILLS, OTIS, 53, M, Merchant,-, MA, 78, 88, CHAS.
MINS, FREDERIC, 35, M, Engineer,-, MA, 293, 293, YORK. In HH of John Steele m 65 born York Dist., SC.
MINS, HORACE, 38, M, Stone mason, -, MA, 289, 289, YORK. In HH of William Montgomery m 23 born Chester Dist., SC.

MITCHELL, ALMUND, 40, M, Clerk, -, MA, 188, 192, RICH. In Hotel.
MITCHELL, HIRAIM, 43, M, Merchant,-, CT, 9, 9, SPART.
MONROE, MARTIN E., 45, M, Merchant,-, RI, 345, 319, CHAS.
MOODIE, A.H., 29, M, Tinplate worker, -,VT, 278, 262, CHAS-.
MOODIE, GEORGE, 28, M, Gas fitter, -, MA, 315, 299, CHAS-. In HH of Saml. A. Nelson m 31 born MA.
MOORE, AUGUSTUS, 30, M, Minister, Epis., -, ME, 320, 304, CHAS-. In HH of L.E. Whilden f 47 born SC.
MOORE, BENJAMIN, 35, M, Machinist, -, MA, 303, 309, RICH.
MOORE, EDWARD, 19, M, Clerk, -, MA, 454, 421, CHAS*. In HH of Sarah Savage f 50 born SC.
MOORE, FRANCIS, 83, F, None listed, -, RI, 454, 421, CHAS*. In HH of Sarah Savage f 50 born SC.
MOORE, JOHN, 46, M, Merchant,-, NH, 22, 22, BEAU+.
MOORE, JOHN E., 17, M, Clerk, -, MA, 454, 421, CHAS*. In HH of Sarah Savage f 50 born SC.
MOORE, MRS., 46, F, None listed, -, NH, 22, 22, BEAU+. In HH of John Moore m 46 born NH.
MOORE, WILLIAM F., 21, M, Merchant,-, MA, 454, 421, CHAS*. In HH of Sarah Savage f 50 born SC.
MORGAN, JESSE, 57, M, Tanner, -, ME, 1900, 1900, SUMT.

MORSE, CYRUS, 69, M, Planter, -, CT, 186, 189, RICK+.
MORSE, REBECCA, 50, F, None listed, -, CT, 186, 189, RICK+. In HH of Cyrus Morse m 69 born CT.
MOSE, JOHN T., 44, M, Farmer, -, ME, 550, 550, HORR.
MOSIER, ELIZA, 14, F, None listed, -, MA, 151, 151, BEAU+. In HH of Dr. R.B. Scriven m l72 born SC..
MOSIER, LAURA, 15, F, None listed, -, MA, 151, 151, BEAU+. In HH of Dr. R.B. Scriven m l72 born SC..
MOSIER, PHILIP, 20, M, None listed, -, MA, 151, 151, BEAU+. In HH of Dr. R.B. Scriven m l72 born SC..
MOSS, JOSEPH R., 47, M, Farmer, -, CT, 504, 504, YORK.
MOURY, ANN D., 50, F, None listed, -, RI, 379, 362, CHAS-. In HH of S. Moury, Jr. m 50 born RI.
MOURY, S., JR., 50, M, Merchant,-, RI, 379, 362, CHAS-.
MULLEN, JAMES, 15, M, Clerk, -, MA, 759, 739, CHAS-. In HH of Harriet E. Miller f 29 born MA.
MULLIGAN, CATHARINE, 60, F, None listed, -, MA, 1725, 1726, EDGE. In HH of A.B. Mulligan m 88 ?, born SC.
MUNROE, G.C., 38, M, Merchant, -, RI, 113, 113, GEOR.
MUNROE, W.J., 35, M, Merchant, -, RI, 113, 113, GEOR. In HH of G.C. Munroe m 38 born RI.
MURDOCK, SARAH S., 37, F, None listed, -, MA, 1193, 1193, YORK. In HH of William

23

Murdock m 38 born Scotland.
MURRAY, MARIAH, 85, F, None listed, -, MA, 1725, 1726, EDGE. In HH of A.B. Mulligan m 88 ?, born SC.
MUTTON, SAML. L., 63, M, Mechanic,-, MA, 1005, 1005, CHES.
MYERS, J.S., 40, M, Tavern keeper, -, MA, 274, 258, CHAS-.

N

NABB, JOHN, 45, M, Mariner, -, MA, 1083, 1060, CHAS-.
NELSON, SAML. A., 31, M, Shoe dealer, -, MA, 315, 299, CHAS-.
NEWELL, EBENEZER, 38, M, Laborer, -,VT, 394, 394, WILL.
NEWELL, J., 34, M, Shoemaker, -, MA, 955, 935, CHAS-. In HH of James Hobson m 49 born MA.
NEWELL, OLIVE T., 36, F, None listed, -,VT, 394, 394, WILL. In HH of Ebenezer B. Newell m 38 born VT.
NEWTON, GILES G.,40, M, Painter, -, CT, 398, 408, RICH.
NICHOLAS, A.G., 32, F, None listed, -, MA, 10, 10, EDGE. In HH of F.M. Nicholas m 34 born SC. A.G. Nicholas born Boston, MA.
NICHOLAS, HENRY, 27, M, Merchant,-,VT, 954, 955, FAIR.
NICHOLS, HORACE E., 36, M, Merchant,-,VT, 238, 243, RICH.
NICHOLS, J. C., 33, M, Merchant,-, ME, 617, 575, CHAS+.
NICHOLS, JAMES, 34, M, Merchant,-, ME, 195, 179, CHAS*.
NICHOLS, JAMES H., 37, M, Merchant,-,VT, 241, 241, CHAS%.
NICHOLS, SARAH, 70, F, None listed, -, MA, 815, 795, CHAS-. In HH of J.D. Wright m 30 born England.
NICHOLS, SARAH, 50, F, None listed, -, MA, 584, 542, CHAS+. In HH of Henry C. Street m 30 born SC.
NICKELSON, CHARLES, 35, M, Farmer, -, ME, 624, 624, EDGE.
NORWOOD, DAVID, 36, M, Carpenter, -, MA, 1070, 1048, CHAS%.
NORWOOD, ELIZA, 30, F, None listed, -, MA, 1070, 1048, CHAS%. In HH of David Norwood m 36 born MA.
NORWOOD, ELLEN, 11, F, None listed, -, MA, 1070, 1048, CHAS%. In HH of David Norwood m 36 born MA.
NORWOOD, RUTH, 8, F, None listed, -, MA, 1070, 1048, CHAS%. In HH of David Norwood m 36 born MA.

O

OAKES, MARGARET G., 35, F, None listed, -, MA, 92, 85, CHAS-. In HH of Z.B. Oakes m 42 born ME.
OAKES, MARY, 62, F, None listed, -, ME, 92, 85, CHAS-. In HH of Z.B. Oakes m 42 born ME.
OAKES, Z.B., 42, M, Broker, -, ME, 92, 85, CHAS-.

OAKLY, EDWARD, 26, M, Stone mason, -, MA, 1723, 1724, EDGE. In HH of Hiram Jordan m 36, landlord, born SC
OBYDON, CATHRN, 17, F, None listed, -, CT, 47, 43, CHAS$. In HH of John Ewing m 50 born MA.
OCHARD, LEVY, 30, M, Engraver,-, MA, 57, 52, CHAS-. In HH of George Garrett m 41 born England.
OLMSTED, LEWIS, 22, M, Clerk, -, CT, 810, 790, CHAS-. In HH of George Cannon m 48 born SC.
OLNEY, G.W., 53, M, Merchant,-, RI, 1010, 987, CHAS%.
OLNEY, OLIVIA, 40, F, None listed, -, MA, 1010, 987, CHAS%. In HH of G.W. Olney m 53 born RI.
OLNEY, STEPHEN, 65, M, Carpenter, -, RI, 1214, 1215, FAIR.
ORILEY, ELIZA, 28, F, None listed, -, MA, 536, 502, CHAS*. In HH of James B. ORiley m 32 born SC.
OSBORN, AMOS W., 60, M, Miller, -, MA, 1369, 1369, CHES.
OSBURN, A.W., 20, M, Brick maker, -, MA, 784, 784, CHES.

P

PACKARD, EBENEZER E., 44, M, Teacher, -, ME, 434, 434, WILL. In HH of Anthony W. Dozier m 48 born SC.
PAINE, CHARLOTTE, 55, F, None listed, -, ME, 492, 496, AND. In HH of Ann Morris f 36 born SC.
PAINE, PHOEBE, 45, F, None listed, -, ME, 492, 496, AND. In HH of Ann Morris f 36 born SC.
PALMER, ASHER, 35, M, Tinner, -, ME, 248, 253, RICH.
PALMER, GEORGIANNA, 25, F, None listed, -, MA, 248, 253, RICH. In HH of Palmer Asher m 35 born ME.
PAMLEY, J., 31, M, Clerk, -, CT, 692, 672, CHAS-. In HH of E.G. Brown m 41 born CT.
PARKER, GEORGE, 37, M, Brick maker, -, CT, 823, 823, KERS. In Hotel.
PARKER, HORRIS, 27, M, Dentist, -, MA, 523, 523, EDGE. In HH of James Dom m 42 born SC.
PARKER, WM., 48, M, Carpenter, -, MA, 387, 351, CHAS.
PARMALLE, M.L., 22, M, Taylor, -, ME, 35, 35, EDGE. In HH of Charles J. Glover m 41 born SC.
PARMELER, W.L., 30, M, Blacksmith, -, CT, 2267, 2267, GREE.
PATTERSON, SAML., 30, M, Printer, -, MA, 315, 299, CHAS-. In HH of Saml. A. Nelson m 31 born MA.
PATTLE, WM., 50, F, Carpenter, -, CT, 208, 208, COLL.
PEARBOON, GEORGE H., 4, M, None listed, -, MA, 131, 131, LEX. In HH of Joseph Pearboon m 29 born NY. George H. Pearboon born Springfield, MA.

PEARBOON, HELEN M., 5, F, None listed, -, MA, 131, 131, LEX. In HH of Joseph Pearboon m 29 born NY. Helen M. Pearboon born Springfield, MA.
PEARBOON, MARY J., 27, F, None listed, -, NH, 131, 131, LEX. In HH of Joseph Pearboon m 29 born NY.
PEASE, J.F., 29, M, Grocer, -, ME, 36, 32, CHAS$.
PECK, JAMES, 44, M, Shoemaker, -, CT, 1269, 1269, LEX.
PECKERELL, LAURA, 37, F, None listed, -, MA, 2294, 2294, GREE. In HH of J.L. Peckerell m 39 born SC.
PECKHAM, JAMES, 53, M, Mechanic, -, CT, 411, 422, RICH.
PELET, D., 25, F, None listed, -, MA, 318, 293, CHAS. In HH of H. Bregnan m 24 born Germany.
PERCIVAL, JOHN, 40, M, Watchman,-, CT, 1005, 982, CHAS%. Under command of Major P. Hagnes, Commanding Officer U.S. Arsenal.
PETERS, JOHN, 52, M, Millwright, -, MA, 416, 416, COLL.
PICKEREL, MARY, 42, F, None listed, -, MA, 347, 349, AND. In HH of Jonathan Pickerel m 53 born SC.
PIERSON, EDWARD, 34, M, Store keeper, -, CT, 692, 672, CHAS-. In HH of E.G. Brown m 41 born CT.
PIPER, H.N., 35, M, Carpenter, -, MA, 88, 88, EDGE. H.N. Piper born Boston, MA.

PLATT, SARAH, 25, F, None listed, -, MA, 25, 25, GEOR+. In HH of George Platt m 30 born NY.
PLUMMER, THOMAS, 44, M, Laborer, -, MA, 1, 1, RICH.
POOL, WM., 79, M, Farmer, -, MA, 651, 651, HORR. In HH of Ann Nixen f 61 born SC.
POPE, SAMUEL, 50, M, Merchant,-, ME, 3, 3, HORR. In HH of Tho. H. Holmes m 40 born SC.
PORTER, JOHN B., 40, M, Physician, -, CT, 23, 21, CHAS$.
POST, R., REV., 68, M, Minister,-,VT, 66, 76, CHAS.
POTTEN, WM. F., 45, M, Prot. Episcopal Clergy, -, MA, 21, 22, AND.
POWER, JOHN, 24, M, Mariner, -, RI, 334, 308, CHAS. In HH of William Bennett m 40 born NY.
POWER, MARY, 2, F, None listed, -, CT, 1088, 1065, CHAS-. In HH of H.S. Hayden m 35 born CT.
POWER, SARAH, 32, F, None listed, -, CT, 1088, 1065, CHAS-. In HH of H.S. Hayden m 35 born CT.
PRATT, GEORGE, 31, M, Engineer,-, MA, 244, 229, CHAS+. In HH of Ellen Pratt f 24 born SC.
PRICE, JOHN, 35, M, Clerk, -, MA, 146, 137, CHAS+. In HH of James Preston m 50 born Ireland.
PROCTOR, CELESTIA, 50, F, None listed, -, MA, 766, 724, CHAS+. In HH of William Proctor m 56 born MA.
PROCTOR, WILLIAM, 56, M, Clerk, -, MA, 766, 724, CHAS+.

PURCE, JAMES, 40, M, Ice Hotel Keeper, -, MA, 146, 137, CHAS+. In HH of James Preston m 50 born Ireland.

Q

QUINLY, LAURENCE, 40, M, Carpenter, -, CT, 1765, 1771, EDGE.

R

RANDALL, THOMAS, 60, M, unkown, -, MA, 706, 706, HORR.
RAVENEL, ABIGAIL MRS., 72, F, None listed, -, RI, 14, 14, CHAS2. In HH of Robert W. Mazyck m 60 born SC.
RAYFORD, G., 60, M, Carpenter, -, RI, 35, 31, CHAS$.
RAYMOND, CHARLES A., 28, M, Baptist Clergyman, -, CT, 1792, 1792, ABB. In HH of William P. Hill m 46, Baptist Clergyman born SC.
READ, BARBAARA, 8, F, None listed, -, RI, 465, 422, CHAS. In HH of Leslie O'Wen m 47 born Ireland.
READ, ELIZABETH P., 68, F, None listed, -, MA, 4, 4, LEX. In HH of Thos. H. Simmons m 55 Physician born SC. Census date stated Sarah E. Simmons born Sommerset, MA.
READ, JOHN,15, M, Confectioner, -, RI, 465, 422, CHAS. In HH of Leslie O'Wen m 47 born Ireland.
READ, THOMAS, 4, M, None listed, -, RI, 465, 422, CHAS. In HH of Leslie O'Wen m 47 born Ireland.
REDLERN, SIMON, 26, M, Mariner, -, RI, 341, 315, CHAS. In HH of William Bellair m 35 born Germany.
REED, ANN M.T., 33, F, None listed, -, RI, 1002, 979, CHAS%. In HH of Gilbert Reed m 32 born RI.
REED, ELLEN W., 11, F, None listed, -, RI, 1002, 979, CHAS%. In HH of Gilbert Reed m 32 born RI.
REED, GILBERT, 32, M, Mechanic,-, RI, 1002, 979, CHAS%.
REED, HIRAM N., 13, M, None listed, -, RI, 1002, 979, CHAS%. In HH of Gilbert Reed m 32 born RI.
REEDER, JANE E., 37, F, None listed, -, MA, 347, 353, RICH.
RICE, HENRY S., 56, M, Notary Public, -, MA, 33, 41, CHAS.
RICH, LOUIS, 36, M, Farmer, -, CT, 1656, 1656, ABB.
RICHARDS, CHRISTIAN P., 33, F, None listed, -,VT, 869, 879, RICH+. In HH of Benjamin Richards m 43 born NY.
RICHARDS, W., 32, M, Editor, -, MA, 721, 701, CHAS-. In Boarding House.
RICK, JOSEPH, 45, M, Brick mason, -, RI, 1573, 1573, SPART.
RIDDELL, J.S., 34, M, Painter, -, MA, 959, 939, CHAS-.
RIDDELL, JANE L.,12, F, None listed, -, MA, 959, 939, CHAS-. In HH of J.S. Riddell m 34 born MA.
RIDDELL, MARY, 29, F, None listed, -, MA, 959, 939, CHAS-.

In HH of J.S. Riddell m 34 born MA.
RIGGS, HARPIN, 33, M, Carriage maker, -, CT, 70, 71, ORNG+.
RING, ISAAC E., 35, M, Blacksmith, -, ME, 425, 425, HORR. In HH of Thos. W. Beatey m 24 born SC.
RIPLEY, ELIZABETH, 65, F, None listed, -, MA, 799, 782, CHAS%. In HH of Thomas S. Jones m 45 born SC.
RIPLEY, N.F., 40, M, Shop keeper, -, MA, 112, 104, CHAS-.
RIPLEY, S.P., 45, M, Merchant,-, CT, 547, 530, CHAS-.
ROBERTSON, R.W., 24, M, Clerk, -, CT, 101, 93, CHAS+. In Boarding House.
ROBINSON, GEO. O., 27, M, Professor of Music, -, NH, 128, 119, CHAS-. In HH of F.W. Saltus m 60 born SC.
ROCHE, ELLEN, 1, F, None listed, -, NH, 804, 787, CHAS%. In HH of John Berry m 35 born Ireland.
ROGERS, CHARLES, 30, M, Shoemaker, -, ME, 348, 348, SUMT. In HH of Robt. P. Rogers m 35 born ME.
ROGERS, ELIZABETH, 25, F, None listed, -, MA, 10, 9, CHAS$. In HH of Sidney Rogers m 25 born NY.
ROGERS, EMMELINE, 19, F, None listed, -, MA, 482, 439, CHAS. In Planters Hotel.
ROGERS, ROBT. P., 35, M, Shoemaker, -, ME, 348, 348, SUMT.
ROGERS, WM., 40, M, Merchant,-, CT, 3, 3, SUMT.
ROOT, LEVI, 32, M, Tinner, -, CT, 275, 281, RICH. In HH of John S. Due m 27 born SC.
ROWAND, ROBT, 43, M, Broker, -, CT, 252, 230, CHAS. Born New Haven, CT.
RUDDOCK, EMILY J., 8, F, None listed, -, CT, 752, 710, CHAS+. In HH of Theodore D. Ruddock m 30 born SC.
RUDDOCK, FRANCIS., 6, M, None listed, -, CT, 752, 710, CHAS+. In HH of Theodore D. Ruddock m 30 born SC.
RUDDOCK, SARAH, 28, F, None listed, -, CT, 752, 710, CHAS+. In HH of Theodore D. Ruddock m 30 born SC.
RUSSEL, JOHN, 31, M, Artist, -, MA, 264, 247, CHAS+.

S

SANDERS, JOHN M.,14, M, None listed, -, MA, 933, 913, CHAS-. In HH of Jos. Sanders m 38 born MA.
SANDERS, JOS., 38, M, Mason, -, MA, 933, 913, CHAS-.
SANDERS, LAVINA, 32, F, None listed, -, MA, 933, 913, CHAS-. In HH of Jos. Sanders m 38 born MA.
SANDFORD, EDWARD, 26, M, Clerk, -, CT, 368, 351, CHAS-. In HH of John Jeffords m 49 born SC.
SCHORB, MARY, 33, F, None listed, -, CT, 491, 491, FAIR. In HH of J.R. Schorb m 31 born Germany.

SCOTT, JOHANNA, 2, F, None listed, -, MA, 26, 23, CHAS$. In HH of William Scott m 30 born Ireland. Johanna Scott listed born Boston {MA}.
SCOTT, TABA., 45, F, None listed, -, MA, 220, 198, CHAS.
SCRIVEN, MRS., 45, F, None listed, -, MA, 151, 151, BEAU+. In HH of Dr. R.B. Scriven m 172 born SC.
SEELY, RICHARD S., 36, M, Episcopal Preacher, -, CT, 769, 770, FAIR.
SEWARD, A., 64, M, Merchant,-, RI, 176, 176, GEOR.
SHARPING, JOHN H., 65, M, Shoemaker, -, MA, 1217, 1217, ABB.
SHAVER, JACOB, 48, M, Farmer, -, MA, 2194, 2194, GREE.
SHAVER, JAY, 19, M, Clerk, -, MA, 2194, 2194, GREE. In HH of Jacob Shaver m 48 born MA.
SHAVER, LUCY, 23, F, None listed, -, MA, 2194, 2194, GREE. In HH of Jacob Shaver m 48 born MA.
SHAVER, SARAH, 47, F, None listed, -, MA, 2194, 2194, GREE. In HH of Jacob Shaver m 48 born MA.
SHELDON, WILLIAM B., 55, M, Farmer, -, RI, 224, 224, LAU.
SHELTON, MALCOLM A., 25, M, Merchant,-, CT, 197, 201, RICH. In HH of Gouveneur M. Thompson m 48 born CT.
SHERMAN, B., 34, M, Miller/sawmill, -, MA, 74, 74, GEOR. In HH of R.E. Fraser m 32 born SC. B. Sherman a Miller at Steam sawmill.
SHERMAN, GEORGE, 50, M, School Teacher, -, MA, 579, 580, AND*.
SIMMINS, THOMAS, 25, M, Mariner, -, MA, 40, 37, CHAS-. Listed as prisoner.
SIMMONS, MARY J.,45, F, None listed, -, RI, 4, 4, LEX. In HH of Thos. H. Simmons m 55 Physician born SC. Census date stated Mary J . Simmons born New Port, RI.
SIMMONS, SARAH E., 24, F, None listed, -, RI, 4, 4, LEX. In HH of Thos. H. Simmons m 55 Physician born SC. Census date stated Sarh E. Simmons born New Port, RI.
SMALL, JOHN, 25, M, Mariner, -, MA, 337, 311, CHAS. In HH of William H. Fowler m 38 running Boarding House born England.
SMILEY, HARRIET, 12, F, None listed, -,VT, 2302, 2302, GREE. In Hotel.
SMILEY, NANCY, 42, F, None listed, -,VT, 2302, 2302, GREE. In Hotel.
SMILEY, T.H., 46, M, Dagartype, -,VT, 2302, 2302, GREE. In Hotel.
SMITH, CALEB, 44, M, None listed, -, MA, 304, 280, CHAS+.
SMITH, E., 39, M, Coach Trimmer, -, MA, 244, 229, CHAS+. In Boarding House rum by Ellen Pratt.
SMITH, HENRY, 36, M, Mariner, -, MA, 362, 333, CHAS. In Boarding House.
SMITH, HENRY, 25, M, Clerk, -, MA, 836, 816, CHAS-. In

Boarding House.
SMITH, JANIUS?, 50, M, Farmer, -, CT, 1273, 1273, GREE.
SMITH, JOHN B., 33, M, Lawyer, -, NH, 68, 68, YORK+. In Hotel.
SMITH, P.F., 42, M, Teacher, -,VT, 880, 860, CHAS-.
SMITH, PHOEBE, 75, F, None listed, -, RI, 577, 535, CHAS+. In HH of Eliza L. Smith f 55 born MD.
SMITH, WALTER, 26, M, Teacher, -, NH, 102, 102, BEAU*. In HH of Martha Davis f 41 born SC.
SPENCER, CHARLES, 29, M, Merchant,-, CT, 2, 2, SUMT.
SPENCER, ISAAC, 45, M, Coach maker, -, CT, 284, 284, YORK.
SPERRY, D.A., 31, M, Mechanic,-, CT, 3, 3, GEOR.
SPERRY, FRANCES, 17, F, None listed, -, CT, 3, 3, GEOR. In HH of D.A. Sperry m 31 born CT.
SPINCER, ELILSHA, 31, M, Merchant,-, CT, 5, 5, SUMT.
SPINK, ALONZO, 14, M, None listed, -, MA, 815, 795, CHAS-. In HH of J.D. Wright m 30 born England.
SPINK, WHITLEY, 31, M, Overseer/Mill, -, RI, 1723, 1724, EDGE. In HH of Hiram Jordan m 36, landlord, born SC.
STAYNE, CHARLOTTE, 25, F, None listed, -, CT, 92, 104, CHAS. In HH of Chs. C. White m 25 born CT.
STEPHENS, ETTA, 4, F, None listed, -, RI, 114, 114, GEOR. In HH of J.G. Stephens m 55 born RI.

STEPHENS, J.G., 55, M, Clerk, -, RI, 114, 114, GEOR.
STEPHENS, JAMES F., 30, M, Clerk, -, RI, 114, 114, GEOR. In HH of J.G. Stephens m 55 born RI.
STEPHENS, SARAH C., 22, F, None listed, -, RI, 114, 114, GEOR. In HH of J.G. Stephens m 55 born RI.
STEVENS, SAMUEL, 42, M, Planter, -, CT, 469, 469, EDGE.
STEVENSON, W., 25, M, Merchant,-, MA, 836, 816, CHAS-. In Boarding House.
STILLMAN, JAMES, 50, M, CH Inspector, -, CT, 310, 294, CHAS-.
STINT, LOUISA, 70, F, None listed, -, CT, 73, 73, CHAS^.
STINT, MINERVA, 34, F, None listed, -, CT, 73, 73, CHAS^. In HH of Louisa Stint f 70 born CT.
STOCKER, CHARLOTTE H., 38, F, None listed, -, ME, 497, 451, CHAS. In Boarding House.
STOCKER, REBECCA, 17, F, None listed, -, CT, 497, 451, CHAS. In Boarding House.
STOWE, SARAH, 50, F, None listed, -, MA, 15, 13, CHAS-. In HH of Silas Stowe m 39 born MA.
STOWE, SILAS, 39, M, Accountant, -, MA, 15, 13, CHAS-.
STRATTON, JAMES H., 37, M, Farmer, -, MA, 980, 957, CHAS%.
STRATTON, SAMUEL E., 34, M, Saddler, -, CT, 89, 90, RICH. Note: dwelling 89/family 90 followed 43/44, apparently copied out of order.
STREET, MARTHA E., 30, F, None listed, -, MA, 584, 542, CHAS+. In HH of Henry C. Street

m 30 born SC.
SWAIN, C.H., 26, M, Teacher, -, CT, 795, 795, KERS. In HH of J.C. Haile m 50 born SC.
SWIFT, HANNAH, 47, F, None listed, -, MA, 470, 428, CHAS. In HH of Thomas B. Swift m 55 born MA.
SWIFT, THOMAS B., 55, M, City Police, -, MA, 470, 428, CHAS.
SWORDS, MARIA, 59, M, Cloth dreper, -, CT, 237, 222, CHAS-. Poor House.

T

TAFT, A.R., 40, M, Merchant., -, MA, 610, 568, CHAS+.
TAYLOR, AUGUSTA, 21, F, None listed, -, CT, 26, 26, EDGE. In HH of W.W. Goodman m 28 born MA.
TAYLOR, C.M., 30, F, None listed, -, MA, 822, 780, CHAS+. In HH of J.H. Taylor m 40 born MA.
TAYLOR, E.J., 25, M, Carriage maker, -, MA, 26, 26, EDGE. In HH of W.W. Goodman m 28 born MA.
TAYLOR, ELIZA, 35, F, None listed, -, MA, 822, 780, CHAS+. In HH of J.H. Taylor m 40 born MA.
TAYLOR, ELLEN, 20, F, None listed, -, MA, 822, 780, CHAS+. In HH of J.H. Taylor m 40 born MA.
TAYLOR, J.H., 40, M, Merchant,-, MA, 822, 780, CHAS+.
THAYER, ANN C., 30, F, None listed, -, MA, 882, 840, CHAS+. In Charleston Hotel.
THAYER, CHARLES J., 53, M, Boot/Shoemaker, -, MA, 511, 515, AND.
THAYER, H. B., 28, M, Merchant,-, MA, 2020, 2026, EDGE. In HH of J.W. Stokes m 45 born SC. H.B. Thayer born Boston, MA.
THAYER, T., 35, M, Merchant,-, MA, 882, 840, CHAS+. In Charleston Hotel.
THOMPSON, ELIZABETH, 32, F, None listed, -, MA, 237, 222, CHAS-. Poor House.
THOMPSON, GOUV-ENEUR {sic} M., 38, M, Merchant,-, CT, 197, 201, RICH.
THOMPSON, HENRY C., 16, M, Clerk, -, CT, 197, 201, RICH. In HH of Gouveneur M. Thompson m 48 born CT.
THORTON, ELLZH., 65, F, None listed, -, MA, 820, 820, KERS. In HH of P. Thorton m 70 born NJ.
TIBBETS, J.D., 41, M, Shoe/bootmaker, -, ME, 43, 43, EDGE.
TOBY, KENNY?, 45, M, Shoe dealer, -, MA, 82, 82, GEOR.
TRASK, JAMES W., 33, M, Merchant,-, MA, 422, 433, RICH.
TROTH, ELIZABETH, 36, F, None listed, -, MA, 73, 73, YORK+. In HH of John T. Lindesay m 25 born York Dist., SC.
TROU, ESTHER D., 25, F, None listed, -, MA, 683, 663, CHAS-. In HH of A.W. Trou m 30 born Bermuda.

TROUT, THOMAS, 50, M, Merchant,-, MA, 870, 850, CHAS-.
TROWBRIDGE, MARVIN, 52, M, Cabinetmaker, -, CT, 2313, 2313, ABB.
TRYON, E., 32, M, Merchant,-, CT, 818, 818, KERS.
TRYON, L.A., 28, F, None listed, -, CT, 818, 818, KERS. In HH of E. Tryon m 32 born CT.
TUCKERMAN, NATHA-NIEL, 57, M, Miller, -, NH, 1017, 1018, FAIR.
TUPPER, DORATHEA, 24, F, None listed, -,VT, 45, 45, SPART. In HH of D.C. Judd m 50 born MA.
TUPPER, TRIS., 60, M, Merchant,-, ME, 254, 232, CHAS.
TUTTLE, GEO. W., 36, M, Baker, -, CT, 779, 759, CHAS-. In HH of John Ogeman m 26 born Germany.
TUTTLE, J.L., REV., 40, M, Minister,-, ME, 233, 211, CHAS. In HH of Charles Love m 40 born Scotland.
TUTTLE, JOSEPH, 36, M, None listed, -, CT, 3, 3, GEOR. In HH of D.A. Sperry m 31 born CT.
TUTTLE, M.A., 45, M, Farmer, -, CT, 40, 40, LANC*.
TUTTLE, SELOMA A., 29, F, None listed, -, CT, 779, 759, CHAS-. In HH of John Ogeman m 26 born Germany.
TWEEDY, WILLIAM, 25, M, Clerk, -, CT, 692, 672, CHAS-. In HH of E.G. Brown m 41 born CT.
TWING, JAMES, 54, M, School Teacher, -, MA, 293, 296, MAR.

TWOMLEY, ENOCH, 32, M, Stone mason, -, NH, 559, 559, UNION. In HH of Charles Gowing m 54 born VT.

U

USHER, JOHN, 50, M, Commercial merchant, -, RI, 2044, 2050, EDGE.
USHER, MARY J., 41, F, None listed, -, CT, 2044, 2050, EDGE. In HH of John Usher m 50 born RI.

W

WADDELL, CATHERINE, 18, F, None listed, -, ME, 534, 570, RICH. In HH of John Waddell m 49 born Ireland.
WADDELL, ROBERT, 20, M, Mechanic, -, ME, 534, 570, RICH. In HH of John Waddell m 49 born Ireland.
WADE, DAVID, 23, M, Mariner, -, MA, 351, 324, CHAS. In Boarding House.
WADE, WILLIAM, 39, M, Mariner, -, MA, 351, 324, CHAS. In Boarding House.
WALKER, GEORGE, 45, M, Boot maker, -, NH, 160, 147, CHAS*.
WALKER, JOHN, 32, M, Clerk, -, MA, 473, 456, CHAS-. In HH of Margaret M. McKenzie f 35 born SC.
WALKER, THOMAS P., 17, F, None listed, -, CT, 396, 406, RICH. In HH of William W. Walker m 42 born SC.

WALLER, WILLARD, 55, M, Engineer,-, CT, 41, 41, GEOR.
WALLEY, WILLIAM, 13, M, None listed, -, MA, 1974, 1980, EDGE. In HH of William Hasy ?, m 26 born MA.
WALLICE, JAMES, 50, M, Mason, -, MA, 1258, 1258, GREE.
WARD, CHARLOTTE, 13, F, None listed, -, CT, 13, 13, EDGE. In HH of Samuel Brooks m 50 born Middlesex, CT. Charlotte Ward born Middlesex, CT.
WARD, E.M., 45, F, Milliner,-, CT, 47, 47, EDGE.
WARD, ELLEN, 12, F, None listed, -, MA, 1723, 1724, EDGE. In HH of Hiram Jordan m 36, landlord, born SC.
WARD, WILLIAM, 29, M, None listed, -, MA, 118, 132, CHAS. In HH of Mary Ward f 26 born SC. William Ward born Boston, MA.
WARD, WILLIAM, 9, M, None listed, -, MA, 118, 132, CHAS. In HH of Mary Ward f 26 born SC. William Ward born Boston, MA.
WARDE, G.W., 43, M, Farmer, -, ME, 40, 40, HORR.
WARREN, EBEN, 22, M, Teacher, -, MA, 31, 32, AND. In HH of Thos. J. Sloan m 20 born SC.
WATSON, DUNHAM, 60, M, Mariner, -, MA, 260, 238, CHAS.
WEAR, HANNAH, 64, F, None listed, -, MA, 508, 474, CHAS*. In HH of John Wear m 78 born England.
WEATHESBY, JOEL, 50, M, Shoe store, -, MA, 540, 523, CHAS-. In Merchants Hotel.
WEAVER, JOHN, 52, M, Farmer, -, RI, 912, 912, GREE.
WEBB, MICHAEL, 58, M, Master mariner, -, ME, 105, 117, CHAS.
WEBB, NEWELL, 32, M, Planter, -, MA, 293, 299, RICK+.??? Is this Pick?? Rich?
WELLS, O.H., 46, M, Printer/editor, -, MA, 2337, 2337, GREE.
WELLS, WILLIS, 55, M, Farmer, -, MA, 2345, 2345, GREE. In HH of J.F. Heim m 33 born Germany.
WEST, C.H., 52, M, Ship chandler, -, MA, 157, 140, CHAS.
WEYMAN, MARGARET, 28, F, None listed, -, MA, 490, 445, CHAS. In HH of Stephen Weyman m 30 born MA.
WEYMAN, STEPHEN, 30, M, Laborer, -, MA, 490, 445, CHAS.
WHALY, ELIZ., 25, F, None listed, -, CT, 660, 660, BARN. In HH of John Whaly m 40 born CT.
WHALY, JOHN, 40, M, Planter, -, CT, 660, 660, BARN.
WHEELER, BARNET F., 35, M, Coach maker, -, CT, 53, 53, YORK+.
WHIPPLE, ARNOLD J., 26, M, Stonecutter, -, RI, 346, 346, YORK. In HH of James Ballou m 37 born RI.
WHITE, ALMERA., 48, F, None listed, -, CT, 92, 104, CHAS. In HH of Chs. C. White m 25 born CT.
WHITE, CHS. C., 25, M, Master Mariner, -, CT, 92, 104, CHAS.
WHITE, D.W., 35, F, None listed, -, MA, 281, 258, CHAS. In HH of Edward B. White m 45 born SC.

WHITE, ELIPHA, 54, M, Clergyman, -, MA, 30, 30, CHAS^.
WHITE, WILLLIAM T., 26, M, Tinner, -, ME, 243, 248, RICH. In HH of John J. Walter m 48 born PA.
WHITMAN, D., 60, M, Cabinet maker, -, MA, 3183, 3183, SPART.
WHITNEY, F.H., 34, M, Soap & Cable Manufacturer,-, MA, 628, 620, CHAS%. Born: Boston, {MA}
WHITRIDGE, JOSHUA, 61, M, Physician, -, RI, 126, 126, CHAS^.
WIER, JULIA E., 22, F, None listed, -, NH, 1809, 1809, ABB. In HH of Ephraim P. Calhoun m 48 born SC.
WIER, PHEOBE, 50, F, None listed, -, NH, 1809, 1809, ABB. In HH of Ephraim P. Calhoun m 48 born SC.
WILCUT, JOSEPH, 33, M, Farmer, -, MA, 1177, 1177, LAU.
WILD, T.B.J., 28, M, Lieut. U.S.A., -, ME, 47, 43, CHAS$. In HH of John Ewing m 50 born MA.
WILLARD, C., 41, M, Farmer, -, CT, 718, 718,HORR.
WILLIAMS, H.H., 46, M, Merchant,-, MA, 1004, 982, CHAS-.
WILLIAMS, JOHN, 25, M, Mariner, -, MA, 40, 37, CHAS-. Listed as prisoner.
WILLIAMS, JOHN J., 61, M, Shoe/Boot maker, -, CT, 1001, 1001, LAU.
WILLINGTON, PETER, 45, M, Shop keeper, -, MA, 133, 124, CHAS-.

WILLIS, HENRY, 58, M, Broker, -, MA, 822, 805, CHAS%.
WILMOT, FRANCES, 8, F, None listed, -, CT, 7, 7, GEOR. In HH of Saml. Wilmot m 55 born CT.
WILMOT, MINERVA, 28, F, None listed, -, CT, 7, 7, GEOR. In HH of Saml. Wilmot m 55 born CT.
WILMOT, SAML., 55, M, Silversmith, -, CT, 7, 7, GEOR.
WILMOT, WM. F., 15, M, None listed, -, CT, 7, 7, GEOR. In HH of Saml. Wilmot m 55 born CT.
WILSON, JOHN, 48, M, Taylor, -, MA, 243, 221, CHAS. Born Boston, MA.
WILSON, MARY, 29, F, None listed, -, ME, 47, 47, KERS. In HH of Thos. Wilson m 28 born Ireland.
WING, FRANCES, 23, M, Manager RR, -, MA, 293, 293, YORK. In HH of John Steele m 65 born York Dist., SC.
WINKLER, A.T., 24, F, None listed, -, RI, 21, 21, BEAU+. In HH of E.J. Winkler m 26 born GA.
WINNSLOWE, GEORGE, 35, M, Mechanic,-, MA, 291, 291, LAU.
WITHINGTON, HIRAM, 35, M, Clerk, -, CT, 177, 177, COLL+.
WOODEN, AUGUST, 45, M, Tanner, -, CT, 1435, 1435, SPART.
WOODEN, CHARLES, 15, M, None listed, -, CT, 1435, 1435, SPART. In HH of August Wooden m 45 born CT.
WOODEN, MARY, 37, F, None listed, -, CT, 1435, 1435, SPART.

In HH of August Wooden m 45 born CT.
WOODEN, WALTER, 18, M, Farmer, -, CT, 1435, 1435, SPART. In HH of August Wooden m 45 born CT.
WOOLEY, AMANDA, 34, F, None listed, -, ME, 424, 383, CHAS+.
WRIGHT, JULIA, 28, F, None listed, -, MA, 815, 795, CHAS-. In HH of J.D. Wright m 30 born England.
WRIGHT, MELESIA, 11, F, None listed, -, MA, 815, 795, CHAS-. In HH of J.D. Wright m 30 born England.
WRINGES, REBECCA, 56, F, None listed, -, MA, 555, 538, CHAS-. In HH of Seth Prior m 37 born SC.
WYLER, ELIZABETH, 39, F, None listed, -, MA, 671, 629, CHAS+. In HH of Vincent Wyler m 47 born England.
WYMAN, J.W., 49, M, MD & Planter, -, MA, 104, 104, BEAU*.

§

Section II

Migration to South Carolina: Mid-Atlantic States, 1850 Census

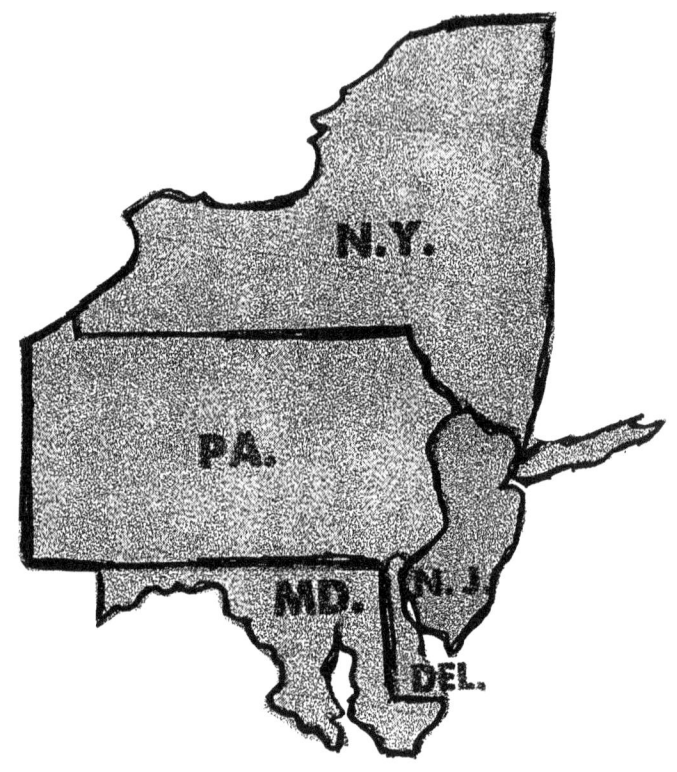

Mid Atlantic States

Abbreviation	State	Population in SC
NY:	New York	892
NJ:	New Jersey	182
PA:	Pennsylvania	358
DE:	Delaware	16
DC:	District of Columbia	30
MD:	Maryland	<u>329</u>
	Total	1792

A

ABRAHAMS, ESTHER, 12, F, None listed, -,NY, 821, 821, SUMT. In HH of Aaron Abrahams m 46 born Poland.
ABRAHAMS, GARROTT, 4, M, None listed, -,NY, 821, 821, SUMT. In HH of Aaron Abrahams m 46 born Poland.
ABRAHAMS, REBECCA, 32, F, None listed, -,NY, 821, 821, SUMT. In HH of Aaron Abrahams m 46 born Poland.
ABY, PETER, 60, M, Mechanic, -, PA, 650, 650, SPART.
ABY, THEBA, 25, F, None listed, -, PA, 650, 650, SPART. In HH of Peter Aby m 60 born PA.
ADAMS, FRANCIS, 10, F, None listed, -,NY, 1067, 1067, PICK+. In HH of Plecidia Adams f 53 born SC.
ADAMS, HARRIOT, 26, F, None listed, -,NY, 782, 762, CHAS-. In HH of Benjamin Lequere m 60 born SC.
ADAMS, W. S., 30, M, Bricklayer, -,NY, 782, 762, CHAS-. In HH of Benjamin Lequere m 60 born SC.
ADAMS, WILLIAM, 45, M, Music teacher, -,NY, 483, 483, LAU.
ADDY, T. CLARK, 39, M, Painter, -,NY, 430, 430, LEX.
ALDEN, MARY, 30, F, None listed, -, MD, 263, 263, KERS. In HH of George Alden m 35 born MA.
ALLASON, THOMAS, 33, M, Sadler, -, NJ, 818, 798, CHAS-.

ALLENDER, BENJAMIN, 44, M, Farmer, -, MD, 1012, 1012, GREE.
ALLISON, GEORGE, 32, M, Shoemaker, -, PA, 473, 431, CHAS.
ALLISON, JAMES, 7, M, None listed, -, PA, 473, 431, CHAS. In HH of George Allison m 32 born PA.
ALLISON, JANE, 24, F, None listed, -, PA, 95, 88, CHAS-. In HH of Samuel Champlin m 60 born PA.
ALLISON, MARY, 24, F, None listed, -,NY, 237, 222, CHAS-. Poor House.
ALLISON, MARY ANN, 24, F, None listed, -, PA, 473, 431, CHAS. In HH of George Allison m 32 born PA.
ALLISON, SUSAN, 9, F, None listed, -, PA, 473, 431, CHAS. In HH of George Allison m 32 born PA.
ALSNER, JOSEPH, 39, M, Seaman, -,NY, 326, 301, CHAS. In HH of William Rollins m 40.
ANDERSON, ANN, 40, F, None listed, -, MD, 2325, 2325, GREE. In HH of Juliet Anderson f 55 born MD.
ANDERSON, ELLEN L., 26, F, None listed, -, NJ, 692, 711, RICH. In HH of Robert C. Anderson m 35 born NJ.
ANDERSON, JULIET, 55, F, None listed, -, MD, 2325, 2325, GREE.
ANDERSON, ROBERT, 29, M, Merchant, -, NJ, 376, 385, RICH. In HH of William L. Reynolds m 22 born SC.

ANDERSON, ROBERT, 29, M, Merchant, -, NY, 202, 206, RICH. In HH of Amos Bostwick m 31 born CT.
ANDERSON, ROBERT, 29, M, Merchant, -, NJ, 376, 385, RICH.
ANDERSON, ROBERT C., 35, M, Merchant, -, NJ, 692, 711, RICH.
ANDERSON, W.W., 61, M, Physician, -, MD, 1215, 1215, SUMT.
ANDREWS, J.W., 40, M, Overseer, -, NY, 40, 37, CHAS.-. Listed as prisoner, date 1850.
ANDREWS, MARGARET, 6, F, None listed, -, NJ, 1088, 1065, CHAS-. In HH of H.S. Hayden m 35 born CT.
ANSELL, CHARLES, 10, M, None listed, -, PA, 816, 796, CHAS-. In HH of John Ansell m 34 born Germany.
ANSELL, JOHN, 7, M, None listed, -, PA, 816, 796, CHAS-. In HH of John Ansell m 34 born Germany.
ANTWERP, ELIZABETH, 21, F, None listed, -, NY, 188, 192, RICH. In Hotel.
ANTWERP, GAWET V., 40, M, Tailor, -, NY, 188, 192, RICH. In Hotel.
ANZALY, E.M., 50, F, None listed, -, NY, 20, 20, KERS. In HH of O.M. Winged m 34 born SC.
APPLEBY, CHARLES, 45, M, Mariner, -, NY, 115, 107, CHAS+. In HH of Thomas Gleave m 32 born England.
ARCHER, BENJAMIN, 40, M, Coach Trimmer, -, NY, 290, 274, CHAS-.
ARNOLD, ANN, 27, F, None listed, -, NY, 20, 23, CHAS. In HH of Rachael Tunno f 70 black born SC.
ARNOLD, LOUISA, 57, F, None listed, -, PA, 575, 558, CHAS-.
ARNOLD, SARAH, 10, F, None listed, -, NY, 20, 23, CHAS. In HH of Rachael Tunno f 70 black born SC.
ASHBY, ALICE, 25, F, None listed, -, NY, 149, 139, CHAS-.
ASHLEY, ABRAM, 77, M, Farmer, -, MD, 1330, 1330, ABB.
ASHLEY, ELINEZAR, 46, M, Farmer, -, MD, 233, 234, AND*.
ASHLEY, MOSES, JR., 78, M, None listed, -, MD, 1318, 1318, ABB.
ASHLEY, SUSAN, 72, F, None listed, -, MD, 1318, 1318, ABB. In HH of Moses Ashley Jr. m 78 born MD.
ASHLEY, WILLIAM, 47, M, Hireling, -, MD, 1368, 1368, ABB.
ATHERTON, JAMES D., 2, M, None listed, -, NJ, 1628, 1628, EDGE. In HH of Thomas Atherton m 24 born England.
AUSTIN, L.A., 26, M, Acct., -, NY, 869, 869, KERS.
AVANTS, N.B., 52, M, Merchant, -, MD, 79, 79, KERS.
AVANTS, N.D., 43, F, None listed, -, MD, 79, 79, KERS. In HH of N.B. Avants m 52 born MD.
AVERY, OTIS, 45, M, Surgeon Dentist, -, NY, 532, 568, RICH. In HH of Shubel Blanding m 55 born MA.

B

BACHMAN, JOHN REV., 59, M, Minister, Lutheran, -, NJ, 787, 770, CHAS%.
BACKMAN, WILLIAM, 27, M, 2C. mate, -, NY, 326, 301, CHAS. In HH of William Rollins m 40 born {-}.
BAILEY, NANCY, 75, F, None listed, -, MD, 248, 248, FAIR. In HH of Andrew McDaniel m 34 born SC.
BAIRD, LOUIS, 30, M, Millwright, -, MD, 462, 462, ABB.
BAKER, H.F., 35, M, Merchant, -, PA, 608, 589, CHAS-.
BAKER, MARY, 26, F, None listed, -, PA, 608, 589, CHAS-. In HH of H.F. Baker m 35 born PA.
BAKER, REGINA, 6, F, None listed, -, PA, 608, 589, CHAS-. In HH of H.F. Baker m 35 born PA.
BANCROFT, CAROLINE, 34, F, None listed, -, NY, 882, 840, CHAS+. In Charleston Hotel.
BANKHEAD, JOHN, 66, M, Planter, -, PA, 835, 835, UNION.
BANKS, C.R., 40, M, Merchant, -, NY, 134, 125, CHAS+. In HH of J.B. Nixon m 31 born NY.
BANKS, SAMUEL, 40, M, Physician, -, NY, 134, 125, CHAS+. In HH of J.B. Nixon m 31 born NY.
BANSKETT, S.E., 40, F, None listed, -, NY, 339, 339, EDGE. IN HH of John Banskett m 50 born NC.
BARBER, THOS., 32, M, Farmer, -, NJ, 313, 313, CHES. In HH of John Furguston m 37 born SC.

BARDEN, REBECCA, 60, F, None listed, -, NJ, 163, 163, CHES. In HH of James Stroud m 34 born SC.
BARKER, MARGARET, 80, F, None listed, -, MD, 191, 191, GREE. In HH of Biddleton Cox m 65 born SC.
BARKER, THOMAS, 22, M, Servant, -, PA, 882, 840, CHAS+. In Charleston Hotel.
BARKERLOO, WILLIAM, 23, M, Clerk, -, NY, 389, 399, RICH.
BARLOW, SAMUEL, 27, M, Laborer, -, NY, 237, 222, CHAS-. Poor House.
BARNES, JAMES, 31, M, Carpenter, -, NY, 1084, 1106, CHAS%.
BARNET, L.S., 40, M, Merchant, -, NY, 482, 439, CHAS. In Planters Hotel.
BARNS, ROBERT, 75, M, None listed, -, PA, 872, 872, YORK.
BARRS, CHARLES, 23, M,, -, NY, 699, 699, HORR.
BARRY, JOHN, 29, M, Seaman, -, NY, 326, 301, CHAS. On Steam Ship Southerner.
BARTELL, F., 40, M, Clerk, -, NY, 937, 917, CHAS-. In Boarding House.
BARTELL, LAURA, 30, F, None listed, -, NY, 937, 917, CHAS-. In Boarding House.
BARTELL, MARY, 38, F, None listed, -, NY, 937, 917, CHAS-. In Boarding House.
BARTLISS, MARY, 68, F, None listed, -, MD, 1012, 989, CHAS%. In HH of W.H. Bartliss m 33 born SC.

BATES, JEHIL, 50, M, Mechanic, -, NY, 12, 12, GEOR.
BEACH, JOSEPH, 37, M, Merchant, -, NY, 1062, 1040, CHAS%.
BEACH, SUSAN, 32, F, None listed, -, NY, 1062, 1040, CHAS%. In HH of Joseph Beach m 37 born NY.
BEAN, WILLIAM H., 31, M, Merchant, -, NJ, 395, 377, CHAS-. In Boarding House.
BEANDON, JOHN, 63, M, Blacksmith, -, PA, 621, 621, YORK.
BEATY, WM. Q., 54, M, Baptist Minister, -, PA, 479, 479, MARL.
BEAUGARD, JOHN, 36, M, Tinner, -, NY, 426, 395, CHAS*. In HH of Thomas Powell m 35 born Scotland.
BECK, ANN, 46, F, None listed, -, PA, 547, 562, RICH. In HH of Charles Beck m 58 born MA.
BECK, MARY S., 8, F, None listed, -, MD, 364, 364, ABB. In HH of James L. Beck m 31 born GA.
BECK, SUSAN M., 29, F, None listed, -, MD, 364, 364, ABB. In HH of James L. Beck m 31 born GA.
BECK, WILLIAM A., 6, M, None listed, -, MD, 364, 364, ABB. In HH of James L. Beck m 31 born GA.
BECKLEY, ANN, 37, F, None listed, -, NY, 778, 761, CHAS%. In HH of Thomas Keegan m 39 born Ireland.
BECKLEY, M., 41, M, Laborer, -, NY, 778, 761, CHAS%. In HH of Thomas Keegan m 39 born Ireland.
BECKLEY, WILLIAM, 6, M, None listed, -, NY, 778, 761, CHAS%. In HH of Thomas Keegan m 39 born Ireland.
BECKMAN, ELIZABETH, 49, F, None listed, -, PA, 330, 313, CHAS-. In HH of John Mealey m 74 born SC. {Note Family No. listed as 350,should be 330}.
BEDELL, CHARLES A., 33, M, None listed, -, NY, 228, 233, RICH. {Page out of order}, follows HH 177/181.
BEEKMAN, CHAS., 30, M, Clerk, -, NY, 692, 672, CHAS-. In HH of E.G. Brown m 41 born CT.
BEHAN, MARGARET, 10, F, None listed, -, NY, 1158, 1137, CHAS%. In HH of Thomas Behan m 40 born Ireland.
BEHAN, MARY, 8, F, None listed, -, NY, 1158, 1137, CHAS%. In HH of Thomas Behan m 40 born Ireland.
BELDEN, A.D., 44, M, Tailor, -, NY, 9, 9, LANC. In Hotel.
BELL, ABNER, 62, M, Wagon maker, -, PA, 27, 27, YORK.
BELL, ISAAC, 72, M, Farmer, -, PA, 2370, 2374, EDGE.
BELL, MARGARET, 33, F, None listed, -, MD, 320, 295, CHAS. In HH of Elizabeth Moore f 37 born PA.
BELL, MARY M., 7, F, None listed, -, PA, 163, 150, CHAS*. In HH of Samuel Bell m 30 born NC.
BELL, SARAH, 25, F, None listed, -, PA, 163, 150, CHAS*. In HH of Samuel Bell m 30 born NC.

BELTON, CATHARINE, 45, F, None listed, -, NJ, 145, 145, BEAU-. In HH of Dr. Charles Belton m 55 born NJ.
BELTON, CHARLES, DR., 55, M, Dr/Planter, -, NJ, 145, 145, BEAU-.
BENNET, JAMES, 56, M, None listed, -, NY, 196, 196, YORK.
BENNETT, CATHERINE, 11, F, None listed, -, NY, 38, 38, SPART. In HH of W.C. Bennett m 37 born NY.
BENNETT, W.C., 37, M, Dentist, -, NY, 38, 38, SPART.
BENNETT, WILLIAM, 40, M, Mariner, -, NY, 334, 308, CHAS.
BENSON, HENRY, 25, M, Lieut. U.S.A., -, NJ, 47, 43, CHAS$. In HH of John Ewing m 50 born MA.
BENTEQUE, DESIREE, 20, F, None listed, -, NY, 105, 102, CHAS*. In HH of William Carpenter m 40 born RI.
BERLIN, R., 30, M, Merchant, -, MD, 93, 93, CHAS%.
BERNARD, HENRY, 12, M, None listed, -, NY, 992, 971, CHAS-. In HH of S.B. Bernard m 38 born France.
BERRY, GILBERT, 6, M, None listed, -, NJ, 236, 241, RICH. In HH of Milo H. Berry m 30 born NJ.
BERRY, JULIA E., 28, F, None listed, -, NY, 236, 241, RICH. In HH of Milo H. Berry m 30 born NJ.
BERRY, M., CAPT., 40, M, Master mariner, -, PA, 326, 301, CHAS. On Steam Ship Southerner.
BERRY, MILO H., 30, M, Cabinetmaker, -, NJ, 236, 241, RICH.
BERRY, WILLIAM, 74, M, Farmer, -, MD, 886, 886, GREE.
BETTS, ELEANOR, 30, F, None listed, -, NY, 367, 340, CHAS*. In HH of Jose Stevens m 60 born Nassau, N.P.
BETTS, JAMES B., 35, M, Merchant, -, NY, 308, 284, CHAS+. In HH of Eliza Selleman f 69 born SC.
BIERFIELD, ISAAC, 45, M, Hotel Keeper, -, NY, 18, 18, NEWB.
BIERFIELD, SARAH, 42, F, None listed, -, NJ, 18, 18, NEWB. In HH of Isaac Bierfield born New YORK.
BIRD, EDWARD, 69, M, None listed, -, PA, 149, 149, YORK*.
BIRD, ELIZABETH, 49, F, None listed, -, MD, 1788, 1788, ABB. In HH of Thomas B. Bird 53 m born Greenwood, TN.
BIRD, SARAH F., 65, F, None listed, -, PA, 438, 396, CHAS.
BISHOP, JOHN, 86, M, Farmer, -, PA, 105, 105, CHES.
BLACK, JOHN, 23, M, Seaman, -, NY, 326, 301, CHAS. On Steam Ship Southerner.
BLACK, WILLIAM, 28, M, Mariner, -, NY, 124, 116, CHAS*.
BLACKENSHIFT, STEPHEN, 27, M, Engineer, -, NY, 113, 105, CHAS+. In HH of Peter Hanschild m 59 born Germany.
BLACKMAN, A., 23, M, Engineer, -, NY, 6, 6, CHAS. A. Blackman born Troy, NY, In HH of Eliza Feckling 51 born SC.
BLACKMAN, ALMIRA, 18, F, None listed, -, NY, 6, 6, CHAS.

Almira Blackman born Troy, NY. HH of Eliza Feckling 51 born SC.
BLACKWOOD, MARIA, 23, F, None listed, -, MD, 285, 262, CHAS. In Planters Hotel.
BLAN, GEO., 64, M, Farmer, -, MD, 861, 861, DARL.
BLAN, MARGARET, 70, F, None listed, -, MD, 861, 861, DARL. In HH of Geo. Blan m 64 born MD.
BLANCHAN, WILLIAM W., 24, M, Clerk, -, NY, 326, 301, CHAS. In HH of William Rollins m 40 born {-}.
BLANCHER, HENRY, 50, M, Ship carpenter, -, NY, 561, 561, HORR. In HH of John Smith m 25 born SC.
BLOOM, ALEXANDER, 36, M, Merchant, -, NY, 61, 55, CHAS+. In HH of Margaret Fancy f 65 mulatto born SC.
BOGART, PETER, 44, M, Laborer, -, NY, 764, 764, SUMT.
BOGGS, ROBERT, 30, M, Clerk, -, NY, 836, 816, CHAS-. In Boarding House.
BOLAN, MATILDA, 33, F, None listed, -, NY, 105, 105, BEAU+. In HH of James Bolan m 66 born SC.
BOLLINGER, WILLIAM, 32, M, Merchant, -, PA, 406, 417, RICH.
BONNER, CHARLES, 38, M, Stone cutter, -, PA, 63, 63, FAIR. In HH of Adna Johnson m 53 born CT.
BONNER, JOHN, 63, M, Carpenter, -, PA, 376, 338, CHAS+.
BONNER, SETH, 36, M, Stonemason, -, PA, 63, 63, FAIR. In HH of Adna Johnson m 53 born CT.
BOOZER, AMELIA, 25, F, None listed, -, PA, 34, 34, NEWB. In HH of David Boozer 55 m born SC.
BOSSWICK, CURRENEE, 21, F, None listed, -, NY, 562, 562, UNION. In HH of James Gage m 37 born SC.
BOSWELL, CATHERINE, 43, F, None listed, -, NY, 44, 44, CHAS2. In HH of Thomas J. Boswell m 51 born NC.
BOSWITH, C.O., 28, F, Teacher, -, NY, 93, 95, AND. In HH of John Hume m 51 born SC.
BOULWARE, BENJAMIN J., 56, M, Planter, -, PA, 941, 942, FAIR.
BOURS, E.N., 25, F, None listed, -, NY, 506, 456, CHAS. In HH of J.B. Bours f 55 born SC.
BOWCY, PRICE, 65, M, Farmer, -, MD, 2283, 2283, ABB.
BOWEN, ELIZABETH, 72, F, None listed, -, MD, 1602, 1602, GREE.
BOWEN, MARY, 84, F, None listed, -, PA, 780, 784, AND. HH of John Stephenson m 52 born SC.
BOWER, GEORGE S., 33, M, Cabinetmaker, -, NY, 194, 198, RICH.
BOWERS, JACOB, 25, M, Seaman, -, NY, 326, 301, CHAS. On Steam Ship Southerner.
BOWIE, CATHARINE, 66, F, None listed, -, MD, 2339, 2339, ABB.
BOWIE, HEZEKIAH, 58, M, Farmer, -, MD, 1577, 1577, ABB.

BOWIE, MARY, 38, F, None listed, -, MD, 2233, 2233, ABB. In HH of James P. Bowie m 41 born SC.
BOWIE, MATILDA, 28, F, None listed, -, MD, 2338, 2338, ABB. In HH of Henry B. Bowie 28 born MD.
BOWLINE, WILLIAM, 19, M, Mariner, -, NY, 41, 38, CHAS-.
BOWMAN, ALEXR. H., 47, M, Capt. Engineer, -, PA, 31, 31, CHAS!.
BOWMAN, ELIZA CLARE, 0, F, None listed, -, PA, 31, 31, CHAS!. In HH of Alexr H. Bowman m 47 born PA. Eliza Clare Bowman age 9/12 yr.
BOWMAN, ELIZABETH, 23, F, None listed, -, MD, 682, 640, CHAS+. In HH of Thomas Bowman m 27 born SC.
BOWMAN, ENLADIY, 5, F, None listed, -, PA, 31, 31, CHAS!. In HH of Alexr H. Bowman m 47 born PA.
BOWMAN, LOUISE, 3, F, None listed, -, PA, 31, 31, CHAS!. In HH of Alexr H. Bowman m 47 born PA.
BOYCE, SYDNEY, 40, M, Millwright, -, NY, 1552, 1552, EDGE.
BOYLE, JAMES, 24, M, Waiter, -, PA, 327, 302, CHAS. On Steam Ship Southerner.
BOYLE, M.A., 9, F, None listed, -, NY, 47, 43, CHAS$. In HH of John Ewing m 50 born MA.
BOYLE, MARY C., 56, F, None listed, -, PA, 868, 826, CHAS+. In HH of Elizabeth Gibson f 80 born Ireland.
BRADFORD, MARIA, 54, F, None listed, -, NJ, 17, 17, COLL. In HH of Jesse Bradford m 60 born MA.
BRADFORD, MARY, 68, F, None listed, -, MD, 1083, 1083, BARN. In HH of Randloph Bradford m 50 born MD.
BRADFORD, MARY, 39, F, None listed, -, MD, 1083, 1083, BARN. In HH of Randloph Bradford m 50 born MD.
BRADFORD, RANDLOPH, 50, M, MD {physician}, -, MD, 1083, 1083, BARN.
BRADLEY, CHARLES, 30, M, Shoe maker, -, NY, 2297, 2297, GREE. Listed as "In Jail".
BRADLEY, MITCHELL, 58, M, Farmer, -, PA, 925, 925, YORK.
BRADSHAW, JOHN, 13, M, None listed, -, NJ, 2338, 2338, GREE. In HH of William Erwin m 32 born Ireland.
BRADY, CATHERINE, 18, F, None listed, -, MD, 165, 155, CHAS-. In HH of Ellen Brady f 39 born Ireland.
BRADY, JAMES, 17, M, None listed, -, MD, 165, 155, CHAS-. In HH of Ellen Brady f 39 born Ireland.
BRADY, MARGARET, 19, F, None listed, -, PA, 165, 155, CHAS-. In HH of Ellen Brady f 39 born Ireland.
BRADY, PHILIP, 22, M, Moulder, -, NY, 165, 155, CHAS-. In HH of Ellen Brady f 39 born Ireland.
BRAN, HENRY, 29, M, Seaman, -, NY, 326, 301, CHAS. In HH of William Rollins m 40 born {-}.

BRANAUGH, EMILY, 25, F, None listed, -, MD, 147, 147, BEAU. In HH of John Fielding m 55 born Ireland.
BRAND, J., 28, M, Millright, -, MD, 11, 11, EDGE. In HH of J.L. Doby m 32, landlord, born SC.
BRANDT, HENRY, 25, M, Mariner, -, NY, 218, 196, CHAS. In HH of Chris. Nelson m 60 born Denmark.
BRANDT, JANE, 53, F, None listed, -, NY, 465, 423, CHAS+. In HH of T.C. Brandt m 55 born Germany.
BRANDT, ROBERT, 10, M, None listed, -, NY, 465, 423, CHAS+. In HH of T.C. Brandt m 55 born Germany.
BRANNACKER, HENRIETTA, 20, F, None listed, -, NY, 412, 371, CHAS+. In HH of Charles Brannacker m 26 born Germany.
BRATTON, JOHN, 55, M, Merchant, -, NY, 882, 840, CHAS+. In Charleston Hotel.
BRAWLEY, J., 30, M, Clerk, -, NY, 831, 811, CHAS-.
BREAKFORD, ALEXR., 30, M, Mariner, -, NY, 362, 333, CHAS. In Boarding House.
BRESIVE, SUSAN, 25, F, None listed, -, MD, 401, 374, CHAS*.
BRIGHTMAN, SOPHIA, 24, F, None listed, -, NY, 318, 292, CHAS*. In HH of William Brightman m 28 born NY.
BRIGHTMAN, WILLIAM, 28, M, Cabinet maker, -, NY, 318, 292, CHAS*.
BRISTOL, JANE M., 22, F, None listed, -, NY, 838, 818, CHAS-. In HH of T.M. Bristol m 30 born CT.
BRITTINGHAM, CELIA, 47, F, None listed, -, NJ, 1145, 1146, FAIR. In HH of Joshua Brittingham m 62 born KY.
BRONSON, MARTHA B., 24, F, None listed, -, PA, 345, 351, RICH. In HH of Hiram C. Bronson m 38 born Ct.
BROOKS, C.M., 44, F, None listed, -, NY, 13, 13, EDGE. In HH of Samuel Brooks m 50 born Middlesex, CT.
BROOKS, S., 34, F, Milliner, -, NJ, 852, 832, CHAS-. In HH of A.G. Parker f 38 born Germany.
BROOM, ANGELICA, 27, F, None listed, -,D.C., 26, 31, CHAS. Born Washington, D.C.. In HH of Moses Levy m 45 taven keeper born SC.
BROOM, JAMES, 30, M, Wharfinger, -,D.C., 26, 31, CHAS. Born Washington, D.C.. In HH of Moses Levy m 45 tavern keeper born SC.
BROW, HARRITT, 60, F, None listed, -, PA, 73, 73, MARL. In HH of B.D. Townsend m 32 merchant born SC.
BROWN, ANN, 36, F, None listed, -, NJ, 420, 403, CHAS-. In HH of Catherine Brown f 65 born NJ.
BROWN, CATHERINE, 65, F, None listed, -, NJ, 420, 403, CHAS-.
BROWN, E.G., JR., 7, M, None listed, -, NY, 692, 672, CHAS-. In HH of E.G. Brown m 41 born CT.
BROWN, EDWARD, 2, M, None listed, -, PA, 1005, 982, CHAS%. Under command of Major P.

Hagnes, Commanding Officer U.S. Arsenal.
BROWN, ELIZA, 48, F, None listed, -, NY, 141, 131, CHAS-.
BROWN, ELIZABETH, 75, F, None listed, -, MD, 1026, 1026, UNION. In HH of William K. Brown m 44 born SC.
BROWN, ELIZABETH, 28, F, None listed, -, PA, 638, 656, RICH. In HH of William S. Brown m 34 born NY.
BROWN, FANNY, 10, F, None listed, -, PA, 638, 656, RICH. In HH of William S. Brown m 34 born NY.
BROWN, HANNAH, 12, F, None listed, -, NJ, 445, 412, CHAS*. In HH of James H. Murrell m 36 born SC.
BROWN, HARRIET D., 44, F, None listed, -, PA, 70, 70, FAIR. In HH of William Alston m 47 born SC. Harriet D. Brown born Philadelphia.
BROWN, JAMES, 87, M, None, -, NJ, 420, 403, CHAS-. In HH of Catherine Brown f 65 born NJ.
BROWN, JOHN, 71, M, Farmer, -, MD, 2068, 2068, SPART.
BROWN, JUDITH, 54, F, None listed, -, NJ, 420, 403, CHAS-. In HH of Catherine Brown f 65 born NJ.
BROWN, JULIA B., 5, F, None listed, -, NJ, 445, 412, CHAS*. In HH of James H. Murrell m 36 born SC.
BROWN, MARY, 45, F, None listed, -, PA, 83, 77, CHAS-.
BROWN, MARY, 31, F, None listed, -, NY, 692, 672, CHAS-. In HH of E.G. Brown m 41 born CT.
BROWN, MARY, 18, F, None listed, -, NY, 338, 312, CHAS. In HH of Henry Pluger m 25 born Germany.
BROWN, N.R.M., 30, M, Teacher, -, NY, 685, 665, CHAS-. In Victoria Hotel.
BROWN, RACHEL, 70, F, None listed, -, MD, 443, 410, CHAS*. In HH of Julius Laidler f 34 born SC.
BROWN, RICHARD, 65, M, Planter, -, MD, 1023, 1023, UNION.
BROWN, THOMAS, 34, M, Laborer, -, NY, 237, 222, CHAS-. Poor House.
BROWN, WILLIAM, 65, M, Planter, -, MD, 1017, 1017, UNION.
BROWN, WILLIAM P., 27, M, Carpenter, -, MD, 2100, 2104, EDGE.
BROWN, WILLIAM S., 34, M, Civil engineer, -, NY, 638, 656, RICH.
BROWN, WILLIAM SR., 84, M, Farmer, -, PA, 291, 291, YORK*.
BRUCE, THOMAS, 78, M, None listed, -, MD, 623, 623, GREE.
BRUESTON, J.A., 46, M, None listed, -, NY, 27, 27, GEOR*.
BRULTE, MARY C., 20, F, None listed, -, PA, 520, 535, RICH. In HH of Alice H. Peers f 45 born England.
BRULTE, SARAH F., 17, F, None listed, -, PA, 520, 535, RICH. In HH of Alice H. Peers f 45 born England.
BRUNSMAN, C., 4, M, None listed, -, NY, 47, 43, CHAS$. In HH of John Ewing m 50 born MA.

BRUSE, WM. C., 44, M, Bank Officer, -, NY, 756, 714, CHAS+.
BUCKMASTER, EDWARD, 38, M, Corn Merchant, -, NY, 2088, 2092, EDGE.
BULL, EDMUND, 31, M, Brass Founder, -, NY, 291, 268, CHAS+.
BULLARD, MARY S., 44, F, None listed, -, NY, 410, 421, RICH. In HH of James J. Mackey m 32 born NY.
BURDET, EMMA, 17, F, None listed, -, NY, 149, 139, CHAS-. In HH of Alice Ashby f 25 born NY.
BURDGESS, ELIZA, 41, F, None listed, -, NY, 684, 703, RICH. In HH of William Burdgess m 39 born SC.
BURK, JOHN, 35, M, Cabinet maker, -, PA, 184, 167, CHAS. In Boarding House. John Burk born Philadelphia, PA.
BURKE, GEO. R., 25, M, Clerk, -, NY, 372, 355, CHAS-.
BURKE, JAMES, 44, M, Carpenter, -, MD, 310, 287, CHAS.
BURKE, JOHN, 30, M, Cabinet maker, -, PA, 986, 965, CHAS-. In HH of John Smyth m 35 born Scotland.
BURNS, JOHN, 20, M, Soda water Mfg., -, PA, 93, 86, CHAS-. In HH of A.P. Smith m 38 born England.
BURT, SAML., 22, M, None listed, -, NY, 717, 717, COLL. In HH of Dr. E.R. Henderson m 45 born SC.
BURTON, ELIZA, 24, F, None listed, -, PA, 137, 127, CHAS-.
BUSBY, G.W., 30, M, Bricklayer, -, NJ, 6, 6, CHAS-.

BUSH, WM., 25, M, Boot Frunder?, -, NY, 391, 355, CHAS. In HH of F.W. Theus m 28 born Germany.
BUTLER, M. J., 48, F, None listed, -, MD, 77, 77, EDGE.

C

CAFFREY, MARY, 28, F, None listed, -, MD, 213, 199, CHAS-. In HH of James Caffrey m 29 born SC.
CAKS, SUSAN, 25, F, None listed, -, MD, 616, 574, CHAS+. In HH of T.M. Caks m 29 born SC.
CALDWELL, ELIZABETH, 17, F, None listed, -, MD, 811, 791, CHAS-. In HH of John Caldwell m 53 born Scotland.
CALDWELL, ELIZABETH, 5, F, None listed, -, MD, 811, 791, CHAS-. In HH of John Caldwell m 53 born Scotland.
CALDWELL, JANE, 14, F, None listed, -, MD, 811, 791, CHAS-. In HH of John Caldwell m 53 born Scotland.
CALDWELL, JOHN, 3, M, None listed, -, MD, 811, 791, CHAS-. In HH of John Caldwell m 53 born Scotland.
CALHOUN, ANZIER, 24, F, None listed, -, NY, 870, 870, PICK+. In HH of Floreide Calhoun f 57 born SC.
CALHOUN, CARNELIA, 26, F, None listed, -,D.C., 870, 870, PICK+. In HH of Floreide Calhoun f 57 born SC.
CALHOUN, JAMES E., 24, M, None listed, -,D.C., 870, 870,

PICK+. In HH of Floreide Calhoun f 57 born SC.
CALHOUN, JOHN C., 27, F, Physician, -,D.C., 870, 870, PICK+. In HH of Floreide Calhoun f 57 born SC.
CAMPBELL, ELIAS, 38, M, Carriage maker, -, NY, 585, 585, MARL.
CAMPBELL, J., 42, M, Blacksmith, -, NJ, 252, 253, ORNG+. In HH of R.B. Flake, m 64, carriage maker born SC.
CAMPBELL, J., 42, M, Blacksmith, -, NJ, 254, 255, ORNG+. In HH of R.B. Flake m 64 born SC.
CAMPBELL, MARY T., 41, F, None listed, -, NY, 51, 51, KERS. In HH of Wm. B. Campbell m 42 born SC.
CAMPBELL, UZAL D., 25, M, Saddler, -, NJ, 277, 283, RICH.
CAMPBHELL, MARY, 60, F, None listed, -, PA, 1473, 1473, ABB. In HH of Bassel Maddox m 46 born SC.
CANE, NOAH, 42, M, Coach maker, -, NJ, 1853, 1853, SUMT.
CANNOVA, F., 38, M, Carpenter, -, PA, 462, 445, CHAS-. In HH of William Patterson m 34 born MD.
CANTLEY, G., 21, M, Merchant, -, NY, 721, 701, CHAS-. In Boarding House.
CANTWELL, MARY ANN, 18, F, None listed, -, NY, 848, 828, CHAS-. In HH of B. Figeroux m 42 born West Indies.
CAPON, WILLIAM H., 33, M, Jailor, -, PA, 420, 431, RICH.
CARMAN, JOHN, 48, M, Shoe maker, -, NJ, 1277, 1278, FAIR.

John Carman born Burlington, NJ.
CARNRIKE, ANDREW K., 35, M, Tailor, -, NY, 233, 238, RICH.
CARNRIKE, ELIZABETH, 22, F, None listed, -, NJ, 233, 238, RICH. In HH of Andrew K. Carnrike m 35 born NY.
CARNRIKE, EMMA J., 2, F, None listed, -, NJ, 233, 238, RICH. In HH of Andrew K. Carnrike m 35 born NY.
CARPENTER, C.F., 47, F, None listed, -, NY, 46, 46, KERS.
CARR, C.D., 40, M, Merchant tailor, -, NY, 519, 485, CHAS*.
CARR, JOHN, 34, M, Printer, -, MD, 165, 152, CHAS*.
CARRINGTON, JAMES, 17, M, Clerk, -, NY, 714, 694, CHAS-. In HH of William Carrington m 48 born England.
CARRINGTON, LOUIS, 12, M, None listed, -, NY, 714, 694, CHAS-. In HH of William Carrington m 48 born England.
CARRINGTON, THERESA, 9, F, None listed, -, NY, 714, 694, CHAS-. In HH of William Carrington m 48 born England.
CARROL, MARY, 71, F, None listed, -, PA, 522, 522, CHES.
CARROLL, ANNA, 26, F, None listed, -, NY, 234, 239, RICH. In HH of William H. Carroll m 31 born VA.
CARRS, ADAM T., 35, M, Printer, -, PA, 241, 246, RICH.
CARRS, ELIZABETH A., 34, F, None listed, -, MD, 241, 246, RICH. In HH of Adam T. Carrs m 35 born PA.
CARRS, JULIAN W., 14, M, None listed, -, MD, 241, 246,

RICH. In HH of Adam T. Carrs m 35 born PA.
CARSTANG, E., 25, F, None listed, -, NY, 845, 825, CHAS-. In HH of B. Lynap m 33 born Ireland.
CARSTANG, MARY E., 23, F, None listed, -, NY, 845, 825, CHAS-. In HH of B. Lynap m 33 born Ireland.
CARTER, DAVID, 29, M, Farming, -, NY, 115, 115, PICK+.
CARTER, ELIZA, 30, F, None listed, -, PA, 136, 127, CHAS+. In HH of John Carter m 35 born PA.
CARTER, JOHN, 35, M, Grain Merchant, -, PA, 136, 127, CHAS+.
CARTER, LAVINA, 23, F, None listed, -, NY, 198, 186, CHAS-. In HH of Emily Timbrook f 49 born PA.
CASEY, SELENA, 13, F, None listed, -, NY, 423, 382, CHAS+. In HH of Mary Casey f 38 born Ireland.
CASTEN, MARY JANE, 9, M, None listed, -, NY, 167, 153, CHAS*. In HH of Lawrence Haberson m 38 born Germany.
CATLINE, ELIZA, 20, F, None listed, -, NY, 994, 973, CHAS-. In HH of J.A. Rutjes m 30 born Holland.
CAUSSE, ROBERT, 47, M, Coach maker, -, NY, 421, 404, CHAS-.
CAVERE, JOSEPHINE, 9, F, None listed, -, NY, 766, 746, CHAS-. In HH of Patrick Hogan m 37 born Ireland.
CAVERE, LOUISA J., 15, F, None listed, -, NY, 766, 746, CHAS-. In HH of Patrick Hogan m 37 born Ireland.
CAVING, JOHN, 72, M, Farmer, -, PA, 176, 176, YORK*.
CAYASS, ANN, 21, F, None listed, -, NY, 661, 619, CHAS+. In HH of Thomas Cayass m 23 born SC.
CELLER, SAMUEL, 3, M, None listed, -, NY, 189, 193, RICH. In HH of Michael Celler m 35 born Prussia.
CHAFFEE, CHARLES, 17, M, Clerk, -, MD, 496, 462, CHAS*. In HH of Nicholas U. Chaffee m 43 born MD. Charles Chaffee born Baltimore, MD.
CHAFFEE, ELIZABETH W., 18, F, None listed, -, MD, 496, 462, CHAS*. In HH of Nicholas U. Chaffee m 43 born MD. Elizabeth W. Chaffee born Baltimore, MD.
CHAFFEE, NICHOLAS U., 43, M, Merchant, -, MD, 496, 462, CHAS*. Born Baltimore, MD.
CHAFFEE, SARAH A., 37, F, None listed, -, MD, 496, 462, CHAS*. In HH of Nicholas U. Chaffee m 43 born MD. Sarah A. Chaffee born Baltimore, MD.
CHALK, CARIL ?, 66, M, Mechanic, -, MD, 1449, 1449, CHES.
CHAMPLIN, ANN E., 30, F, Inspector, -, PA, 95, 88, CHAS-. In HH of Samuel Champlin m 60 born PA.
CHAMPLIN, SAMUEL, 60, M, Inspector, -, PA, 95, 88, CHAS-.
CHANDLER, A. AMELIA, 42, F, None listed, -, NY, 505, 505, FAIR. In HH of Mason Chandler

m 48 born NY.
CHANDLER, ANTONNETTE, 11, F, None listed, -, NJ, 505, 505, FAIR. In HH of Mason Chandler m 48 born NY. Antonette Chandler born Newark, NJ.
CHANDLER, MARY T., 15, F, None listed, -, NJ, 505, 505, FAIR. In HH of Mason Chandler m 48 born NY. Mary T. Chandler born Newark, NJ.
CHANDLER, MASON, 48, M, Harness maker, -, NY, 505, 505, FAIR.
CHANDLER, WILLIAM N., 13, M, None listed, -, NJ, 505, 505, FAIR. In HH of Mason Chandler m 48 born NY. William N. Chandler born Newark, NJ.
CHANNER, CATHERINE E., 45, F, None listed, -, NY, 398, 359, CHAS+. In HH of Ann Griner f 43 born NY.
CHAPIN, MARTIN, 29, M, Clerk, -, NY, 303, 309, RICH. In Hotel, Davis Caldwell m 51 proprietor.
CHARLEEN, JOHN C., 24, M, Shoemaker, -, PA, 300, 306, RICH. In Boarding House.
CHARLON, CATHARINE, 14, F, None listed, -, NY, 1036, 1014, CHAS%. In HH of John Charlon m 22 born SC.
CHARLON, MARY, 33, F, None listed, -, NY, 1036, 1014, CHAS%. In HH of John Charlon m 22 born SC.
CHARTAN, C.L., 30, M, Carpenter, -, NJ, 56, 56, KERS.
CHASE, N.H., 28, M, Store clerk, -, NY, 1003, 1003, EDGE. In HH of Robt. Anderson m 35,
merchant, born SC.
CHASTLE, WEST, 26, M, Seaman, -, NY, 326, 301, CHAS. On Steam Ship Southerner.
CHICHESTER, E., 19, M, Clerk, -, NY, 721, 701, CHAS-. In Boarding House.
CHOATE, MARIANA, 22, F, None listed, -, NY, 274, 248, CHAS*. In HH of J.C. Jervey m 30 born SC.
CHRISTIE, G.W., 30, M, Merchant, -, PA, 22, 22, GEOR.
CHURCH, JOS. F., 26, M, Plumber, -, NY, 67, 67, CHAS%. In HH of Francis Church f 26 born SC.
CHURCHILL, CHARLES B., 37, M, Merchant/clerk, -, NY, 2393, 2400, EDGE. In HH of Levi Churchill m 40 born NY.
CHURCHILL, LEVI, 40, M, Merchant/clerk, -, NY, 2393, 2400, EDGE.
CINCLARE, CATHARINE, 2, F, None listed, -, NY, 174, 174, BEAU*. In HH of Peter Cinclare m 30 born NY.
CINCLARE, PETER, 30, M, Mechanic, -, NY, 174, 174, BEAU*.
CINCLARE, REBECCA, 3, F, None listed, -, NY, 174, 174, BEAU*. In HH of Peter Cinclare m 30 born NY.
CINCLARE, SARAH, 23, F, None listed, -, NY, 174, 174, BEAU*. In HH of Peter Cinclare m 30 born NY.
CINCLARE, TANILLE, 0, F, None listed, -, NY, 174, 174, BEAU*. In HH of Peter Cinclare m 30 born NY. Tanille Cinclare

age 2/12 yr.
CLARK, CALEB, 46, M, Physician, -, MD, 531, 531, FAIR
CLARK, CHARLES, 60, M, Druggist, -, NY, 70, 62, CHAS+.
CLARK, FREDERICK, 25, M, Clerk, -, NY, 685, 665, CHAS-. In Victoria Hotel.
CLARK, H.B., 29, M, Saddler, -, MD, 139, 439, LAU.
CLARK, ROBERT A., 17, M, Merchant, -, NY, 545, 528, CHAS-.
CLARK, SARAH, 78, F, None listed, -, PA, 444, 444, YORK*.
CLARK, WILLIAM, 48, M, None listed, -, MD, 531, 531, FAIR. In HH of Caleb Clark m 46 born MD.
CLARKE, ISABELLA F., 12, F, None listed, -, NY, 1765, 1769, EDGE. In HH of Joseph Clarke m 51 born Scotland.
CLARKE, JENNETT, 17, F, None listed, -, NY, 1765, 1769, EDGE. In HH of Joseph Clarke m 51 born Scotland.
CLARKE, JOHN M., 37, M, Merchant, -, NJ, 2263, 2277, EDGE.
CLARKE, MARY, 21, F, None listed, -, MD, 202, 189, CHAS-. In HH of Grace Piexolla f 30 born SC.
CLARKSON, WILLIAM, 56, M, Physician, -, NJ, 58, 58, CHAS^.
CLAYTON, EDWD., 20, M, Machinist, -, NY, 462, 445, CHAS-. In HH of William Patterson m 34 born MD.
CLAYTON, F., 25, M, Carpenter, -, MD, 46, 46, SPART. In HH of D.B.P. Moorman m 30 born NC.

CLAYTON, JOHN W., 9, M, None listed, -, MD, 576, 534, CHAS+. In HH of William C. Clayton m 40 born MD.
CLAYTON, MARGARET JANE, 17, F, None listed, -, MD, 576, 534, CHAS+. In HH of William C. Clayton m 40 born MD.
CLAYTON, PAMELIA ANN, 12, F, None listed, -, MD, 576, 534, CHAS+. In HH of William C. Clayton m 40 born MD.
CLAYTON, VINCENT A., 22, M, Printer, -, MD, 576, 534, CHAS+. In HH of William C. Clayton m 40 born MD.
CLAYTON, WILLIAM, 20, M, Carpenter, -, MD, 576, 534, CHAS+. In HH of William C. Clayton m 40 born MD.
CLAYTON, WILLIAM C., 40, M, Printer, -, MD, 576, 534, CHAS+.
CLEARY, SARAH, 18, F, None listed, -, NY, 167, 158, CHAS+. In Boarding House.
CLEMENT, PRISSILLA, 76, F, None listed, -, MD, 245, 246, AND*. In HH of Isaac Clement m 73 born VA.
CLIFTON, A.J., 25, M, 1st mate, -, NY, 326, 301, CHAS. In HH of William Rollins m 40 born {not listed}.
CLIFTON, AGNESS, 34, F, None listed, -, MD, 1189, 1168, CHAS%. In HH of William Lightburn m 44 born Ireland.
CLIFTON, AGNESS, 12, F, None listed, -, MD, 1189, 1168, CHAS%. In HH of William Lightburn m 44 born Ireland.

CLIFTON, JAMES, 14, M, None listed, -, MD, 1189, 1168, CHAS%. In HH of William Lightburn m 44 born Ireland.
CLIFTON, JOHN, 9, M, None listed, -, MD, 1189, 1168, CHAS%. In HH of William Lightburn m 44 born Ireland.
CLIFTON, JULIA, 6, F, None listed, -, MD, 1189, 1168, CHAS%. In HH of William Lightburn m 44 born Ireland.
CLIFTON, MARGARET, 4, F, None listed, -, MD, 1189, 1168, CHAS%. In HH of William Lightburn m 44 born Ireland.
CLIFTON, RAYMOND, 39, M, Engineer, -, MD, 1189, 1168, CHAS%. In HH of William Lightburn m 44 born Ireland.
CLINKSCALE, FRANCES, 63, M, Farmer, -, MD, 1026, 1026, ABB.
CLINKSCALE, JOHN, 70, M, Farmer, -, MD, 1325, 1325, ABB.
CLINKSCOLES, WILLIAM F., 73, M, Farmer, -, MD, 26, 26, AND*.
COCHRAN, HANNAH, 89, F, None listed, -, PA, 834, 834, ABB.
COCHRAN, JAMES, 59, M, Printer, -, PA, 217, 222, RICH. {Page out of order}, follows HH 177/181.
COCKEROFF, LOUISA, 20, F, None listed, -, NY, 158, 158, EDGE. In HH of John H. Hughes m 48 born SC.
CODDING, G.T., 43, M, Teacher, -, NY, 237, 222, CHAS-. Poor House.
COE, CHESTER S., 40, M, Planter, -, NY, 31, 31, CHAS3.
COGDELL, MARY, 64, F, None listed, -, NY, 881, 839, CHAS+. In HH of The Honorable R.B. Gilchrist m 53 born SC.
COHEN, NANCY, 60, F, None listed, -, MD, 1001, 1001, UNION. In HH of Thomas Cohen m 60 born TN.
COLBURN, J. HY., 35, M, Clerk, -, NY, 836, 816, CHAS-. In Boarding House.
COLBURN, JOHN, 24, M, Teacher, -, NY, 426, 427, ORNG+. In HH of Henry L. Smoke m 44 born SC.
COLBURN, JOHN, 24, M, Teacher, -, NY, 426, 427, ORNG+. In HH of Henry L. Smoke m 44 born SC.
COLE, GEO. F., 45, M, Music Store, -, MD, 676, 656, CHAS-.
COLEMAN, MARTHA J., 4, F, None listed, -, NY, 139, 129, CHAS-. In HH of Hugh Stoop m 60 born Ireland.
COLES, BENJ. T., 38, M, Merchant, -, NY, 237, 237, CHAS3.
COLLINS, ALICIA, 11, F, None listed, -, NY, 218, 195, CHAS*. In HH of Daniel Collins m 44 born Ireland.
COLLINS, CAROLINE, 13, F, None listed, -, NY, 472, 430, CHAS+. In HH of James N. Collins m 40 born Ireland.
COLLINS, CAROLINE, 12, F, None listed, -, NY, 609, 567, CHAS+. In HH of James Collins m 50 born Ireland.

COLLINS, CATHERINE, 2, F, None listed, -, MD, 270, 251, CHAS+. In HH of Richard M. Collins m 40 born Ireland.
COLLINS, EMMA, 16, F, None listed, -, NY, 609, 567, CHAS+. In HH of James Collins m 50 born Ireland.
COLLINS, GEORGIANA, 6, F, None listed, -, NY, 472, 430, CHAS+. In HH of James N. Collins m 40 born Ireland.
COLLINS, HARRIOT B., 10, F, None listed, -, NY, 472, 430, CHAS+. In HH of James N. Collins m 40 born Ireland.
COLLINS, JAMES, 10, M, None listed, -, NY, 609, 567, CHAS+. In HH of James Collins m 50 born Ireland.
COLLINS, JANE, 14, F, None listed, -, NY, 609, 567, CHAS+. In HH of James Collins m 50 born Ireland.
COLLINS, JOHN, 18, M, Blacksmith, -, NY, 609, 567, CHAS+. In HH of James Collins m 50 born Ireland.
COLLINS, MARGERY, 13, F, None listed, -, NY, 218, 195, CHAS*. In HH of Daniel Collins m 44 born Ireland.
COLLINS, MARY JANE, 16, F, None listed, -, NY, 472, 430, CHAS+. In HH of James N. Collins m 40 born Ireland.
COLLINS, MATILDA, 37, F, None listed, -, NY, 472, 430, CHAS+. In HH of James N. Collins m 40 born Ireland.
COLLINS, THOMAS, 29, M, Boot Frunder?, -, NY, 391, 355, CHAS. In HH of F.W. Theus m 28 born Germany.
CONKLIN, M.C., 39, M, Gun smith, -, NY, 29, 29, GEOR.
CONNOR, MARGARET, 9, F, None listed, -, NY, 91, 92, RICH. Note: apparently out of dwelling and family order. pg. 3 In HH of James Connor m 32 born Ireland.
CONROY, AUGUSTUS, 28, M, Seaman, -, NY, 326, 301, CHAS. On Steam Ship Southerner.
CONWAY, A., 36, M, Printer, -, NJ, 1826, 1826, SUMT.
CONWAY, ANN, 56, F, None listed, -, NJ, 1826, 1826, SUMT. In HH of A. Conway m 36 born NJ.
COOK, JOHN P., 60, M, Merchant, -, PA, 334, 340, RICH. In HH of Coleman A. Walker m 23 born SC.
COOK, TRUMAN, 40, M, Engineer, -, NY, 439, 422, CHAS-.
COOKE, EMMA, 6, F, None listed, -, MD, 124, 116, CHAS*. In HH of William Black m 28 born NY. Emma Cooke born Baltimore, MD.
COOKE, HORATIO, 33, M, Physician, -, NY, 1889, 1895, EDGE.
COOPER, OLIVER, 40, M, None, -, NJ, 542, 557, RICH. Date 1833 by name. In Lunatic Asylum.
COPP, ELLEN L., 22, F, None listed, -, MD, 819, 777, CHAS+. In HH of James Taylor m 30 born England.
CORDES, LOUISA, 41, F, None listed, -, PA, 421, 404, CHAS-. In HH of Robert Causse m 47 born NY.

CORNESKEY, ELIZA, 50, F, None listed, -, PA, 529, 512, CHAS-. In HH of T.T. Seymour m 32 born Burmudas.
CORNISH, CATHERINE D., 31, F, None listed, -, NY, 265, 267, AND. In HH of A.H. Cornish m 36 born MA.
CORNISH, ELIZABETH B., 6, F, None listed, -, NY, 265, 267, AND. In HH of A.H. Cornish m 36 born MA.
CORNISH, KATHERINE R., 8, F, None listed, -, NY, 265, 267, AND. In HH of A.H. Cornish m 36 born MA.
CORSON, JAMES, 60, M, Ship Mas?, -, PA, 36, 36, GEOR.
COUARTRIGHT, ISAAC, 30, M, Tailor, -, NJ, 766, 766, ABB. In HH of Agness M Kingsmore f 56 born England.
COURSAY, THOMAS, 20, M, Seaman, -, NY, 326, 301, CHAS. On Steam Ship Southerner.
COURTNEY, ANN, 30, F, None listed, -, NY, 262, 262, CHAS%. In HH of John Courtney m 40 born NY.
COURTNEY, ELIZA, 43, F, None listed, -, NY, 383, 366, CHAS-. In HH of E.S. Courtney m 55 born SC.
COURTNEY, JOHN, 40, M, None listed, -, NY, 262, 262, CHAS%.
COUSTER, JULIA L., 31, F, None listed, -, NJ, 32, 32, YORK+. In HH of Jeremiah Couster m 47 born NC.
COWPERTHWARTE, E.R., 36, M, Furniture store, -, NY, 764, 722, CHAS+.

COX, HANNAH, 25, F, None listed, -, NY, 2314, 2314, GREE. In HH of T.M. Cox m 37 born SC.
CRAFTS, SARAH E., 54, F, None listed, -, PA, 849, 829, CHAS-.
CRAMER, MARY L., 35, F, None listed, -, MD, 366, 328, CHAS+. In HH of Geo. W. Cramer m 40 born SC.
CRAVEN, ALFRED, 28, M, Watchmaker, -, PA, 68, 68, YORK+. In Hotel. Born Philadelphia, PA.
CRAVEN, EMMA, 15, F, None listed, -, PA, 68, 68, YORK+. In Hotel. Born Philadelphia, PA.
CRAVEN, LOUISE, 17, F, None listed, -, PA, 68, 68, YORK+. In Hotel. Born Philadelphia, PA.
CRAVEN, VIRGINIA, 12, F, None listed, -, PA, 68, 68, YORK+. In Hotel. Born Philadelphia, PA.
CRAWFORD, WILLIAM, 31, M, Tavern keeper, -, NY, 28, 33, CHAS.
CRAWLY, MARTIN, 49, M, Coach maker, -, MD, 771, 771, ABB.
CREMER, DAVID, 49, M, Shoe maker, -, NJ, 520, 520, FAIR.
CREMER, ELIZABETH, 46, F, None listed, -, NJ, 520, 520, FAIR. In HH of David Cremer m 49 born NJ.
CREMER, JANE, 82, F, None listed, -, NJ, 520, 520, FAIR. In HH of David Cremer m 49 born NJ.
CROAKER, WILLIAM, 36, M, Mariner, -, NY, 334, 308, CHAS. In HH of William Bennett m 40

born NY.
CROGAN, ELLEN, 4, F, None listed, -, NY, 193, 181, CHAS+. In HH of Peter Crogan m 30 born Ireland.
CROMLAY, ANNA, 18, F, None listed, -, NY, 122, 113, CHAS+. In HH of Daniel Cromlay m 50 born Ireland.
CROMLAY, FANNY, 8, F, None listed, -, PA, 122, 113, CHAS+. In HH of Daniel Cromlay m 50 born Ireland.
CROMLAY, SUSAN, 20, F, None listed, -, NY, 122, 113, CHAS+. In HH of Daniel Cromlay m 50 born Ireland.
CROSS, WILLIAM T., 22, M, Clerk, -, MD, 470, 485, RICH. In Hotel
CROWEL, ISRAEL, 66, M, Shoemaker, -, NJ, 668, 703, PICK.
CROWEL, ISRAEL, 62, M, Shoe maker, -, NY, 432, 455, PICK.
CROWEL, ISRAEL, 60, M, Shoemaker, -, NJ, 668, 703, PICK.
CRUMP, JOHN D., 30, M, Mariner, -, NY, 362, 333, CHAS. In Boarding House.
CUMMINS, HARMAN, 96, M, Farmer, -, MD, 772, 776, AND.
CUMPSTY, ELIZABETH, 17, F, None listed, -, NY, 1642, 1642, EDGE. In HH of William Cumpsty m 51 born England.
CUNNINGHAM, ELLEN, 20, F, None listed, -, NY, 992, 971, CHAS-. In HH of S.B. Bernard m 38 born France.
CUNNINGHAM, JAMES, 23, M, Seaman, -, NY, 326, 301, CHAS. On Steam Ship Southerner.

CURLES, ELLEN, 20, F, None listed, -, NY, 678, 636, CHAS+. In HH of John Curles m 25 born Germany.
CURRAN, J., 28, M, Merchant, -, NY, 624, 605, CHAS-. In HH of Julia Jacobs f 45 born SC.
CURRAN, MARY, 25, F, None listed, -, NY, 624, 605, CHAS-. In HH of Julia Jacobs f 45 born SC.
CURRY, WILLIAM, 23, M, Carpenter, -, MD, 816, 774, CHAS+. In Boarding House.
CURTIS, LUPSON, 36, M, Minister, -, NY, 564, 564, UNION. In HH of William Clowing m 52 born SC.

D

DALEY, ELIZABETH, 20, F, None listed, -, PA, 338, 312, CHAS. In HH of Henry Pluger m 25 born Germany.
DALEY, JOHN A., 30, M, Merchant, -, NY, 476, 434, CHAS. In HH of M.M. Stewart f 40, runs boarding house, born SC.
DALLISON, LOUISA, 24, F, None listed, -, NY, 751, 731, CHAS-. In HH of Jos. B. Dallison m 27 born England.
DALLWIG, ELIZA, 23, F, None listed, -, MD, 988, 967, CHAS-.
DALLWIG, LEWIS WM., 12, M, None listed, -, MD, 988, 967, CHAS-. In HH of Eliza Dallwig f 23 born MD.
DALLWIG, THOMAS, 16, M, Clerk, -, MD, 988, 967, CHAS-. In HH of Eliza Dallwig f 23 born MD.

DARBY, MARY, 90, F, None listed, -, MD, 986, 990, AND. In HH of James Darby m 53 born SC.
DARLINGTON, J.W., 26, M, Moulding, -, NY, 53, 53, GEOR.
DARLINGTON, RACHEL, 24, F, None listed, -, NY, 53, 53, GEOR. In HH of J.W. Darlington m 26 born NY.
DARROW, FRED., 32, M, Coach Trimmer, -, NY, 23, 23, NEWB. In HH of J. Wilson 33 m Hotel Keeper born SC.
DAVENPORT, ROBERT, 28, M, Bookbinder., -, MD, 379, 390, RICH.
DAVID, E.T., 40, M, Farmer, -, NY, 1292, 1292, EDGE.
DAVIDS, A. J., 38, M, Painter, -, NY, 546, 512, CHAS*. In HH of Solomon Knepley m 58 born PA.
DAVIDS, MATILDA, 27, F, None listed, -, MD, 546, 512, CHAS*. In HH of Solomon Knepley m 58 born PA.
DAVIS, CALVIN, 28, M, Bricklayer, -, NY, 428, 397, CHAS*. In HH of Glenn Carr f 37 mulatto born SC.
DAVIS, E.T., 30, M, None listed, -, NY, 8, 8, EDGE. In HH of H.R. Spann m 31 born SC.
DAVIS, ELIZABETH, 3, F, None listed, -, NJ, 694, 713, RICH. In HH of Cornelius Davis m 30 born CT.
DAVIS, F.H., 23, F, None listed, -, NY, 428, 397, CHAS*. In HH of Glenn Carr f 37 mulatto born SC.
DAVIS, HENRY, 46, M, Mechanic, -, MD, 430, 441, RICH.
DAVIS, JOHN, 33, M, Brickmason, -, NY, 454, 454, EDGE.
DAVIS, JOHN B., 64, M, Sadler, -, PA, 237, 222, CHAS-. Poor House.
DAVIS, LEVI, 72, M, Farmer, -, MD, 402, 403, AND*.
DAVIS, LOUISA, 24, F, None listed, -, NJ, 694, 713, RICH. In HH of Cornelius Davis m 30 born CT.
DAVIS, LYDIA, 63, F, None listed, -, MD, 401, 402, AND*.
DAVIS, MALVINA, 1, F, None listed, -, NJ, 694, 713, RICH. In HH of Cornelius Davis m 30 born CT.
DAVIS, MATTHEW, 50, M, Shoemaker, -, NY, 215, 220, RICH.
DAVIS, SAMUEL, 70, M, Farmer, -, MD, 283, 292, PICK.
DAVIS, THOMAS, 18, M, Painter, - DC, 23, 23 m Hotel Keeper born SC. Thomas Davis listed as born in Washington, D.C.}
DAVIS, ZACHARIAH, 72, M, Farmer, -, MD, 394, 395, AND*.
DAVISON, ELIZABETH, 74, F, None listed, -, MD, 1120, 1120, UNION. In HH of Samuel Davison m 85 born VA.
DAY, JOSEPH, 27, M, Engineer, -, PA, 526, 526, CHES. In HH of G.F. Kennedy m 39, Hotel Keeper, born SC.
DAY, OLIVIA, 45, F, None listed, -, NY, 829, 809, CHAS-. In HH of Fisher Day m 56 born MA.
DE C. MENADE, 28, M, Carpenter, -, NY, 654, 613, CHAS+. In HH of George Beckman m 45 born Sweden.

DE LEON, HARRIETTA, 45, F, None listed, -, NY, 871, 871, KERS.
DEANE, THOMAS, 75, M, Farmer, -, MD, 770, 774, AND.
DEAT, JACOB M., 44, M, Farmer, -, PA, 134, 134, YORK*.
DEDRIC, ALLEN, 27, M, Teacher, -, NY, 1792, 1792, ABB. In HH of William P. Hill m 46, Baptist Clergyman born SC.
DELANO, D., 29, M, Priv. U.S.A., -, NY, 47, 43, CHAS$. In HH of John Ewing m 50 born MA.
DELLA, NANCY, 76, F, None listed, -, MD, 725, 725, UNION.
DELPORTE, LOUIS, 7, M, None listed, -, NY, 639, 598, CHAS+. In HH of Simon Delporte m 34 born France.
DENNY, ANNA, 16, F, None listed, -, NY, 170, 153, CHAS. In HH of John Young m 23 born SC.
DENTON, RICHARD W., 26, M, Attorney, -, PA, 447, 447, LAU. In HH of Richard Denton m 48 born England.
DESSAN, REBECCA, 12, F, None listed, -, PA, 668, 648, CHAS-. In HH of Jonathan Zachariah m 58 born Poland.
DEWLEY, WILLIAM, 6, M, None listed, -, NY, 921, 898, CHAS%. In HH of John Dewley m 32 born Ireland.
DEXTER, ISARA, 25, M, Seaman, -, NY, 326, 301, CHAS. In HH of William Rollins m 40 born {-}.
DIAL, SUSANNA, 44, F, None listed, -, PA, 602, 619, RICH. In HH of William H. Dial m 48 born Germany.
DICKERSON, JACOB, 24, M, Mechanic, -, NJ, 949, 949, CHES. In HH of A.J. Roddy m 35 born SC.
DICKINS, RAWLINS, 40, M, Mariner, -, NY, 334, 308, CHAS. In HH of William Bennett m 40 born NY.
DICKSON, MARY, 80, F, None listed, -, MD, 965, 965, ABB. In HH of William Dickson m 48 born SC.
DICKSON, MARY, 70, F, None listed, -,DE, 683, 718, PICK. In HH of Andrew Dickson m 36 born SC.
DICKSON, MARY, 70, F, None listed, -,DE, 683, 718, PICK. In HH of Andrew Dickson m 36 born SC.
DILL, EDWARD, 66, M, Farmer, -,DE, 1017, 1017, GREE.
DOILE, WILLIAM, 68, M, Farmer, -, MD, 13, 13, PICK.
DOLE, MARY ANN, 20, F, None listed, -, MD, 47, 43, CHAS$. In HH of John Ewing m 50 born MA.
DONNELLY, DAN, 13, M, None listed, -, NY, 39, 34, CHAS+. In HH of Dennis Connelly m 44 born Ireland.
DONNELLY, JANE, 11, F, None listed, -, NY, 289, 263, CHAS*. In HH of Patrick Donnelly m 38 born Ireland.
DONNELLY, MARY, 15, F, None listed, -, NY, 39, 34, CHAS+. In HH of Dennis Connelly m 44 born Ireland.
DONNELLY, RICHARD, 9, M, None listed, -, NY, 289, 263, CHAS*. In HH of Patrick Donnelly m 38 born Ireland.

DONNELLY, SAML., 42, M, Minister, O.S., -, NY, 359, 359, KERS.
DOSENBURY, SAML., 58, M, Minister, -, NY, 422, 422, HORR. In HH of G.W. Dosenbery m 30 born NC.
DOTEN, JNO., 30, M, Tavern keeper, -, MD, 1265, 1265, DARL.
DOTEY, THOMAS, 23, M, Porter, -, NY, 923, 903, CHAS-. In HH of James Williams m 29 born NY.
DOUGHERTY, JANE A., 7, F, None listed, -, NJ, 226, 212, CHAS-. In HH of William M. Dougherty m 45 born NY.
DOUGHERTY, JOHN G., 15, M, None listed, -, NJ, 226, 212, CHAS-. In HH of William M. Dougherty m 45 born NY.
DOUGHERTY, WILLIAM M., 45, M, Gas fitter, -, NY, 226, 212, CHAS-.
DOUGLAS, JANE, 17, F, None listed, -, NY, 673, 653, CHAS-. In HH of J.G. Newcomb m 27 born NY.
DOUGLAS, JOSEPH, 44, M, Tailor, -, NY, 495, 449, CHAS.
DOUGLAS, LEVI, 21, M, Gilder, -, NY, 495, 449, CHAS. In HH of Joseph Douglas m 44 born NY.
DOUGLASS, RACHEL, 50, F, None listed, -, NJ, 1426, 1432, Mar. In HH of John Douglass 50 b. Scotland.
DOUNAN, HENRY, 5, M, None listed, -, NY, 47, 43, CHAS$. In HH of John Ewing m 50 born MA.
DOWLING, MARGARET, 12, F, None listed, -, NY, 167, 158, CHAS+. In Boarding House.

DOWNES, CAROLINE E., 18, F, None listed, -, NY, 154, 144, CHAS-. In HH of Catherine Gordon f 28 born MA.
DOYLE, CATHARINE, 40, F, None listed, -, MD, 2336, 2336, ABB. In HH of Richard P. Doyl m 42 born MD.
DOYLE, JOHN, 14, M, Carpenter, -, NY, 111, 106, CHAS*. In Boarding House.
DOYLE, MARGARET, 21, F, None listed, -, MD, 128, 128, BEAU+. In HH of Michael Doyle m 30 born Ireland.
DOYLE, RICHARD P., 49, M, Croper, -, MD, 2336, 2336, ABB.
DOYLEY, SUSAN, 18, F, None listed, -, NY, 851, 831, CHAS-. In HH of E. Knowles f 30 born England.
DRAIN, MARGARET, 13, F, None listed, -,D.C., 695, 653, CHAS+. In HH of Samuel Burke m 27 born SC. Margaret Drain born Washington, D.C.
DRAKE, JAMES P., 25, M, Blacksmith, -, NY, 38, 33, CHAS+. In Boarding House.
DRAYTON, DIANA, 28, F, None listed, B, NY, 475, 433, CHAS+. In HH of Sarah Drayton m 45 black born NY.
DRAYTON, HARRIOT, 10, F, None listed, M, NY, 475, 433, CHAS+. In HH of Sarah Drayton m 45 black born NY.
DRAYTON, PATIENCE, 11, F, None listed, M, NY, 475, 433, CHAS+. In HH of Sarah Drayton m 45 black born NY.
DRAYTON, SARAH, 45, F, None listed, B, NY, 475, 433,

CHAS+.
DREKER, DO?, 62, M, Planter, -, MD, 153, 153, UNION.
DRUMMOND, WM., 40, M, Blacksmith, -, NY, 1045, 1045, BARN.
DRYER, FREDERICK, 37, M, Clerk, -, NY, 98, 90, CHAS+. In HH of E.H. Margenhoff m 39 born Germany.
DUFORT, AMELIA, 31, F, None listed, -, PA, 482, 478, CHAS%. In HH of A. Dufort m 31 born SC.
DUFREES, JOHN, 40, M, Clerk, -, NY, 1147, 1126, CHAS%.
DUFREES, JOHN, 16, M, Clerk, -, NY, 1147, 1126, CHAS%. In HH of John Dufrees m 40 born NY.
DUFREES, MARY ANN, 36, F, None listed, -, NY, 1147, 1126, CHAS%. In HH of John Dufrees m 40 born NY.
DUNKIN, B.F., HONBLE, 56, M, Chancellor, -, PA, 16, 16, CHAS%.
DUNLAP, ELIZA, 42, F, None listed, -, NY, 656, 636, CHAS-. In HH of James Dunlap m 60 born Ireland.
DUNLAP, MARGARET, 15, F, None listed, -, NY, 656, 636, CHAS-. In HH of James Dunlap m 60 born Ireland.
DUNLAP, WILLIAM, 73, M, None listed, -, NJ, 351, 325, CHAS*.
DUNWOODY, SAMUEL, 70, M, Methodist Clergyman, -, PA, 2105, 2105, ABB.
DUVAL, MARY, 37, F, None listed, -, MD, 541, 500, CHAS+. In HH of John Sharleyson m 39 born Ireland.
DYKES, ALFRED, 24, M, None listed, -, NY, 841, 821, CHAS-. In HH of Samuel Dykes m 40 born England.
DYKES, CHARLOTTE, 30, F, None listed, -, NY, 841, 821, CHAS-. In HH of Samuel Dykes m 40 born England.
DYKES, MARY, 11, F, None listed, -, PA, 841, 821, CHAS-. In HH of Samuel Dykes m 40 born England.

E

EAST, MARY JANE, 35, F, None listed, -, NY, 425, 394, CHAS*.
EASTWICK, FRANCIS A., 16, F, None listed, -, PA, 383, 393, RICH. In HH of William S. Wood m 30 born SC.
EATON, HOMER, 25, M, Clerk, -, PA, 68, 69, RICH. In HH of Edward Harris m 66 born VA.
EDWARDS, JOHN, 30, M, Coalpasser, -, NY, 326, 301, CHAS. In HH of William Rollins m 40 born {-}. In crew of the Steam Ship Isabel.
EDWARDS, JOHN, 26, M, Seaman, -, NY, 326, 301, CHAS. In HH of William Rollins m 40 born {-}.
EDWARDS, WILLIAM, 30, M, Shoemaker, -, NY, 190, 174, CHAS*.
ELLET, JAS. M. E., 38, M, Farmer, -, PA, 1529, 1529, CHES.
ELLIOT, E., 35, M, Mechanic, -, MD, 523, 523, CHES.

ELLIS, L.B., 23, F, None listed, -, NY, 868, 868, SUMT. In HH of John Nettles, Sr. m 40 born SC.
ELLIS, MARY, 70, F, None listed, -, MD, 144, 144, YORK.
ELLIS, PHOEBE ANN, 30, F, None listed, -, PA, 719, 677, CHAS+.
ELLIS, ST. JOHN, 29, M, Tin smith, -, NY, 55, 55, GEOR. Note: name may be Ellis St. John
ELLISON, B.B., 51, M, Tailor, -, MD, 1398, 1398, CHES.
ELRED, GEORGE, 23, M, Mercht., -, NJ, 57, 57, GEOR.
EMANUEL, CHARLOTTE, 9, F, None listed, -, NY, 390, 373, CHAS-. In HH of N. Emanuelo m 56 born England.
EMANUEL, EDWIN, 17, M, Clerk, -, NY, 61, 61, GEOR. In HH of Nathan Emanuel m 36 born VA.
EMANUEL, L.G., 26, M, Shop keeper, -, NY, 56, 56, GEOR.
EMANUEL, LAFAYETTE, 21, M, Baker, -, NY, 61, 61, GEOR. In HH of Nathan Emanuel m 36 born VA.
EMANUEL, ROSETTA, 10, F, None listed, -, NY, 390, 373, CHAS-. In HH of N. Emanuelo m 56 born England.
EMANUEL, SARAH, 45, F, None listed, -, NY, 390, 373, CHAS-. In HH of N. Emanuelo m 56 born England.
ENGLISH, ELIZA A., 35, F, None listed, -, NJ, 956, 956, SUMT. In HH of Thos. English m 44 born SC.
ENIX, ELIZABETH, 32, F, None listed, -, PA, 2237, 2237, GREE.
In HH of William Enix m 48 born VA.
ENSTON, DANL. E., 27, M, Clerk, -, PA, 80, 74, CHAS-. In HH of Wm. Enston m 42 born England.
ERTZBURGER, N.H., 32, M, Carriage Maker, -, NY, 209, 211, AND.
ERVAN, HANNAH, 25, F, None listed, -, NJ, 658, 638, CHAS-. In HH of John Ervan m 60 born PA.
ERVAN, JOHN, 60, M, Silversmith, -, PA, 658, 638, CHAS-.
ERVAN, PHOEBE, 40, F, None listed, -, NJ, 658, 638, CHAS-. In HH of John Ervan m 60 born PA.
ERVAN, WILLIAM, 30, M, Silversmith, -, NJ, 658, 638, CHAS-. In HH of John Ervan m 60 born PA.
EVANS, CAWARD, 50, M, Mechanic, -, PA, 834, 835, AND*.
EVANS, ELLEN, 38, F, None listed, -, PA, 834, 835, AND*. In HH of Caward Evans m 50 born PA.
EVANS, GRACY, 63, F, None listed, -, MD, 766, 767, AND*. In HH of Aaron Holland m 35 born SC.
EVANS, ISAAC, 36, M, Blacksmith, -, MD, 209, 197, CHAS+.
EVANS, JOSEPH, 31, M, Servant, -, NY, 882, 840, CHAS+. In Charleston Hotel.
EVANS, LEVI, 9, M, None listed, -, PA, 834, 835, AND*. In HH of Caward Evans m 50 born PA.
EVANS, MARGARET, 40, F, None listed, -, NJ, 237, 222,

CHAS-. Poor House.
EVANS, ROBERT, 27, M, Servant, -, NY, 882, 840, CHAS+. In Charleston Hotel.
EWART, ANNA, 26, F, None listed, -, NY, 260, 265, RICH. In HH of John Ewart m 58 born England.
EWART, MARY H., 23, F, None listed, -, NY, 260, 265, RICH. In HH of John Ewart m 58 born England.

F

FAGAN, TONEY, 12, M, None listed, -, NY, 486, 444, CHAS+. In HH of Dennis Fagan m 48 born Ireland.
FAHM, SARAH S., 33, F, None listed, -, NY, 251, 251, BEAU+. IN HH of Jacob Fahm m 71 born SC.
FAIR, JAMES, 63, M, Farmer, -, PA, 33, 33, GREE.
FAIRCHILD, MARY, 5, F, None listed, -, PA, 877, 856, CHAS-. In HH of Rufus Fairchild m 40 born PA.
FAIRCHILD, RUFUS, 40, M, Tavern keeper, -, PA, 877, 856, CHAS-.
FALLS, ALEXANDER, 38, M, Merchant, -, NY, 385, 395, RICH.
FALLS, SARAH E., 28, F, None listed, -, NY, 385, 395, RICH. In HH of Alexander Falls m 38 born NY.
FANNESTOCK, W., 28, M, Tobacconist, -, PA, 1208, 1187, CHAS%. In HH of John Herron m 38 born SC.
FANNING, F.D., 43, M, Merchant, -, NY, 755, 713,

CHAS+.
FARMER, HENRY, 40, M, Seaman, -, NJ, 326, 301, CHAS. On Steam Ship Southerner.
FARREL, ELIZABETH, 23, F, None listed, -, NY, 314, 298, CHAS-. In HH of Sarah Mallery f 40 born CT.
FARVIS, THOMAS, 74, M, Farmer, -,DE, 816, 816, YORK.
FAVRIS, MARY, 84, F, None listed, -,DE, 821, 821, YORK. In HH of James Favris m 82 born York Dist., SC.
FAYETTE, WILLIAM W., 29, M, Clerk, -, NY, 685, 704, RICH.
FELT, LEMUEL, 50, M, Tailor, -, PA, 1871, 1871, ABB. In HH of Maximilian Hutchinson m 62 born SC.
FEREBEE, MARGARET, 33, F, None listed, -, NY, 86, 86, BEAU+. In HH of John Ferebee m 54 born SC.
FERGUSON, CATHERINE, 10, F, None listed, -, NY, 440, 423, CHAS-. In HH of John Ferguson m 54 born Ireland.
FERGUSON, JANE, 12, F, None listed, -, NY, 440, 423, CHAS-. In HH of John Ferguson m 54 born Ireland.
FERGUSON, ROBERT, 8, M, None listed, -, NY, 440, 423, CHAS-. In HH of John Ferguson m 54 born Ireland.
FINLEY, FREDERICK, 21, M, None listed, -, MD, 121, 126, PICK. In HH of Henry Witmire m 80 born MD.
FINLEY, FREDERICK, 21, M, Farmer, -, MD, 121, 126, PICK. In HH of Henry Witmire m 80 born

MD.
FINNIGAN, JOHON, 40, M, Tailor, -, MD, 71, 65, CHAS-. In HH of Catherine Gibson f 39 born SC.
FISCHER, FELIX, 8, M, None listed, -, NY, 189, 172, CHAS. In HH of F. Fischer m 32 born France.
FISCHER, FRANCISCO, 6, F, None listed, -, NY, 189, 172, CHAS. In HH of F. Fischer m 32 born France.
FISCHER, FREDERICK, 4, M, None listed, -, NY, 189, 172, CHAS. In HH of F. Fischer m 32 born France.
FITZGERALD, MARY, 1, F, None listed, -, NY, 410, 372, CHAS. In HH of George Redmond m 26 born Ireland.
FLAGG, DOROTHEA, 9, F, None listed, -, NY, 420, 379, CHAS+. In HH of Patrick Flagg m 40 born Ireland.
FLAGG, SUSAN, 12, F, None listed, -, NY, 420, 379, CHAS+. In HH of Patrick Flagg m 40 born Ireland.
FLEMING, ALFRED W., 22, M, Clerk, -, PA, 15, 15, CHAS%. In HH of Robert Adger m 36 born SC.
FLEMING, L., 40, M, Merchant, -, NY, 882, 840, CHAS+. In Charleston Hotel.
FLEMING, R.T., 39, F, None listed, -, NY, 882, 840, CHAS+. In Charleston Hotel.
FLEMMING, JAMES, 60, M, Carpenter, -, PA, 2, 2, CHAS$.
FLINN, HANNAH, 18, F, None listed, -, NY, 220, 197, CHAS*. In HH of Nicholas Boesch m 28 born Switzerland.
FLINN, JOHN, 45, M, Tailor, -, NY, 514, 464, CHAS.
FLODORER, MARY JANE, 28, F, None listed, -, NY, 529, 495, CHAS*. In HH of John Flordorer m 58 born Sweden.
FONDER, C.Y., 22, M, Clerk, -, NY, 837, 817, CHAS-. In HH of George Oates m 55 born England.
FOOTMAN, W.C., 54, M, Farmer, -, PA, 38, 38, Will.
FORA, JOSEPHINE, 36, F, None listed, -, MD, 79, 73, CHAS-. In HH of Lewis Fora m 42 born Minorca.
FORCE, B.W., 45, M, Merchant, -, NJ, 516, 475, CHAS+.
FORD, JOHN, 18, M, Laborer, -, NY, 188, 192, RICH. In Hotel.
FORD, JOSEPH W., 40, M, Shoe maker, -, MD, 743, 723, CHAS-.
FORD, THOS., 34, M, Mariner, -, NY, 351, 324, CHAS. In Boarding House.
FORLEY, ELIZABETH, 30, F, None listed, -, PA, 886, 863, CHAS%. In HH of Joseph Forley m 34 born SC.
FORSHAW, HARRIET A., 40, F, None listed, -,D.C., 144, 148, RICH. D.C.: District of Columbia. Note: {Page out of order}. follows HH 88/87.
FORTER, JOHN A., 28, M, Meth. Clergyman, -, NY, 80, 80, MARL.
FOSHET, DON ALOUSO, 32, M, Mail contractor, -, NY, 95, 95, COLL.
FOWLER, ANNE, 30, F, None listed, -, NY, 337, 311, CHAS. In

HH of William H. Fowler m 38 running Boarding House born England.
FOWLER, MARY, 22, F, None listed, -, NY, 337, 311, CHAS. In HH of William H. Fowler m 38 running Boarding House born England.
FRANCES, EDWARD, 7, M, None listed, -, NY, 347, 309, CHAS+. In HH of John Francis m 44 born England.
FRANCES, FRANCES, 23, F, None listed, -, NY, 347, 309, CHAS+. In HH of John Francis m 44 born England.
FRANCES, RICHARD, 11, M, None listed, -, NY, 347, 309, CHAS+. In HH of John Francis m 44 born England.
FRANKLIN, LOUISA, 17, F, None listed, -, NY, 149, 139, CHAS-. In HH of Alice Ashby f 25 born NY.
FRANKLIN, STEPHEN, 51, M, Hatter, -, MD, 565, 562, AND. In HH of Stephen Haney m 44 Hatter born SC.
FRELAND, DANIEL, 28, M, Merchant, -, NJ, 1213, 1213, ABB. In HH of Abram Walker m 37 born NC.
FRILLINGS, ABBEY, 26, F, None listed, -, NJ, 232, 237, RICH. In HH of Edward Frillings m 31 born England.
FRILLINGS, SARAH P., 4, F, None listed, -, NJ, 232, 237, RICH. In HH of Edward Frillings m 31 born England.
FRULAND, J.M.C., 33, M, Merchant, -, NY, 1072, 1072, EDGE.
FRUSSEL, HOENSLEY, 78, M, Farmer, -, MD, 57, 57, AND*.
FULLER, R.M., 36, M, Merchant, -, NY, 1004, 1004, EDGE.
FURGUSON, JAMES T., 63, M, Farmer, -, PA, 5, 5, CHES.
FURRMAN, JAMES, 53, M, Shop keeper, -, NY, 319, 294, CHAS.
FUTTON, ANNIE S., 86, F, None listed, -, MD, 2, 2, YORK+.

G

GABLE, JANE, 22, F, None listed, -, NY, 1724, 1727, EDGE. In HH of R.W. Gable lm 33 born SC.
GABRON, JUDY, 47, F, None listed, -, NY, 872, 871, KERS.
GAGE, JAMES W., 40, M, Carpenter, -, NY, 1818, 1818, ABB.
GAITHER, JAMES W., 29, M, Jeweller, -,D.C, 599, 616, RICH.
GALLAWAY, MARY, 26, F, None listed, -, NY, 679, 659, CHAS-.
GAMAGE, EDWARD, 38, M, Merchant, -, NY, 251, 229, CHAS. In HH of John Lee m 58 mulatto, hotel keeper, born SC.
GAMAGE, ESTHER, 35, M, None listed, -, NY, 251, 229, CHAS. In HH of John Lee m 58 mulatto, hotel keeper, born SC.
GANNON, MICHAEL, 8, M, None listed, -, NY, 274, 254, CHAS+. In HH of Roger Gannon m 30 born Ireland.

GANTT,?, RICHARD, 85, M, None listed, -, MD, 1240, 1240, GREE.
GARBER, ELIZA, 60, F, None listed, -, NY, 473, 439, CHAS*. In HH of S. Wierfelder m 30 born Germany.
GARDNER, JAS. N., 44, M, Physician, -, NY, 140, 140, ORNG*.
GARDNER, PHOEBE N, 69, F, None listed, -, NY, 140, 140, ORNG*. In HH of Jas. N. Gardner m 44, physician, born NY.
GARDNER, PHOEBE N., 69, F, None listed, -, NY, 140, 140, ORNG*. In HH of Jas. N. Gardner m 44 born NY.
GARDNER, SAMUEL, 47, M, Baker, -, MD, 428, 439, RICH.
GARRISON, ANN, 73, F, None listed, -, PA, 431, 431, YORK.
GASSAWAY, BENJAMIN, 68, M, Farmer, -, MD, 302, 303, AND*.
GASTHER, RACHEL, 80, F, None listed, -, MD, 1421, 1421, YORK. In HH of Sarah Bradshaw f 40 born Fairfield Dist., SC.
GAWLY, GEO. B., 49, M, School teacher, -, NY, 648, 648, SUMT.
GEARTY, WM., 45, M, Merchant, -, PA, 181, 181, EDGE*.
GEVINS?, MARY, 80, F, None listed, -, PA, 1306, 1306, YORK. In HH of Samuel Gevins? m 84 born NC.
GIBSON, WM. H., 50, M, Wharfinger, -, PA, 374, 347, CHAS*. In HH of Harriot Gray f 45 born SC.
GIFFER, MARY, 36, F, None listed, -, NY, 471, 437, CHAS*. In HH of Hans Giffer m 44 born Denmark.
GIFFORD, MARY, 40, F, None listed, -, NY, 870, 870, KERS.
GILBERT, ELIZ. MRS., 45, F, None listed, -, NJ, 53, 53, COLL.
GILBERT, MARY, 83, F, None listed, -, NY, 2250, 2250, GREE. In HH of J.H. Benidick m 54 born CT.
GILBERT, MARY, 81, F, None listed, -, NY, 27, 27, RICH.
GILCHRIST, MARY, 52, M, None listed, -, NY, 881, 839, CHAS+. In HH of The Honorable R.B. Gilchrist m 53 born SC.
GILDER, J.L., 50, M, Physician, -, PA, 876, 876, NEWB.
GILLARD, JAMES R., 30, M, Preacher, Pres., -, PA, 806, 807, FAIR.
GILLMAN, B.B. MRS., 28, F, None listed, -, MD, 5, 5, AND. In HH of William Hubbard m 51, Innkeeper, born SC.
GILMORE, E.P., 36, M, Farmer, -, NY, 94, 94, LEX. Census states E.P. Gilmore m 36 born Patterson, New Jersey.
GILT, JOHN, 34, M, Carpenter, -, PA, 1163, 1142, CHAS%. Born Philadelphia, {PA}
GLADDEN, CATHARINE, 41, F, None listed, -,D.C., 1174, 1175, FAIR. In HH of John Gladden m 57 born SC. Catharine born Washington, D.C.
GLAZE, SARAH, 36, F, None listed, -, PA, 528, 487, CHAS+. In HH of Augustus Wilman m 33 born SC.
GLEASON, ELIZABETH, 33, F, None listed, -, PA, 836, 816,

CHAS-.
GLEASON, JANE ANN, 28, F, None listed, -, NY, 311, 295, CHAS-. In HH of John E. Gleason m 28 born PA.
GLEASON, JOHN E., 28, M, Professor of Music, -, PA, 311, 295, CHAS-.
GLEASON, SARAH CATHERINE, 3, F, None listed, -, NY, 311, 295, CHAS-. In HH of John E. Gleason m 28 born PA.
GLOVER, MARY J., 20, F, None listed, -, NY, 1814, 1820, EDGE. In HH of John Glover m 24 born SC.
GODDARD, N.B., 31, M, Farmer, -, MD, 911, 911, DARL.
GODMAN, H.R., 24, M, Physician, -, PA, 448, 448, LAU.
GOLDBERG, RACHEL, 9, F, None listed, -, PA, 638, 597, CHAS+. In HH of Jacob Goldberg m 38 born Germany.
GOLDBERG, REBECCA, 7, F, None listed, -, PA, 638, 597, CHAS+. In HH of Jacob Goldberg m 38 born Germany.
GONZALLUS, JOHN, 4, M, None listed, -, NY, 327, 296, CHAS+. In HH of Sarah Logan f 45 born SC.
GONZALLUS, MATILDA, 6, F, None listed, -, NY, 327, 296, CHAS+. In HH of Sarah Logan f 45 born SC.
GONZALLUS, WILLIAM, 0, M, None listed, -, NY, 327, 296, CHAS+. In HH of Sarah Logan f 45 born SC. William Gonzzallus age 8/12 yr.
GOODMAN, A.S., 21, F, None listed, -, NY, 26, 26, EDGE. IN HH of W.W. Goodman m 28 born MA.
GOODMAN, HENRY, 44, M, Labourer, -, PA, 1837, 1843, EDGE.
GOODWIN, ARTHUR G., 25, M, Merchant, -, NY, 470, 485, RICH. In HH of Henry Medlock m 23 born SC.
GOODWIN, GEORGE, 38, M, Clerk, -, NJ, 911, 891, CHAS-.
GOODWIN, MARY, 32, F, None listed, -, NJ, 911, 891, CHAS-. In HH of George Goodwin m 38 born NJ.
GORDON, JOHN, 40, M, Grocer, -, NY, 149, 149, CHAS%.
GORDON, THOMAS, 24, M, Merchant, -, NJ, 504, 504, FAIR. In HH of J.F. Gamble m 42, hotel keeper, born NC. Thomas Gordon born Newark, NJ. At the Winnsboro Hotel.
GORMAN, JOHN, 23, M, Teacher, -, NY, 94, 96, AND.
GOSNILE, JOSHUA, 93, M, Laborer, -, MD, 691, 691, GREE.
GOSSETT, CATHARINE, 80, F, None listed, -, MD, 1245, 1245, UNION. In HH of Elijah Gossett m 50 born SC.
GOUBER, A., 3, M, None listed, -, NY, 47, 43, Cash$. In HH of John Ewing m 50 born MA.
GOVENEUR, ELIZABETH, 14, F, None listed, -, NY, 383, 347, CHAS. In HH of Peter Goveneur m 44 born France.
GOWING, RODNEY, 24, M, Clerk, -, NY, 559, 559, UNION. In HH of Charles Gowing m 54 born VT.

GRADY, MARY T., 30, F, None listed, -, NY, 983, 962, CHAS-. In HH of James Grady m 40 born SC.
GRAHAM, ELIZABETH, 30, F, None listed, -, PA, 84, 84, BEAU. IN HH of Richardson Graham m 35 born Ireland.
GRAHAM, MARTHA, 22, F, None listed, -, PA, 801, 801, SUMT. In HH of John Q. Graham m 32 born Ireland.
GRANDY, HARRIOT, 28, F, None listed, -, NY, 248, 233, CHAS-.
GRANT, MARY, 24, F, None listed, -, NY, 824, 804, CHAS-. In HH of N.S. King m 39 born NY.
GRAY, JOHN S., 57, M, Merchant, -, PA, 423, 434, RICH.
GRAY, LOUISA, 13, F, None listed, -, NY, 849, 807, CHAS+. In HH of Chris Gray m 40 born Germany.
GREEN, ANN E., 20, F, None listed, -, PA, 450, 450, FAIR. In HH of Daniel H. Kerr m 65 born PA.
GREEN, REBECCA, 35, F, None listed, -, PA, 2021, 2027, EDGE. In HH of John Green m 40 born Germany.
GREER, ELIZABEATH, 23, M, None listed, -, NY, 186, 169, CHAS. In HH of Wm. Greer m 25 born Ireland.
GREER, MARY JANE, 24, F, None listed, -, NY, 202, 189, CHAS-. In HH of Grace Piexolla f 30 born SC. **GRICE, GEO. D.**, 21, M, Clerk, -, NJ, 822, 802, CHAS-.
GRIFFIN, DAVID F., 27, M, School teacher, -, NY, 1998, 1995, EDGE.
GRIFFIN, HANNAH, 23, F, None listed, -, NY, 1998, 1995, EDGE. In HH of David F. Griffin m 27 born NY.
GRIMBALL, E.B., 18, F, None listed, -, NY, 27, 27, CHAS*. In HH of J.B. Grimball m 50 born SC.
GRINER, ANN, 43, F, None listed, -, NY, 398, 359, CHAS+.
GRISWOLD, CAROLINE, 16, F, None listed, -, NY, 663, 655, CHAS%. In HH of Mary J.'On {sic} Kentock f 45 born SC.
GROSS, JOHN, 67, M, None listed, -, PA, 679, 671, CHAS%.
GROVE, CHARLES, 26, M, Clerk, -, PA, 369, 342, CHAS*.
GROVES, JOSEPH, 82, M, Farmer, -, MD, 1191, 1191, ABB.
GRUBER, WM. H., 33, M, Plasterer, -, MD, 771, 729, CHAS+.
GUINORAN, JOHN, 65, M, Watchmaker, -, NY, 1973, 1979, EDGE.

H

HADDOCK, JOHN, 40, M, Farmer, -, PA, 1394, 1394, CHES.
HAFSETT, MICHAEL, 21, M, Seaman, -, NY, 326, 301, CHAS. On Steam Ship Southerner.
HAGNES, P., MAJOR, 40, M, Command Officer U.S. Arsenal, -,D.C, 1005, 982, CHAS%. Born : District of Columbia.
HAIGHT, ASHLEY A., 25, M, Printer, -, NY, 558, 574, RICH.
HAISTIE, JOHN, 35, M, Merchant, -, NY, 453, 453, LAU.

HALL, HENRY, 22, M, Clerk, -, NY, 211, 216, RICH.
HALL, JAMES, 43, M, Merchant, -, PA, 105, 106, RICH. Note: {Page out of order}. follows HH 146/150.
HALMAN, M., 34, M, Clerk, -, NY, 379, 344, CHAS. In HH of N.R. Schineder m 32 born Germany.
HAMILTON, CAROLINE, 47, F, None listed, -, NY, 277, 261, CHAS-. In HH of Alexander Hamilton m 52 born SC.
HAMILTON, ELIZABETH, 30, F, None listed, -, MD, 370, 370, EDGE. In HH of John B. Hamilton m 45 born SC. Elizabeath Hamilton born Baltimore, MD.
HAMILTON, JANE, 22, F, None listed, -, PA, 693, 694, FAIR. In HH of Robert Brice m 58 born SC.
HAMILTON, THOMAS, 92, M, Farmer, -, PA, 891, 892, AND*. In HH of Davis K. Hamilton m 56 born SC.
HAMNER, JAMES, 47, M, Nonek, -, MD, 470, 485, RICH. In Hotel
HAMPTON, E.A., 23, M, Coach maker, -, NJ, 2312, 2312, GREE. In HH of E.M. Gower m 36 born ME.
HANCE, WILLIAM, 45, M, Saddler, -, PA, 1208, 1208, LAU.
HANCKEL, C.M., REVD., 64, M, Protestant .Episcopal Minister, -, PA, 1114, 1091, CHAS-.
HARBERT, ELIZA, 33, F, None listed, -, NY, 546, 547, AND*. In HH of Frederic Harbert m 39 born Germany.
HARD, B.F., 69, M, Planter, -, NY, 938, 918, CHAS-.
HARDIN, MARY, 86, F, None listed, -, MD, 1173, 1173, CHES.
HARDY, ISAAC, 75, M, None, B, MD, 1242, 1242, UNION.
HARE, ROBT. W., 37, M, Merchant, -, PA, 517, 476, CHAS+.
HARINGTON, C.F., 34, M, Waggon maker, -, NY, 2064, 2071, EDGE.
HARKIN, JOHN, 15, M, None listed, -, PA, 538, 553, RICH. In HH of John Harkin m 48 born Ireland.
HARKIN, MICHAEL, 13, M, None listed, -, PA, 538, 553, RICH. In HH of John Harkin m 48 born Ireland.
HARRAL, ST.M, 33, F, None listed, -, NY, 958, 938, CHAS-. In HH of William Harral m 37 born NY.
HARRAL, WILLIAM, 37, M, Apothecary, -, NY, 958, 938, CHAS-.
HARRINGTON, CAROLINE, 19, F, None listed, -, NY, 882, 840, CHAS+. In Charleston Hotel.
HARRINGTON, FRANCES, 25, F, None listed, -, NY, 937, 917, CHAS-. In Boarding House.
HARRIS, A.B., 13, F, None listed, -, MD, 47, 43, CHAS$. In HH of John Ewing m 50 born MA.
HARRIS, ANNA, 80, F, None listed, -, MD, 297, 299, AND. In HH of Sarah G. Harris f 50 born SC.
HARRIS, CATHERINE, 30, F, None listed, -, MD, 47, 43, CHAS$. In HH of John Ewing m 50 born MA.

HARRIS, H.J., 11, M, None listed, -, MD, 47, 43, CHAS$. In HH of John Ewing m 50 born MA.
HARRIS, MATHIAS, 51, M, Clergyman, P.E., -, MD, 47, 43, CHAS$. In HH of John Ewing m 50 born MA.
HARRIS, RICHARD, 28, M, Mariner, -, MD, 334, 308, CHAS. In HH of William Bennett m 40 born NY.
HARRIS, WILLIAM, 65, M, None listed, -, NJ, 598, 598, YORK. In HH of Elesinga W. Smith m 49 born York Dist., SC.
HARRISON, NANCY, 80, F, None listed, -, NJ, 863, 903, PICK.
HARRISON, NANCY, 80, F, None listed, -, NJ, 863, 903, PICK.
HARROD, GEORGE, 26, M, Labourer, -, PA, 1736, 1737, EDGE. In HH of Samuel Cook m 57 born SC.
HART, H.N., 28, F, None listed, -, NJ, 412, 395, CHAS-. In HH of H.N. Hart m 36 born Ireland.
HARTPENS, CATHERINE, 40, F, None listed, -, NJ, 408, 368, CHAS+. In HH of Elijah Hartpens m 44 born NJ.
HARTPENS, ELIJAH, 44, M, Laborer, -, NJ, 408, 368, CHAS+.
HARTPENS, ELIZA, 12, F, None listed, -, NJ, 408, 368, CHAS+. In HH of Elijah Hartpens m 44 born NJ.
HARTZ, MARY, 4, F, None listed, -, NY, 26, 24, CHAS-. In HH of F.P. Hartz m 40 born Germany.
HARVEY, MARIA, 38, F, None listed, -, PA, 795, 753, CHAS+.
HASGOOD, SALOME, 22, F, None listed, -, NY, 46, 46, BEAU. In HH of William A. Morcock m 46 born SC, Susan Morecock runs boardinghouse.
HASGOOD, SARAH, 20, F, None listed, -, NY, 46, 46, BEAU. In HH of William A. Morcock m 46 born SC, Susan Morecock runs boardinghouse.
HASKELL, ELIZA S., 26, F, None listed, -, NY, 177, 177, YORK. In HH of Samuel Moore m 58 born York Dist., SC.
HASKELL, ISAAC, 32, M, Joiner, -, NY, 42, 42, BEAU.
HATFIELD, ELIZABETH, 56, F, None listed, -, NY, 7, 7, CHAS. In HH of Mary Richisby f 50 born NY.
HAVELAND, W., 24, M, Clerk, -, NY, 836, 816, CHAS-. In Boarding House.
HAVEN, ELIZA, 45, F, None listed, -, NY, 362, 324, CHAS+.
HAWLEY, RICHMOND, 25, M, Merchant, -, NY, 196, 200, RICH.
HAWTHORN, ANN E., 24, F, None listed, -, NJ, 472, 487, RICH. In HH of Henry Hawthorn m 29 born Canada.
HAYDEN, CALVIN, 55, M, Planterer, -, NY, 95, 96, ORNG+.
HAYDEN, CALVIN, 55, M, Planter, -, NY, 95, 96, ORNG+.
HAYNA, ANNA, 16, F, None listed, -, PA, 848, 828, CHAS-. In HH of B. Figeroux m 42 born West Indies.
HAYNE, MARGARETTA, 24, F, None listed, -, PA, 103, 101, CHAS*. In HH of R.B. Hayne f 55 born SC.
HAYS, CHARLES, 26, M,

Waggon maker, -, MD, 269, 269, FAIR.
HAZELIUS, HULD C., 63, F, None listed, -, NJ, 65, 65, LEX. In HH of E.L. Hazelius m 72 Lutheran Clergy born Prussia.
HEART, ELIZA D., 33, F, None listed, -,D.C., 239, 224, CHAS-. Born Washington, D.C.. In HH of John Heart m 44 born PA.
HEART, JOHN, 44, M, Editor Charles{ton} Mer{?}y, -, PA, 239, 224, CHAS-.
HEISE, HARRIET A., 33, F, None listed, -, MD, 681, 700, RICH. In HH of James R. Heise m 38 born D.C..
HEISE, JAMES R., 38, M, RR Officer, -,D.C., 681, 700, RICH.
HEISE, JOHN H., 39, M, Confectioner, -,D.C., 384, 394, RICH.
HEISE, MARION, 8, F, None listed, -, MD, 681, 700, RICH. In HH of James R. Heise m 38 born D.C..
HEISE, MARY E., 15, F, None listed, -,D.C., 681, 700, RICH. In HH of James R. Heise m 38 born D.C..
HENDERSON, J.P?, 36, M, Carpenter, -, PA, 2303, 2303, GREE. In Hotel.
HENRY, ARABELLA, 80, F, Farmer, -,DE, 328, 328, YORK*.
HENSOLL, W., 19, M, Clerk, -, NY, 379, 344, CHAS. In HH of N.R. Schineder m 32 born Germany.
HENSON, REBECCA, 73, F, None listed, -, MD, 1000, 1000, GREE. In HH of John Henson m 75 born VA.
HERBEMONT, ALEXANDER H., 58, M, Clerk Court App, -, NY, 622, 640, RICH. Clerk Court Appeals.
HERBERT, PHOEBE, 45, F, None listed, -, NY, 185, 174, CHAS+. In HH of Michael Herbert m 39 born France.
HERBERT, WILLIAM C., 30, M, Painter, -, MD, 346, 308, CHAS+. In Boarding House.
HERVING, JAMES, 43, M, Merchant, -, MD, 551, 534, CHAS-.
HEWOT, JOSEPH, 47, M, Hotel keeper, -, NY, 3, 3, CHAS$.
HICKEY, DANIEL, 28, M, Servant, -, NY, 882, 840, CHAS+. In Charleston Hotel.
HICKMIN, M.E., 49, M, Canter, -,DE, 100, 100, GEOR.
HIGMAN, ABRAHAM, 5, M, None listed, -, NY, 165, 169, RICH. In HH of John W. Higman m 32 born England.
HIGMAN, ANNA A., 7, F, None listed, -, NY, 165, 169, RICH. In HH of John W. Higman m 32 born England.
HILL, ELIZA, 19, F, None listed, -, NY, 38, 33, CHAS+. In Boarding House.
HILL, JOHN, 47, M, Merchant, -, PA, 141, 132, CHAS+.
HILL, JOHN W., 25, M, Carriage builder, -, NY, 38, 33, CHAS+. In Boarding House.
HILL, MARGARET, 40, F, None listed, -, PA, 141, 132, CHAS+. In HH of John Hill m 47 born PA.
HILL, ROLAND, 12, M, None listed, -, NY, 2195, 2202, EDGE.

In HH of James Hill m 44 born England.
HILL, WALTER, 17, M, Carpenter, -, NY, 2195, 2202, EDGE. In HH of James Hill m 44 born England.
HILLEBRANT, JOHN W., 55, M, Hireling, -, NY, 425, 425, ABB. In HH of Alexander Scott m 50 born SC.
HINCLEY, WILLIAM, 22, M, Seaman, -, NY, 326, 301, CHAS. On Steam Ship Southerner.
HISLOP, JOHN, 35, M, Cotton Presser, -, MD, 693, 651, CHAS+. In HH of William Hislop m 43 born MD.
HISLOP, WILLIAM, 43, M, Cotton presser, -, MD, 693, 651, CHAS+.
HITCHCOCK, WILLIAM, 34, M, Proprietor Stable, -, NY, 450, 463, RICH.
HOAGLAND, CHARLES, 30, M, Saddler, -, NJ, 295, 301, RICH.
HOBBS, HENRY, 7, M, None listed, -, NY, 409, 392, CHAS-. In HH of William Hobbs m 45 born England.
HODGE, SAMUEL, 84, M, Planter, -, PA, 1288, 1288, UNION.
HODGES, MARY, 42, F, None listed, -,D.C., 264, 266, AND. D.C. {District of Columbia}.
HOFF, JOHN C., 60, M, Stationer, -, PA, 298, 275, CHAS.
HOFFMAN, CHRISA., 20, F, Milliner, -, PA, 852, 832, CHAS-. In HH of A.G. Parker f 38 born Germany.
HOLLISTER, MARY, 46, F, None listed, -, NY, 293, 299, RICH. In HH of Howel W. Hollister m 48 born CT.
HOLMES, AMELIA L., 34, F, None listed, -, MD, 73, 83, CHAS. In HH of James G. Holmes m 52 born SC.
HOLMES, WATSON, 36, M, Carpenter, -, NY, 62, 62, Orng.
HOLMES, WATSON, 36, M, Carpenter, -, NY, 61, 62, ORNG.
HOLMES, Z.L., 35, M, Minister, -, NY, 1334, 1334, LAU.
HOOD, ELIZA, 45, F, None listed, -, NY, 427, 396, CHAS*.
HOOD, MARY, 73, F, None listed, -, MD, 1228, 1228, YORK. In HH of John P. Hood m 30 born York Dist., SC.
HOPKIN, ANNY, 22, F, None listed, -, MD, 1446, 1446, SPART. In HH of William Hopkin m 91 born MD.
HOPKIN, DINA, 26, F, None listed, -, MD, 1446, 1446, SPART. In HH of William Hopkin m 91 born MD.
HOPKIN, JAMES, 27, M, None listed, -, MD, 1446, 1446, SPART. In HH of William Hopkin m 91 born MD.
HOPKIN, NANCY, 62, F, None listed, -, MD, 1446, 1446, SPART. In HH of William Hopkin m 91 born MD.
HOPKIN, S.A., 19, F, None listed, -, MD, 1446, 1446, SPART. In HH of William Hopkin m 91 born MD.
HOPKIN, WILLIAM, 91, M, Farmer, -, MD, 1446, 1446, SPART.
HOPKINS, JOHN SENR., 59, M, Farmer, -, MD, 264, 265,

AND*.
HOPKINSON, JAMES, 36, M, Planter, -, NJ, 97, 97, CHAS^.
HOPSON, LINUS F., 30, M, Saddler, -, NY, 390, 400, RICH.
HORSEY, RACHEL, 68, F, None listed, -, MD, 704, 704, YORK. In HH of David Horsey m 68 born VA.
HORTON, JOEL W., 34, M, Farmer, -, MD, 139, 139, EDGE.
HORTON, THOMAS, 75, M, Merchant, -, NY, 939, 919, CHAS-. In HH of George Thomson m 60 born SC.
HOSHELL, JESSE, 40, M, Tanner, -, MD, 399, 399, FAIR. In HH of Samuel Jackson m 40 born SC.
HOUGHTON, H.C., 25, F, None listed, -, NY, 533, 537, AND. In Hotel.
HOWARD, VIRGINIA, 18, F, None listed, -, NY, 32, 29, CHAS-. In HH of Ellen Gillet f 60 born VA
HOWELL, GEHUGH, 45, M, Farmer, -, NY, 1170, 1170, GREE.
HOWELL, JOSIAH, 80, M, Farmer, -, NJ, 306, 306, EDGE. In HH of Jacob Wright m 45 born SC.
HOWELL, STEPHEN M., 30, M, Saddler, -, NJ, 279, 285, RICH.
HOWTON, HENRY, 25, M, Waiter, -, NY, 326, 301, CHAS. In HH of William Rollins m 40 born {-}. In crew of the Steam Ship Isabel.
HOXIE, NORTON A., 27, M, Merchant, -, NY, 618, 636, RICH.
HOYT, EPHRAIM S., 39, M, Carpenter, -, NY, 30, 30, RICH.

HUGGINS, M., 58, M, None listed, -, NY, 13, 13, SPART.
HUGHES, MAHALE, 80, M, None listed, -, MD, 690, 725, PICK. In HH of John Hughes m 45 born SC.
HULL, ANN, 60, F, None listed, -, NJ, 1992, 1998, EDGE. In HH of Josiah J. Bryson m 35 born TN.
HUNITCH, EDWARD H., 28, M, Druggist, -, PA, 392, 402, RICH.
HUNITCH, FRANCIS, 25, F, None listed, -, PA, 392, 402, RICH. In HH of Edward H. Hunitch m 28 born PA.
HUNT, MARTHA E., 50, F, None listed, -, MD, 470, 485, RICH. In HH of Alfred M. Hunt m 50 born NC.
HUNTER, ETHELINDA, 28, F, None listed, -, PA, 16, 17, AND. In HH of Mary Hunter f 50 born PA.
HUNTER, MANDANNA, 30, F, None listed, -, PA, 16, 17, AND. In HH of Mary Hunter f 50 born PA.
HUNTER, MARY, 50, F, None listed, -, PA, 16, 17, AND.
HUNTER, SARAH, 64, F, None listed, -, PA, 538, 538, PICK+. In HH of Wm. Hunter m 31 born SC.
HUNTER, SUSAN, 18, F, None listed, -, NJ, 476, 491, RICH. In HH of Johnson Hunter m 24 born Ireland.
HURDLE, EDWARD, 32, M, Carpenter, -, NY, 237, 222, CHAS-. Poor House.
HURLBUT, F.C., 16, F, None listed, -, PA, 582, 540, CHAS+. In HH of M.A. Hurlbut f 49 born NJ.

HURLBUT, M.A., 49, F, None listed, -, NJ, 582, 540, CHAS+.
HURLBUT, MARY JANE, 18, F, None listed, -, PA, 582, 540, CHAS+. In HH of M.A. Hurlbut f 49 born NJ.
HURST, ROBERT, 22, M, None listed, -, NY, 673, 653, CHAS-. In HH of J.G. Newcomb m 27 born NY.
HURST, WILLIAM, 22, M, Confectioner, -, NY, 673, 653, CHAS-. In HH of J.G. Newcomb m 27 born NY.
HUTCHENS, CLARA, 21, F, None listed, -, MD, 499, 453, CHAS. In HH of Eliza O. Hanlin f 58 born SC.

I

IDE, JOSEPH E., 34, M, Stonecutter, -, PA, 350, 350, YORK.
ISAACS, A., 28, M, Merchant, -, NY, 5, 5, AND. In HH of William Hubbard m 51, Innkeeper, born SC.

J

JACKSON, M.A., 33, F, None listed, -, NJ, 290, 290, CHES. In HH of Wm. H. Jackson m 57 born SC.
JACOBI, GEORGIANA S., 14, F, Merchant, -, NY, 694, 674, CHAS-. In HH of W.J. Jacobi m 53 born Prussia.
JACOBS, FERDINAND, 11, M, None listed, -, MD, 297, 297, CHAS%. In HH of Ferdind Jacobs m 40 born VA.

JARVIS, AUGUSTUS S., 24, M, Saddler, -, NJ, 347, 353, RICH. In HH of Jane E. Reeder f 37 born MA.
JEFFORDS, E.W., 50, F, None listed, -, NJ, 404, 364, CHAS+. In HH of James Marsh m 78 born NJ.
JENKENS, DOROTHEA, 70, F, None listed, -, MD, 437, 460, PICK.
JENKENS, DOROTHEA, 68, F, None listed, -, MD, 656, 690, PICK. In HH of Archibald Jenkens m 29 born SC.
JENKINS, ADAM H., 33, M, Planter, -, DE, 442, 442, COLL.
JENNINGS, MARGARET, 11, F, None listed, -, NY, 141, 129, CHAS*. In HH of William Jennings m 30 born SC.
JERVEY, JOS. E.V., 7, M, None listed, -, NJ, 685, 643, CHAS+. In HH of Thomas D. Jervey m 32 born NC.
JOHNSON, A., 32, M, Priv. U.S.A., -, NY, 47, 43, CHAS$. In HH of John Ewing m 50 born MA.
JOHNSON, CAROLINE, 19, F, None listed, -, NY, 32, 29, CHAS-. In HH of Ellen Gillet f 60 born VA.
JOHNSON, ELIZA, 13, F, None listed, -, NY, 227, 232, RICH. {Page out of order}, follows HH 177/181. In HH of Giles M. Johnson m 38born NJ.
JOHNSON, EMILY F., 9, F, None listed, -, NY, 227, 232, RICH. {Page out of order}, follows HH 177/181. In HH of Giles M. Johnson m 38born NJ.

JOHNSON, GEORGE, 26, M, Seaman, -, NY, 326, 301, CHAS. On Steam Ship Southerner.
JOHNSON, GILES M., 38, M, Clerk, -, NJ, 227, 232, RICH. {Page out of order}, follows HH 177/181.
JOHNSON, JANE M., 63, F, None listed, -, MD, 1007, 1007, CHES.
JOHNSON, MAHALA, 36, F, None listed, -, NY, 227, 232, RICH. {{Page out of order}, follows HH 177/181}. In HH of Giles M. Johnson m 38 born NJ.
JOHNSON, REBECCA, 35, F, None listed, -, PA, 259, 237, CHAS. In HH of James Johnson m 36 born Germany.
JOHNSTON, ANN, 60, F, Seamstress, -, MD, 22, 26, CHAS.
JOHNSTON, ELIZA P., 29, F, None listed, -, NY, 240, 245, RICH. In HH of William B. Johnston m 32 born Ireland.
JOHNSTON, ROBT., 21, M, Clerk, -, NY, 127, 118, CHAS+. In Boarding House.
JOICE, JOBE, 38, M, Printer, -, NY, 1723, 1724, EDGE. In HH of Hiram Jordan m 36, landlord, born SC.
JONES, ANNA, 46, F, None listed, -, NY, 499, 465, CHAS*. In HH of John Jones m 50 born NY.
JONES, CATHERINE, 29, F, None listed, -, NY, 559, 517, CHAS+. In HH of Edward Jones m 32 born NY.
JONES, E.D., 9, M, None listed, -, NY, 60, 60, EDGE. IN HH of Oratio Blease m 46 born England.
JONES, EDWARD, 32, M, Gass Fitter, -, NY, 559, 517, CHAS+.
JONES, EMMA, 24, F, None listed, -, PA, 321, 296, CHAS. In HH of Samuel Jones m 40 born SC.
JONES, JOHN, 65, M, Planter, -, MD, 1319, 1319, EDGE.
JONES, JOHN, 50, M, Clerk, -, NY, 499, 465, CHAS*.
JONES, JOHN, 28, M, Laborer, -, MD, 1197, 1176, CHAS%. In Boarding House.
JONES, JOHN, 27, M, Book binder, -, NY, 499, 465, CHAS*. In HH of John Jones m 50 born NY.
JONES, JOHN L., 50, M, Ship chandler, -, NY, 173, 156, CHAS.
JONES, MATILDA, 19, F, None listed, -, NJ, 32, 29, CHAS-. In HH of Ellen Gillet f 60 born VA.
JONES, NANCY, 80, F, None listed, -, PA, 71, 71, YORK. In HH of James L. Jones born York Dist., SC.
JONES, OLLIVER, 50, M, Labourer, -, PA, 2086, 2093, EDGE.
JONES, RACHEL, 40, F, None listed, -, NY, 57, 58, ORNG+. In HH of James Jones m 40 born England.
JONES, WILLIAM, 12, M, None listed, -, NY, 559, 517, CHAS+. In HH of Edward Jones m 32 born NY.
JONES, WILLIAM HENRY, 40, M, Master mariner, -, NY, 202, 185, CHAS*.
JOSEPHS, LOUISA, 20, F, None listed, -, NY, 90, 102, CHAS. In HH of S.J. Josephs m 22 born Italy.

JOUDON, ELIZABETH, 25, F, None listed, -, NY, 198, 186, CHAS-. In HH of Emily Timbrook f 49 born PA.
JUMPER, MARTHA J., 57, F, None listed, -, NY, 608, 625, RICH. In HH of Walter Van Wart m 27 born NY.
JUNE, DANIEL R., 52, M, Physician/planter, -, NY, 210, 210, FAIR.
JUST, MARGARET, 50, F, None listed, -, PA, 460, 443, CHAS-. In HH of George Just m 65 born Germany.

K

KAY, ELIZABETH, 62, F, None listed, -, MD, 848, 848, ABB. In HH of James J. Kay m 63 born VA.
KEELER, T.H., 53, M, Millwright, -, NY, 81, 81, GREE.
KEENAN, ELIZABETH, 60, F, None listed, -, NY, 2, 2, CHAS-. In HH of James Moorhead m 50 born Ireland.
KELLY, CAROLINE, 25, F, None listed, -, NY, 1663, 1663, BARN. In HH of Geo. Kelly m 35 born NY.
KELLY, GEO., 35, M, Miller, -, NY, 1663, 1663, BARN.
KELLY, MARGARET, 10, F, None listed, -, NY, 331, 298, CHAS+. In HH of James McCormick m 31 born Ireland.
KELLY, MARY, 20, F, Servant, -, NY, 45, 53, CHAS. In HH of Wilmot DeSanfure m 28, Attorney at Law, born SC.
KELLY, THOMAS, 46, M, Boot maker, -, NY, 232, 210, CHAS.
KELLY, WILLIAM, 62, M, Farmer, -,DE, 55, 55, GREE.
KENNARD, JOHN, 51, M, Teacher, -, PA, 237, 222, CHAS-. Works in Poor House.
KENNEDY, JAMES, 33, M, Clerk, -, NY, 495, 449, CHAS. In HH of Joseph Douglas m 44 born NY.
KENNY, CATHERINE, 12, F, None listed, -, NY, 279, 259, CHAS+. In HH of James Kenny m 43 born Ireland.
KENNY, MARY JANE, 14, F, None listed, -, NY, 279, 259, CHAS+. In HH of James Kenny m 43 born Ireland.
KERN, FANNY, 32, F, None listed, -, NY, 237, 222, CHAS-. Poor House.
KERR, DANIEL H., 65, M, Planter, -, PA, 450, 450, FAIR.
KERR, WILLIAM, 50, M, Shoe maker, -, PA, 450, 450, FAIR. In HH of Daniel H. Kerr m 65 born PA.
KETCHAM, WILLIAM., 38, M, Landlord, -, NJ, 1987, 1990, EDGE.
KETCHUM, A.H., 30, M, Painter, -, PA, 124, 115, CHAS+. In Boarding House.
KETCHUM, JOEL, 41, M, Merchant, -, NY, 240, 240, CHAS%.
KING, AMELIA, 7, F, None listed, -, NY, 1088, 1066, CHAS%. In HH of James K. King m 40 born NY.
KING, ANN E., 36, F, None listed, -, NY, 1088, 1066, CHAS%. In HH of James K. King

m 40 born NY.
KING, CAROLINE, 9, F, None listed, -, NY, 1088, 1066, CHAS%. In HH of James K. King m 40 born NY.
KING, ELIZABETH M., 17, F, None listed, -, NY, 1088, 1066, CHAS%. In HH of James K. King m 40 born NY.
KING, EMILY, 11, F, None listed, -, NJ, 824, 804, CHAS-. In HH of N.S. King m 39 born NY.
KING, JAMES K., 40, M, Carpenter, -, NY, 1088, 1066, CHAS%.
KING, JOHN, 12, M, None listed, -, NY, 1088, 1066, CHAS%. In HH of James K. King m 40 born NY.
KING, N.S., 39, M, Shop keeper, -, NY, 824, 804, CHAS-.
KING, RUTH S., 19, F, None listed, -, NY, 369, 378, RICH. In HH of Gilbert T. Snowden m 56 born NJ.
KINGMAN, HANNAH, 88, F, None listed, -, NY, 198, 186, CHAS-. In HH of Emily Timbrook f 49 born PA.
KINGSTAND, E.W., 40, M, Merchant, -, NJ, 2310, 2310, GREE. In HH of John Eretenden m 67 born CT.
KINGSTAND, ISAAC, 5, M, None listed, -, NY, 2310, 2310, GREE. In HH of John Eretenden m 67 born CT.
KINGSTAND, JOHN, 7, M, None listed, -, NJ, 2310, 2310, GREE. In HH of John Eretenden m 67 born CT.
KLINE, ABRAHAM L., 35, M, Clerk, -, NJ, 368, 377, RICH.

KLINE, MARIA, 54, F, None listed, -, NJ, 368, 377, RICH. need to find whose HH she is in.368/377 {{Page out of order}.}..
KNAPP, FRANCES, 45, F, None listed, -, MD, 406, 389, CHAS-. In HH of William M. Smith m 32 born SC.
KNEFF, B., 31, M, Physician, -, PA, 804, 762, CHAS+.
KNEPLEY, SOLOMON, 58, M, Customs Inspector, -, PA, 546, 512, CHAS*.
KNEPLEY, SUSAN J., 47, F, None listed, -, MD, 546, 512, CHAS*. In HH of Solomon Knepley m 58 born PA.
KNOWLES, MARY, 20, F, None listed, -, NY, 198, 186, CHAS-. In HH of Emily Timbrook f 49 born PA.
KNOX, CATHERINE, 69, F, None listed, -, NY, 1089, 1066, CHAS-.
KNOX, GEORGE, 88, M, Farmer, -,DE, 232, 232, YORK*.
KNOX, SARAH ANN, 36, F, None listed, -, MD, 651, 610, CHAS+. In HH of William P. Knox m 38 born SC.
KNUST, GEORGE, 27, M, Clerk, -, PA, 447, 430, CHAS-. In HH of Sarah Knust f 67 born PA.
KNUST, SARAH, 67, F, None listed, -, PA, 447, 430, CHAS-.
KOETTER, CHARLES, 32, M, Planter, -, NY, 397, 397, SUMT.
KURTZ, JANE T., 28, F, None listed, -,D.C., 30, 30, CHAS!. In HH of John D. Kurtz m 30 born District of Columbia.

KURTZ, JOHN D., 30, M, Lt. W. Engineer, -,D.C., 30, 30, CHAS!. District of Columbia

L

LACASTO, JULIA ANN, 47, F, None listed, -, NY, 776, 734, CHAS+. In HH of Adolphus LaCasto m 51 born SC.
LADD, PATIENCE, 40, F, None listed, -, NY, 542, 557, RICH. Date 1838 by name. In Lunatic Asylum.
LALANE, J.A., JR., 29, M, Suger maker, -, NY, 142, 126, CHAS. In HH of J.A. Lalane m 60 born St. Domingo.
LALANE, PETER B., 32, M, Bank Officer, -, NY, 417, 389, CHAS*.
LAMBERT, MARTHA, 29, F, None listed, -, NY, 850, 808, CHAS+. In HH of Robert Lambert m 43 born Ireland.
LAND, ELIZABETH, 80, F, None listed, -, MD, 74, 74, SPART. In HH of H.A.W. Land m 43 born SC.
LANHAM, JOSIAH, 65, M, Planter, -, MD, 1255, 1255, EDGE.
LARK, CHARLES, 14, M, None listed, -, PA, 937, 937, PICK+. In HH of Charles Lark m 34 born Germany
LARKIN, CATHERINE, 15, F, None listed, -, NY, 124, 115, CHAS+. In HH of Catherine Larkin m 34 born Ireland.
LARKIN, JANE N., 13, F, None listed, -, NY, 124, 115, CHAS+. In HH of Catherine Larkin m 34 born Ireland.
LARKIN, MICHAEL, 33, M, Seaman, -, NY, 326, 301, CHAS. On Steam Ship Southerner.
LA ROUSSELLIERE, ISABELLA, 23, F, None listed, -, PA, 675, 655, CHAS-. In HH of T.H. LaRousselliere m 29 born SC.
LATIMER, CLEMENT, 68, M, Farmer, -, MD, 1499, 1499, ABB.
LATTA, ELIZA D., 55, F, None listed, -, PA, 878, 888, Rich+. In HH of Robert Latta m 67 born Ireland.
LAWSON, FREDERICK, 20, M, Seaman, -, NY, 326, 301, CHAS. On Steam Ship Southerner.
LAWSON, HIRAM T., 28, M, Tinner, -, NY, 772, 772, ABB.
LEADER, MARY, 77, F, None listed, -, NY, 193, 181, CHAS-.
LEAMAN, HENRIETTA, 6, F, None listed, -, PA, 411, 370, CHAS+. In HH of Jeannet Leaman f 40 born England.
LEAMAN, MITCHELL, 7, M, None listed, -, PA, 411, 370, CHAS+. In HH of Jeannet Leaman f 40 born England.
LEDYARD, JOHN, 22, M, Clerk, -, NY, 385, 395, RICH. In HH of Alexander Falls m 38 born NY.
LEDYARD, SARAH, 60, F, None listed, -, NY, 385, 395, RICH. In HH of Alexander Falls m 38 born NY.
LEE, FRANCIS, 62, F, None listed, -, MD, 72, 72, KERS.
LEGARD, LAVINA, 51, F, None listed, M, NY, 473, 431, CHAS+. In HH of Susan Legard f 18 mulatto born NY.

LEGARD, SUSAN, 18, F, None listed, M, NY, 473, 431, CHAS+.
LEGG, WILLIAM, 32, M, Taylor, -, MD, 8, 8, EDGE. In HH of H.R. Spann m 31 born SC.
LEGG, WISLEY, 25, M, Taylor, -, MD, 8, 8, EDGE. In HH of H.R. Spann m 31 born SC.
LENAR, PAMELIA, 29, F, None listed, -, MD, 400, 360, CHAS+. In HH of Joseph Lenar m 32 born Italy.
LEORELL?, ANN, 15, F, None listed, -, NY, 46, 46, BEAU. In HH of William A. Morcock m 46 born SC, Susan Morecock runs boardinghouse.
LESHER, MARY A., 27, F, None listed, -, PA, 208, 212, RICH. In HH of Susanna Lesher f 56 born PA.
LESHER, SUSANNA, 56, F, None listed, -, PA, 208, 212, RICH.
LESLY, LOUISA, 47, F, None listed, -, PA, 789, 789, ABB. In HH of David Lesly m 51 born SC.
LEVERTON, JAS., 50, M, Shoemaker, -, MD, 6, 6, LANC.
LEVY, CATHERINE, 20, F, None listed, -, NJ, 271, 239, CHAS. In HH of Orlando Levy m 24 born SC.
LEVY, ELIZA., 40, F, None listed, -, NY, 26, 31, CHAS. In HH of Moses Levy m 45 taven keeper born SC.
LEVY, H., 55, M, Merchant, -, NY, 50, 50, KERS.
LEVY, S.B., 28, M, Merchant, -, NY, 50, 50, KERS. In HH of H. Levy m 55 born NY.

LEWELL, HARRIOT, 40, F, None listed, -, NY, 238, 213, CHAS*. In HH of Robert Wotherspoon m 55 born Scotland.
LEWIS, WILLIAM, 34, M, Cabinet maker, -, PA, 2043, 2049, EDGE.
LHOMDIEU, O., 31, M, Artist, -, NJ, 843, 823, CHAS-.
LIDDONS, LAURENCE, 25, M, Clerk, -, NY, 728, 708, CHAS-. In HH of Maria Spencer f 63 born England.
LIMEHONER, BEN, 25, M, Miller, -, NY, 1664, 1664, BARN. In HH of John Limehoner m 35 born NY.
LIMEHONER, JOHN, 35, M, Miller, -, NY, 1664, 1664, BARN.
LITTLE, DAVID, 28, M, Mariner, -, NY, 38, 33, CHAS+. In Boarding House.
LOCKWOOD, ELIZABETH S., 30, F, None listed, -, MD, 11, 11, SPART. Elizabeth born Baltimore, MD. In HH of William Lockwood m 42 born England.
LOCKWOOD, JOHN, 9, M, None listed, -,D.C., 11, 11, SPART. John born Columbia {D.C.}. In HH of William Lockwood m 42 born England.
LOCKWOOD, SARAH A., 13, F, None listed, -, MD, 11, 11, SPART. Sarah A. born Baltimore, MD. In HH of William Lockwood m 42 born England.
LONG, ANDREW K., 39, M, Gass fitter, -, PA, 128, 120, CHAS*.
LONG, CAROLINE, 38, F, None listed, -, PA, 128, 120, CHAS*. In HH of Andrew K. Long m 39 born

LONG, CATHERINE, 8, F, None listed, -, PA, 128, 120, CHAS*. In HH of Andrew K. Long m 39 born PA.
LONG, JANE, 5, F, None listed, -, PA, 128, 120, CHAS*. In HH of Andrew K. Long m 39 born PA.
LONG, JOHN, 18, M, Gass Fitter, -, PA, 128, 120, CHAS*. In HH of Andrew K. Long m 39 born PA.
LONG, MARY, 12, F, None listed, -, PA, 128, 120, CHAS*. In HH of Andrew K. Long m 39 born PA.
LONG, RICHARD, 10, M, None listed, -, PA, 128, 120, CHAS*. In HH of Andrew K. Long m 39 born PA.
LONG, SOPHIA, 28, F, None listed, -, NY, 290, 264, CHAS*. In HH of Emma Long f 60 born SC.
LONG, WILLIAM, 14, M, Plumber, -, PA, 128, 120, CHAS*. In HH of Andrew K. Long m 39 born PA.
LONGMAN, JAMES H., 25, M, Artist, -, NY, 303, 309, RICH.
LONGSBERRY, B., 48, M, Saddler, -, PA, 51, 51, LANC*. In HH of D. Morrow m 53 born NC. B. Longsberry born Philadelphia, PA.
LOOMIS, CYRENUS, 45, M, Marshall SC Collage, -, NY, 656, 675, RICH.
LOVE, MARY ANN, 30, F, None listed, -, NY, 233, 211, CHAS. In HH of Charles Love m 40 born Scotland.
LOVELY, MARIA, 14, F, None listed, -, NY, 68, 69, RICH. In HH of Edward Harris m 66 born VA.
LOVETT, ELIZABETH, 25, F, None listed, -, NY, 350, 323, CHAS. In HH of William Lovett m 49 born NC.
LUBY, THOMAS, 20, M, Blacksmith, -, NJ, 436, 447, RICH. In Boarding House.
LUTHA, ROLAND, 35, M, Capt. U.S.A., -, PA, 47, 43, CHAS$. In HH of John Ewing m 50 born MA.
LYMAN, LEVI, 24, M, Superintendant Spinning, -, NY, 1622, 1622, EDGE.
LYNCH, F.C., 53, M, Tailor, -, PA, 257, 242, CHAS-.
LYON, JOHN, 41, M, Merchant/taylor, -, NJ, 6, 6, EDGE. Born in Espen, NJ.
LYON, JOHN, 22, M, Clerk, -, NY, 467, 450, CHAS-. In HH of Martha Mitchell f 30 born SC.
LYONS, ELIZABETH, 32, F, None listed, -, PA, 495, 510, RICH. In HH of Henry Lyons m 44 born SC.
LYONS, HENRY, 25, M, Clerk, -, NY, 351, 324, CHAS. In Boarding House.
LYONS, JACOB C., 43, M, Merchant, -, PA, 181, 185, RICH. {{Page out of order}.}, follows HH 135/139.
LYONS, LOUISA, 37, F, None listed, -, PA, 181, 185, RICH. {Page out of order}, followss HH 135/139. In HH of Jacob C. Lyons m 43born PA.

M

MACKEY, ALICE S., 6, F, None listed, -, NY, 410, 421, RICH. In HH of James J. Mackey m 32 born NY.
MACKEY, JAMES J., 32, M, Gunsmith, -, NY, 410, 421, RICH.
MACKEY, JAMES J., 1, M, None listed, -, NY, 410, 421, RICH. In HH of James J. Mackey m 32 born NY.
MACKEY, MARY C., 8, F, None listed, -, NY, 410, 421, RICH. In HH of James J. Mackey m 32 born NY.
MACKEY, SARAH L., 4, F, None listed, -, NY, 410, 421, RICH. In HH of James J. Mackey m 32 born NY.
MACKEY, SARAH S., 26, F, None listed, -, NY, 410, 421, RICH. In HH of James J. Mackey m 32 born NY.
MADDEN, RICHARD, 60, M, Farmer, -, MD, 2307, 2307, ABB.
MAGUIRE, JULIA, 5, F, None listed, -, NY, 397, 395, CHAS%. In HH of John Maguire m 34 born Ireland.
MAGUIRE, SIMON, 8, M, None listed, -, NY, 397, 395, CHAS%. In HH of John Maguire m 34 born Ireland.
MAHONEY, JOHN JR., 16, M, Waiter, -, NY, 326, 301, CHAS. On Steam Ship Southerner.
MAHONEY, REBECCA, 9, F, None listed, -, NY, 634, 615, CHAS-. In HH of Dennis Mahoney m 42 born Ireland.
MAHOONEY, JOHN, 8, M, None listed, -, NY, 558, 516, CHAS+. In HH of Patrick Mahooney m 44 born Ireland.
MAIN, A.R., 50, M, Merchant, -, NY, 438, 397, CHAS+.
MALLERY, EZEKIAH, 25, M, Mariner, -, NY, 314, 298, CHAS-. In HH of Sarah Mallery f 40 born CT.
MALLET, GEORGE, 7, M, None listed, -, NY, 109, 101, CHAS+. In HH of Frederick Mallet m 36 born France.
MALONEY, JOHN, 35, M, Packer, -, NY, 90, 83, CHAS-. In HH of Margaret Larkin m 60 born Ireland.
MANOR, RICHARD, 28, M, None listed, -, NY, 35, 35, YORK*. In HH of Peter Morgan m 81 born VA.
MANSFIELD, JOANNAH, 10, F, None listed, -, NY, 1219, 1219, EDGE. Note: out of order after fam. 1221 In HH of Tarry Mansfield m 40 born Ireland.
MAPILLON, LAURA, 24, F, None listed, -, MD, 469, 466, CHAS%. In HH of Felice Mapillon m 59 born France.
MARINDA, ADEL, 2, F, None listed, -, NY, 633, 591, CHAS+. In HH of Archy Marinda m 26 born NC.
MARKHAM, JOHN, 24, M, Seaman, -, NY, 326, 301, CHAS. On Steam Ship Southerner.
MARKIE, ANN, 4, F, None listed, -, NY, 304, 288, CHAS-. In HH of C.T. Dunham m 29 born MA.
MARQUIS, JAMES, 35, M, Engineer, -, PA, 328, 328, CHAS%.

MARSH, ELIZABETH, 76, F, None listed, -, NJ, 404, 364, CHAS+. In HH of James Marsh m 78 born NJ.
MARSH, JAMES, 78, M, Ship Wright, -, NJ, 404, 364, CHAS+.
MARTIN, AMANDA, 22, F, None listed, -, PA, 97, 95, CHAS*. In HH of Eliza Martin f 54 born England.
MARTIN, AUGUSTUS, 12, M, None listed, -, NY, 369, 369, BEAU-. In HH of Charles R. Martin m 25 born NY.
MARTIN, CHARLES R., 25, M, Teacher, -, NY, 369, 369, BEAU-.
MARTIN, ELIZA, 19, F, None listed, -, PA, 97, 95, CHAS*. In HH of Eliza Martin f 54 born England.
MARTIN, ELOISE, 32, F, None listed, -, PA, 304, 278, CHAS*. In HH of W.E. Martin m 35 born SC.
MARTIN, EMMA, 24, F, None listed, -, PA, 97, 95, CHAS*. In HH of Eliza Martin f 54 born England.
MARTIN, HENRY, 27, M, Carpenter, -, PA, 97, 95, CHAS*. In HH of Eliza Martin f 54 born England.
MARTIN, MELTON, 14, M, None listed, -, NY, 369, 369, BEAU-. In HH of Charles R. Martin m 25 born NY.
MARTIN, SARAH, 23, F, None listed, -, NY, 369, 369, BEAU-. In HH of Charles R. Martin m 25 born NY.
MASON, CHARLES M., 18, M, None listed, -, NY, 822, 802, CHAS-. In HH of Geo. D. Grice m 21 born NJ.
MASON, GEORGE T., 27, M, Merchant, -, MD, 32, 32, RICH.
MASTERSON, JAMES, 16, M, None listed, -, NY, 47, 43, CHAS$. In HH of John Ewing m 50 born MA.
MASTERSON, MARTHA, 9, F, None listed, -, NY, 47, 43, CHAS$. In HH of John Ewing m 50 born MA.
MASTERSON, MICHAEL, 3, M, None listed, -, NY, 47, 43, CHAS$. In HH of John Ewing m 50 born MA.
MATTHEWS, MARGARET, 65, F, None listed, -, MD, 1120, 1120, YORK. In HH of Samuel Matthews m 67 born VA.
MAXON, DAVID N., 38, M, Seaman, -, NY, 326, 301, CHAS. On Steam Ship Southerner.
MAY, ELIZA, 10, F, None listed, -, NY, 110, 102, CHAS+. In HH of John May m 30 born Ireland.
MAY, JOHN, 14, M, None listed, -, NY, 110, 102, CHAS+. In HH of John May m 30 born Ireland.
MAYFIELD, MARGARET, 88, F, None listed, -, PA, 187, 188, AND*. In HH of James McCoy m 35 born SC.
MAYSEY, THOMAS, 55, M, Shoe maker, -, PA, 239, 217, CHAS. In HH of John Drummond m 50 born Scotland.
MCADAMS, ELIZABETH, 66, F, None listed, -, PA, 710, 710, UNION. In HH of John McKeown m 53 born SC.
MCCADDEN, J.S., 43, M, Shoe Dealer, -, PA, 90, 82, CHAS+.

MCCALLISTER, JOHN, 87, M, None listed, -, MD, 858, 859, AND*. In HH of Andrew McCallister m 60 born NC.
MCCANTS, ANDREW, 11, M, None listed, -,D.C., 995, 996, FAIR. In HH of James J. McCants m 36 born SC. Andrew McCants born Washington, D.C.
MCCARTHY, F.J., 39, M, Attorney at Law, -, NJ, 78, 78, BEAU+.
MCCAUDLES, L., 30, M, Teacher, -, NJ, 854, 854, KERS.
MCCAVE, EDWARD, 9, M, None listed, -, NY, 359, 321, CHAS+. In HH of James McCave m 48 born Ireland.
MCCAVE, GEORGE, 14, M, None listed, -, NY, 359, 321, CHAS+. In HH of James McCave m 48 born Ireland.
MCCAVE, ISABELLA, 44, F, None listed, -, PA, 359, 321, CHAS+. In HH of James McCave m 48 born Ireland.
MCCAVE, JOHN, 17, M, Clerk, -, PA, 359, 321, CHAS+. In HH of James McCave m 48 born Ireland.
MCCHISNY, E.C., 22, F, None listed, -, NY, 570, 570, CHES. In HH of C.D. Melton 30 born SC.
MCCLELLAN, JOHN, 58, M, Farmer, -, MD, 1680, 1680, ABB.
MCCLENAHEN, C.L., 15, M, None listed, -, MD, 676, 656, CHAS-. In HH of Geo F. Cole m 45 born MD.
MCCULLY, ELIZA M., 35, F, None listed, -,D.C., 480, 495, RICH. In HH of John McCully m 50 born SC.
MCCUSKER, E., 23, F, None listed, -, PA, 560, 560, CHES. In HH of E. McCusker m 25 born Ireland.
MCCUTCHIN, HUGH, 20, M, Seaman, -, NY, 326, 301, CHAS. On Steam Ship Southerner.
MCDONALD, J.B., 39, F, None listed, -,D.C., 12, 12, KERS. Born Washington, D.C.. In HH of C.A. McDonald m 48 born SC.
MCDONALD, M., 21, F, None listed, -, NY, 1105, 1105, CHES. In HH of James D. Crawford m 52 born SC.
MCDOWALL, J.S., 28, M, Clerk, -, PA, 852, 832, CHAS-. In HH of A.G. Parker f 38 born Germany.
MCDOWALL, SUSAN, 34, F, None listed, -, NJ, 84, 84, KERS. In HH of Wm. D. McDowell m 43 born Scotland.
MCFEAT, ELIZABETH P., 61, F, None listed, -, NJ, 386, 396, RICH.
MCGEE, JOHN S., 26, M, Carriage maker, -, NJ, 611, 628, RICH. In HH of Richard S. Pomeroy m 30 born NY.
MCGILL, JOHN, 74, M, Farmer, -, PA, 919, 919, YORK.
MCGIVLEY, JERUSHA, 71, F, None listed, -, NJ, 150, 138, CHAS*. In HH of Samuel McGivley m 64 born PA.
MCGIVLEY, SAMUEL, 64, M, Iron dealer, -, PA, 150, 138, CHAS*.
MCGOWAN, JOHN, 99, M, Brickmason, -, NY, 168, 168, UNN+.
MCHENRY, K?, 28, M, Printer, -, NY, 553, 553, CHES. In HH of Mary Gill m 44 born SC.

MCINNERNY, JAMES, 12, M, None listed, -, NY, 17, 16, CHAS$. In HH of Michael McInnerny m 45 born Ireland.
MCINNERNY, MICHAEL, 10, M, None listed, -, NY, 17, 16, CHAS$. In HH of Michael McInnerny m 45 born Ireland.
MCKELVY, JOHN, 85, M, None, -, PA, 1169, 1169, CHES. In HH of Valentine Atkinson m 50 born SC.
MCKENSIE, GEO. T., 25, M, Sadler, -, NY, 478, 436, CHAS. In HH of R.B. McKensie m 30 born Ireland.
MCKENZIE, ADELINE, 33, F, None listed, -, NY, 402, 413, RICH. In HH of John McKenzie m 40 born Scotland.
MCKENZIE, ANNA, 9, F, None listed, -, NY, 402, 413, RICH. In HH of John McKenzie m 40 born Scotland.
MCKENZIE, MARY, 13, F, None listed, -, NY, 402, 413, RICH. In HH of John McKenzie m 40 born Scotland.
MCKENZIE, W., 35, M, Merchant, -, NY, 482, 439, CHAS. In Planters Hotel.
MCKINNEY, DANIEL, 74, M, Farmer, -, NY, 102, 102, PICK+.
MCKNIGHT, ROBERT A., 29, M, Printer, -, NY, 610, 627, RICH.
MCKNIGHT, ROBERT W., 2, M, None listed, -, NY, 610, 627, RICH. In HH of Robert A. McKnight m 29 born NY.
MCKNIGHT, SARAH C., 23, F, None listed, -, NY, 610, 627, RICH. In HH of Robert A. McKnight m 29 born NY.
MCKNIGHT, WILLIAM J., 3, M, None listed, -, NY, 610, 627, RICH. In HH of Robert A. McKnight m 29 born NY.
MCLURE, E.E., 15, M, None listed, -, NJ, 534, 534, CHES. In HH of Thomas McLure m 65 born NC.
MCLURE, J.J., 22, M, Lawyer, -, NJ, 534, 534, CHES. In HH of Thomas McLure m 65 born NC.
MCMAHON, ANNA, 16, F, None listed, -, NY, 445, 457, RICH. In HH of James McMahon m 58 born Ireland.
MCMAKIN, MARY, 25, F, None listed, -, NY, 64, 64, SPART. In HH of Andrew McKen {sic} m 28 born SC.
MCMANES, NATHANIEL, 20, M, None, -, MD, 325, 300, CHAS.
MCMANUS, CATHERINE, 14, F, None listed, -, NY, 4, 4, CHAS$. In HH of Mary McManus f 38 born Ireland
MCNANCE, MARGARET, 35, F, Stuardess, -, NY, 326, 301, CHAS. In HH of William Rollins m 40 born {-}.
MCNANCE, MARY, 9, F, None listed, -, NY, 326, 301, CHAS. In HH of William Rollins m 40 born {-}.
MCNULTY, WM., 42, M, Postman, -, NY, 111, 111, GEOR.
MCRICE, WM. THE HONBLE, 49, M, Judge City Court., -, NY, 58, 57, CHAS*.
MCRILEY, CATHERINE, 18, F, None listed, -, NY, 223, 199, CHAS*. In HH of Elizabeth Lawrence f 42 born SC.

MEAD, ANN, 8, F, None listed, -, NY, 136, 126, CHAS-. In HH of Rosa Stien f 22 born Germany.
MEAD, CAROLINE, 3, F, None listed, -, NY, 136, 126, CHAS-. In HH of Rosa Stien f 22 born Germany.
MEAD, ELIZABETH, 10, F, None listed, -, NY, 136, 126, CHAS-. In HH of Rosa Stien f 22 born Germany.
MEAD, MARGARET, 36, F, None listed, -, NY, 136, 126, CHAS-. In HH of Rosa Stien f 22 born Germany.
MEALEY, MARY, 84, F, None listed, -, PA, 330, 313, CHAS-. In HH of John Mealey m 74 born SC. {Note Family No. listed as 350, should be 330}
MEDON, ELIZABETH, 36, F, None listed, -, NY, 805, 785, CHAS-.
MEDON, PHOEBE J., 18, F, None listed, -, NY, 805, 785, CHAS-. In HH of Elizabeth Medon f 36 born NY.
MELOY, JOHN, 28, M, Blacksmith, -,D.C., 55, 55, EDGE. John Meloy listed as born Alex, D.C.. {most likely /Washington, D.C.}
MEMMINGER, MARY, 37, F, None listed, -, NJ, 1103, 1080, CHAS-. In HH of C.G. Memminger m 47 born Germany.
MERCER, CHARLOTTE, 34, F, None listed, -, NY, 882, 840, CHAS+. In Charleston Hotel.
MERKHERDT, AUGUSTINA, 5, F, None listed, -, NY, 1022, 999, CHAS%. In HH of M. Merkherdt m 23 born Germany.
MERKHERDT, MARIA, 3, F, None listed, -, NY, 1022, 999, CHAS%. In HH of M. Merkherdt m 23 born Germany.
MEYER, CAROLINE, 16, F, None listed, -, MD, 419, 378, CHAS+. In HH of Frederick C. Meyer m 54 born Germany.
MEYER, HENRY, 12, M, None listed, -, MD, 419, 378, CHAS+. In HH of Frederick C. Meyer m 54 born Germany.
MEYER, M., 14, M, None listed, -, MD, 419, 378, CHAS+. In HH of Frederick C. Meyer m 54 born Germany.
MIDDLETON, ANN, 26, F, None listed, -, PA, 848, 828, CHAS-. In HH of B. Figeroux m 42 born West Indies.
MIDDLETON, EURETTA, 45, F, None listed, -, NY, 77, 87, CHAS. In HH of Thomas Middleton m 55 born SC.
MILAN, FRANCIS, 5, F, None listed, -, NY, 278, 258, CHAS+. In HH of John Milan m 30 born Ireland.
MILAN, SUSANNAH, 9, F, None listed, -, NY, 278, 258, CHAS+. In HH of John Milan m 30 born Ireland.
MILES, EMILY, 14, F, None listed, -, PA, 608, 589, CHAS-. In HH of H.F. Baker m 35 born PA.
MILES, SAMUEL S., 45, M, Store keeper, -, NY, 172, 158, CHAS*.
MILLER, DAVID, 65, M, Merchant, -, PA, 6, 6, SPART. Born Philadelphia, PA.
MILLER, GEORGE, 68, M, Planter, -, MD, 185, 185, EDGE.

MILLER, JEROME M., 34, M, Police Officer, -, NY, 609, 626, RICH.
MILLER, JULIA M., 24, F, None listed, -, NY, 65, 65, LEX. In HH of E.L. Hazelius m 72 Lutheran Clergy born Prussia.
MILLER, WILLIAM, 20, M, Sail maker, -, MD, 159, 150, CHAS+. In HH of Z. Miller m 46 born MD.
MILLER, Z., 46, M, Sail maker, -, MD, 159, 150, CHAS+.
MILLIKEN, MARY JANE, 28, F, None listed, -, PA, 224, 211, CHAS+. In HH of William Milliken m 45 born PA.
MILLIKEN, SARAH, 8, F, None listed, -, MD, 224, 211, CHAS+. In HH of William Milliken m 45 born PA.
MILLIKEN, WILLIAM, 45, M, Merchant, -, PA, 224, 211, CHAS+.
MILLS, CLARK, 32, M, Artist, -, NY, 118, 131, CHAS.
MITCHELL, GEORGE, 37, M, Merchant, -, NY, 937, 917, CHAS-. In Boarding House.
MITCHELL, HARRIET, 18, F, None listed, -, NY, 937, 917, CHAS-. In Boarding House.
MITTAG, A., 47, F, None listed, -, NY, 19, 19, LANC. In HH of J.F.G. Mittag m 47 born MD.
MITTAG, J.F.G., 47, M, Lawyer, -, MD, 19, 19, LANC.
MITZ, SARAH, 20, F, None listed, -, NJ, 1751, 1756, EDGE. In HH of Joseph Wooley m 52 born England.
MIXEN, CATHARINE, 35, F, None listed, -, NY, 241, 241, BEAU*. In HH of John A. Mixen m 29 born NY.
MIXEN, JESSIE, 21, M, Farmer, -, NY, 241, 241, BEAU*. In HH of John A. Mixen m 29 born NY.
MIXEN, JOHN A., 29, M, Farmer, -, NY, 241, 241, BEAU*.
MIXEN, REBECCA, 7, F, None listed, -, NY, 241, 241, BEAU*. In HH of John A. Mixen m 29 born NY.
MIXEN, WILLIAM, 15, M, Farmer, -, NY, 241, 241, BEAU*. In HH of John A. Mixen m 29 born NY.
MONSEAU, ADOLPHUS, 30, M, Laborer, -, NY, 585, 577, CHAS%.
MONTGOMERY, A., 35, M, None listed, -, NY, 21, 19, CHAS$.
MONTGOMERY, BENJAMIN, 64, M, Laborer, -, MD, 1628, 1628, YORK.
MONTGOMERY, CHARLES, 23, M, Clerk, -, MD, 1065, 1042, CHAS-. In HH of Andrew Montgomery m 56 born Ireland.
MONTGOMERY, ELINOR, 72, F, None listed, -, MD, 874, 874, YORK. In HH of Hillory Montgomery m 73 born MD.
MONTGOMERY, HILLARY, 73, M, None listed, -, MD, 874, 874, YORK.
MONTGOMERY, JOHN, 28, M, Watchmaker, -, MD, 1065, 1042, CHAS-. In HH of Andrew Montgomery m 56 born Ireland.
MONTGOMERY, PRISCILLA, 45, F, None listed, -, MD, 1065, 1042, CHAS-. In HH of Andrew Montgomery m 56 born Ireland.

MOORE, ALFRED, 51, M, Blacksmith, -,DE, 509, 513, AND.
MOORE, ELIZABETH, 37, F, None listed, -, PA, 320, 295, CHAS.
MOORE, OLIVER, 25, M, Farmer, -,D.C., 58, 58, CHAS!. {District of Columbia}.
MORDALE, THODORE, 32, M, Cabinet maker, -, NY, 2303, 2303, GREE. In Hotel.
MORGAN, RUTH, 56, F, None listed, -, MD, 986, 963, CHAS%. In HH of Benjn. Morgan m 48 born SC.
MORGAN, RUTH, 50, F, None listed, -, MD, 159, 146, CHAS*. In HH of Benjamin Morgan m 50 born SC.
MORRIS, F.M., 19, F, None listed, -, NY, 476, 434, CHAS. In HH of M.M. Stewart f 40, runs boarding house, born SC.
MORRIS, GEORGIANA, 20, F, None listed, -, NY, 1054, 1031, CHAS-. In HH of Julia Morris f 48 born NY.
MORRIS, JULIA, 48, F, None listed, -, NY, 1054, 1031, CHAS-.
MORRIS, MALVINA, 23, F, None listed, -, NY, 1054, 1031, CHAS-. In HH of Julia Morris f 48 born NY.
MORRIS, REBECCA, 88, F, None listed, -, PA, 239, 241, AND. In HH of Samuel Morris m 66 born SC.
MORRIS, W.R., 15, M, None listed, -, NY, 476, 434, CHAS. In HH of M.M. Stewart f 40, runs boarding house, born SC.
MORROW, ELIZABETH, 108, F, None listed, -, PA, 1062, 1066, AND. In HH of Thomas Skilton m 68 born SC.
MORSE, A.A., 30, M, Minister, Presbyterian, -, NJ, 29, 29, SPART.
MOSES, ANABELLA, 11, F, None listed, -, NY, 1859, 1859, SUMT. In HH of M. Moses m 42 born SC.
MOSES, CATHARINE, 40, F, None listed, -, PA, 1859, 1859, SUMT. In HH of M. Moses m 42 born SC.
MOSES, F.J., 46, M, Lawyer, -, PA, 1858, 1858, SUMT.
MOSES, FRANKLIN J., 13, M, None listed, -, NY, 1859, 1859, SUMT. In HH of M. Moses m 42 born SC.
MOSES, MYER, 17, F, None listed, -, NY, 1859, 1859, SUMT. In HH of M. Moses m 42 born SC.
MOSES, ZALEGNIAN P., 15, M, None listed, -, NY, 1859, 1859, SUMT. In HH of M. Moses m 42 born SC.
MOULTON, L.V., 40, M, Merchant, -, PA, 882, 840, CHAS+. In Charleston Hotel.
MULLER, CHARLES, 0, M, None listed, -, NY, 196, 180, CHAS*. In HH of Lewis Muller m 31 born Germany. Charles Muller age 4/12 yr.
MULLER, ELLEN, 7, F, None listed, -, NY, 196, 180, CHAS*. In HH of Lewis Muller m 31 born Germany.
MULLER, FREDERICK, 5, M, None listed, -, NY, 196, 180, CHAS*. In HH of Lewis Muller m 31 born Germany.

MULLER, LUDWICK, 2, M, None listed, -, NY, 196, 180, CHAS*. In HH of Lewis Muller m 31 born Germany.
MULLIKIN, BENJAMIN, 81, M, Farmer, -, MD, 1038, 1039, AND*. Name noted as Mullikin in pencil on document.
MUNS, JAMES, 34, M, Mariner, -, PA, 351, 324, CHAS. In Boarding House.
MUNSON, ALBERT, 45, M, Merchant, -, NJ, 376, 359, CHAS-. In HH of Mathew Ryan m 36 born Ireland
MURCHISON, ELIZA C., 55, F, None listed, -, NY, 1472, 1472, SUMT. In HH of Charles H. Durant m 22 born SC.
MURRAY, JOHN ALEXR., 18, M, Machinist, -, MD, 539, 522, CHAS-. In HH of Eliza Wilson f 39 born Ireland.
MURRAY, MARGARET, 28, F, None listed, -, NY, 318, 293, CHAS. In HHof H. Bregnan m 24 born Germany.
MURRY, JOHN, 6, M, None listed, -, PA, 2300, 2300, GREE. In HH of Thomas Murry m 40 born Ireland.
MURTIHY(?), A., 23, M, Tailor, -, PA, 9, 9, LANC. In Hotel.
MYERS, GEORGE M., 10, M, None listed, -, MD, 290, 274, CHAS-. In HH of Benjamin Archer m 40 born NY.
MYERS, JACOB B., 8, M, None listed, -, MD, 290, 274, CHAS-. In HH of Benjamin Archer m 40 born NY.

N

NATHAN, FRANK, 21, M, Shoemaker, -, NJ, 217, 194, CHAS*. In HH of Nathan Myer m 50 born Poland.
NATHAN, MOSES, 28, M, Tailor, -, NJ, 217, 194, CHAS*. In HH of Nathan Myer m 50 born Poland.
NEAL, MARGARET, 88, F, None listed, -, MD, 1378, 1378, YORK.
NEAL, WILLIAM, 35, M, Carpenter, -, NY, 14, 13, CHAS+.
NELLES, P.D., 30, M, Cooper, -, NY, 107, 100, CHAS-.
NELSON, ANN MARIA, 26, F, None listed, -, NY, 314, 298, CHAS-. In HH of Sarah Mallery f 40 born CT.
NELSON, MARY E., 25, F, None listed, -, NY, 218, 196, CHAS. In HH of Chris. Nelson m 60 born Denmark.
NEVIT, WILLIAM, 66, M, Farmer, -, MD, 173, 174, AND*.
NEWCOMB, CORNELIUS, 5, M, None listed, -, NY, 673, 653, CHAS-. In HH of J.G. Newcomb m 27 born NY.
NEWCOMB, J.G., 27, M, Confectioner, -, NY, 673, 653, CHAS-.
NEWCOMB, JOHN T., 9, M, None listed, -, NY, 237, 222, CHAS-. Poor House.

NEWCOMB, WILLIAM, 13, M, None listed, -, NY, 673, 653, CHAS-. In HH of J.G. Newcomb m 27 born NY.
NEWMAN, ATLANTA, 29, F, None listed, -, NJ, 1415, 1415, SUMT. In HH of Jackson Newman m 35 born SC.
NICHOLS, JOSHUA, 30, M, Planter, -,D.C., 840, 798, CHAS+. Born George Town, D.C.
NICHOLS, MARY H., 30, F, None listed, -, NY, 238, 243, RICH. In HH of Horacea E. Nichols m 36 born VT.
NICHOLS, S.M., 23, F, None listed, -, PA, 86, 86, EDGE. IN HH of R.H. Nichols m 47 born England.
NICHOLSON, M., 16, F, None listed, -, NY, 1146, 1125, CHAS%. In HH of Harris Simons m 43 born Ireland. Marie Ramsay Simons age 8/12 yr.
NICKLE, A.J., 23, F, None listed, -, NY, 293, 293, KERS. In HH of John Brown m 54 born SC.
NICKLE, M.E., 21, F, None listed, -, NY, 293, 293, KERS. In HH of John Brown m 54 born SC.
NIVVER, JANE, 27, F, None listed, -, NY, 805, 785, CHAS-. In HH of Elizabeth Medon f 36 born NY.
NIXON, J.B., 31, M, Printer, -, NY, 134, 125, CHAS+.
NOLEN?, JAMES, 78, M, Farmer, -, MD, 854, 854, GREE.
NOLEN?, SARAH, 68, F, None listed, -, PA, 854, 854, GREE. In HH of James Nolen? m 78 born MD.

NORRIS, EDWARD, 11, M, None listed, -, NY, 788, 746, CHAS+. In HH of William Norris m 28 born Ireland.
NORRIS, JOSEPH, 16, M, Clerk, -, NY, 788, 746, CHAS+. In HH of William Norris m 28 born Ireland.
NORTHROP, L.B., JR., 11, M, None listed, -, NY, 526, 492, CHAS*. In HH of C.B. Northrop m 37 born SC.
NORTON, ANNA, 22, F, None listed, -, NY, 844, 824, CHAS-. In HH of Rachel Norton f 26 born NY.
NORTON, MARGARET, 14, F, None listed, -, NY, 844, 824, CHAS-. In HH of Rachel Norton f 26 born NY.
NORTON, RACHEL, 26, F, None listed, -, NY, 844, 824, CHAS-.
NORTON, SARAH, 19, F, None listed, -, NY, 844, 824, CHAS-. In HH of Rachel Norton f 26 born NY.
NOWELL, RICHARD, 31, M, Carpenter, -, NY, 768, 751, CHAS%.

O

O'DONNEL, BRIDGET, 12, F, None listed, -, NY, 394, 392, CHAS%. In HH of John O'Connel m 45 born Ireland.
O'DONNEL, CATHERINE, 10, F, None listed, -, NY, 394, 392, CHAS%. In HH of John O'Connel m 45 born Ireland.
O'HERN, ANN, 45, F, None listed, -, NJ, 542, 557, RICH. Date

1830 by name. In Lunatic Asylum.
O'NEAL, ELIZABETH, 85, F, None listed, -, PA, 145, 145, YORK*. In HH of John Wilson m 67 born VA.
OAKES, JONATHAN, 34, M, Seaman, -, NY, 326, 301, CHAS. On Steam Ship Southerner.
OAKLEY, R.S., 50, M, Druggist, -, PA, 855, 835, CHAS-.
OAKLEY, W.C., 36, M, Merchant, -, NY, 482, 439, CHAS. In Planters Hotel.
OATES, ISABELLA, 19, F, None listed, -, NY, 837, 817, CHAS-. In HH of George Oates m 55 born England.
OGLES, JOHN, 43, M, Farmer, -, PA, 422, 422, UNION.
OHARA, MARGARET, 8, F, None listed, -, NY, 183, 172, CHAS+. In HH of W. Vironee m 50 born SC.
OLIVER, BARNEY, 7, M, None listed, -, NY, 205, 205, CHAS%. In HH of Ann Oliver f 31 born Europe.
OLIVER, ELIZABETH, 12, F, None listed, -, NY, 1005, 982, CHAS%. Under command of Major P. Hagnes, Commanding Officer U.S. Arsenal.
OLIVER, JANUS, 14, M, None listed, -, NY, 1005, 982, CHAS%. Under command of Major P. Hagnes, Commanding Officer U.S. Arsenal.
OLIVER, JOHN, 7, M, None listed, -, NY, 205, 205, CHAS%. In HH of Ann Oliver f 31 born Europe.
OLIVER, JULIA, 3, F, None listed, -, NY, 1005, 982, CHAS%. Under command of Major P. Hagnes, Commanding Officer U.S. Arsenal.
OLIVER, LILLY, 15, F, None listed, -, NY, 205, 205, CHAS%. In HH of Ann Oliver f 31 born Europe.
ONEAL, MARIA, 38, F, None listed, -, NY, 127, 118, CHAS+. In Boarding House.
ONEELL, MARY ANN, 27, F, None listed, -, PA, 356, 328, CHAS. In HH of J.F. ONeell 33 m born SC.
ORCHARD, SAMUEL, 40, M, None listed, -, NY, 275, 255, CHAS+. In HH of William Perry m 45 born PA.
ORR, ELIZABETH, 89, F, None listed, -, PA, 829, 829, UNION. In HH of William Orr m 54 born Scotland.
OWENS, ALFRED, 6, M, None listed, B, NY, 474, 432, CHAS+. In HH of Smart Owens m 50 black born NY.
OWENS, DOLLY, 12, F, None listed, B, NY, 474, 432, CHAS+. In HH of Smart Owens m 50 black born NY.
OWENS, HANNAH, 40, F, None listed, B, NY, 474, 432, CHAS+. In HH of Smart Owens m 50 black born NY.
OWENS, RICHARD, 4, M, None listed, B, NY, 474, 432, CHAS+. In HH of Smart Owens m 50 black born NY.
OWENS, SMART, 50, M, Carpenter, B, NY, 474, 432, CHAS+.

P

PACKINGHAM, SAMUEL, 45, M, Stonecutter, -, PA, 665, 684, RICH.
PAGETT, JAMESS, 28, M, Planter, -, PA, 234, 234, FAIR. In HH of George W. Hagain m 35 born NC.
PAGETT, WILLIAM, 65, M, Farmer, -, MD, 691, 692, AND*.
PAITE, MARY A., 77, F, None listed, -, MD, 2334, 2334, ABB.
PARCELL, JOSEPH, 50, M, Merchant, -, NY, 882, 840, CHAS+. In Charleston Hotel.
PARCELL, THOMAS, 45, M, Merchant, -, NY, 882, 840, CHAS+. In Charleston Hotel.
PARK, FREDERICK, 26, M, Carpenter, -, NY, 959, 939, CHAS-. In HH of J.S. Riddell m 34 born MA.
PARK, JAMES, 25, M, Clerk, -, NY, 244, 229, CHAS+. In Boarding House run by Ellen Pratt.
PARKER, MARGARET A., 17, F, Milliner, -, PA, 852, 832, CHAS-. In HH of A.G. Parker f 38 born Germany.
PARKER, MARY, 60, F, None listed, -,DE, 319, 319, CHAS%. In HH of P.G. Parker m 52 born SC.
PARROTT, GEORGE, 48, M, Merchant, -, MD, 2393, 2397, EDGE.
PARSELL, W.N., 42, M, Cabinet maker, -, NY, 809, 789, CHAS-.
PARSON, H.H., 36, M, Clerk, -, NY, 270, 254, CHAS-. In HH of Thomas E. Baker m 50 born VA.
PARSON, MARGETTA, 27, F, None listed, -, NY, 665, 665, BARN. In HH of Seth Parson m 28 born NY.
PARSON, SETH, 28, M, Taylor, -, NY, 665, 665, BARN.
PATTERSON, WILLIAM, 50, M, Clerk, -, PA, 371, 344, CHAS*.
PATTERSON, WILLIAM, 34, M, Carpenter, -, MD, 462, 445, CHAS-.
PATTON, ELLEN, 32, F, None listed, -, NY, 237, 222, CHAS-. Poor House.
PAULK, ELIZABETH, 74, F, None listed, -, PA, 984, 984, UNION. In HH of William J. Page m 62 born VA.
PEACE, WASHINGTON, 27, M, Student, -, PA, 683, 702, RICH. Student at Theological Seminary.
PEALER, JOSEPH, 35, M, Dentist, -, PA, 180, 180, EDGE*.
PEARBOON, JOSEPH, 29, M, Manufacturer, -, NY, 131, 131, LEX.
PECKHAM, THOMAS., 45, M, Overseer, -, NJ, 1735, 1738, EDGE. In HH of Benj. P. Battles m 29 born MA.
PEERS, ADELINE, 11, F, None listed, -, NY, 402, 413, RICH. In HH of John McKenzie m 40 born Scotland.
PEERS, ALICE, 14, F, None listed, -, NY, 402, 413, RICH. In HH of John McKenzie m 40 born Scotland.
PELLEFER, JOSEPH P., 38, M, Seaman, -, NY, 326, 301, CHAS. On Steam Ship Southerner.
PELTON, GROVE A., 32, M, Merchant, -, NY, 421, 432, RICH.

PERKINS, BENJAMIN, 38, M, Blacksmith, -, NY, 176, 166, CHAS-. In HH of Elizabeth Uray f 22 born NC.
PERRY, C., 30, M, Engineer, -, PA, 346, 308, CHAS+. In Boarding House.
PERRY, H.M., 22, F, None listed, -, NY, 86, 86, EDGE. IN HH of R.H. Nichols m 47 born England.
PERRY, JANE, 21, F, None listed, -, NY, 751, 731, CHAS-. In HH of Jos. B. Dallison m 27 born England.
PERRY, WILLIAM, 45, M, Customs Inspector, -, PA, 275, 255, CHAS+.
PETERSON, ELIZABETH, 39, F, None listed, -, NY, 28, 35, CHAS. In HH of Christian Peterson m 39 born Sweden.
PETIT, HANNAH, 22, F, None listed, -, NY, 142, 130, CHAS*. In HH of James Petit m 30 born SC.
PHILBY, ELIZABETH, 91, F, None listed, -, PA, 1053, 1053, UNION. In Poor House.
PHILIPS, GEORGE, 20, M, Carpenter, -, NY, 1753, 1758, EDGE. In HH of W.R. Gunten m 38 born SC.
PHILIPS, GEORGE, 19, M, Mechanic, -, NY, 420, 420, BARN. In HH of John Philips m 40 born NY.
PHILIPS, JOHN, 75, M, Farmer, -, MD, 89, 91, AND.
PHILIPS, JOHN, 40, M, Mechanic, -, NY, 420, 420, BARN.
PHILIPS, KEZIAH, 73, F, None listed, -, MD, 650, 650, GREE. In HH of Eber Wooton m 38 born SC.
PHILLIPS, ADDISON R., 34, M, Merchant, -, NY, 376, 385, RICH. In HH of William L. Reynolds m 22 born SC.
PHILLIPS, BARNA L., 16, M, Merchant Clerk, -, NY, 1971, 1977, EDGE. In HH of Abraam Levig m 30 born Poland.
PHILSON, WILLIAM, 58, M, Farmer, -, PA, 339, 339, LAU.
PICKERING, E.B., 63, F, None listed, -, NJ, 51, 51, KERS. In HH of Wm. B. Campbell m 42 born SC.
PIERSON, J.W., 22, M, Merchant, -, NY, 833, 813, CHAS-. In HH of James S. Roberts m 29 born SC.
PIERSON, MADORA, 11, F, None listed, -, NY, 692, 672, CHAS-. In HH of E.G. Brown m 41 born CT.
PIERSON, MARY, 19, F, None listed, -, NY, 833, 813, CHAS-. In HH of James S. Roberts m 29 born SC.
PIERSON, PHILIP, 49, M, O.S.P. Clergyman, -, NY, 1655, 1655, SUMT.
PIERSON, SARAH, 34, F, None listed, -, NY, 692, 672, CHAS-. In HH of E.G. Brown m 41 born CT.
PIKE, WILLIAM, 65, M, Laborer, -, MD, 1257, 1257, GREE.
PILIRS, JAMES, 22, M, Clerk, -, NY, 127, 118, CHAS+. In Boarding House.
PINKHAM, THOS., 20, M, Daguereotypeist, -, NY, 1726, 1727, EDGE. In HH of Alexander Hunter m 46, landlord, born VA.

PLATT, GEORGE, 30, M, Schoolmaster, -, NY, 25, 25, GEOR+.
PLATT, GEORGE, 25, M, Tailor, -, NJ, 198, 202, RICH. In HH of Joel Stevenson m 51 born MD.
PLUMMER, CHS., 70, M, None listed, -, MD, 612, 612, DARL. In HH of Chs. W. Plummer m 27 born NC.
POMEROY, RICHARD S., 30, M, Carriage maker, -, NY, 611, 628, RICH.
PONESS, ALEX., 76, M, Farmer, -, MD, 2098, 2098, LAU.
PORCHER, MARY A., 40, F, None listed, -, MD, 302, 279, CHAS. In HH of Peter Porcher m 48 born SC.
PORTER, EMMA A., 32, F, None listed, -,D.C., 636, 617, CHAS-. Born Washington, D.C.. In HH of W.D. Porter m 39 born SC.
PORTER, JAMES, 24, M, Seaman, -, NY, 326, 301, CHAS. On Steam Ship Southerner.
POSEY, MARTHA, 65, F, None listed, -, MD, 790, 790, ABB. In HH of James H. Tusten m 49 born NY.
POST, V. AMANDA, 21, F, None listed, -, NY, 1998, 1995, EDGE. In HH of David F. Griffin m 27 born NY.
POTTER, S.V., 22, F, None listed, -, PA, 311, 287, CHAS+. In HH of Deas H. Kenny m 31 born Germany.
POWELL, ELIZA, 30, F, None listed, -, PA, 2239, 2239, GREE. In HH of Thomas Powell m 60 born England.
POWELL, JOHN V., 32, M, Carpenter, -, NY, 1093, 1070, CHAS-.
POWELL, THOMAS, 30, M, Steward, -, NY, 326, 301, CHAS. In HH of William Rollins m 40 born {-}.
POWER, J.N., 38, M, Clerk, -, NY, 1088, 1065, CHAS-. In HH of H.S. Hayden m 35 born CT.
POWERS, P.N., 36, M, Merchant, -, NY, 2256, 2256, GREE.
PRATHER, JAMES W., 68, M, Farmer, -, MD, 429, 429, ABB.
PRENTICE, MARIA, 45, F, None listed, -, NY, 26, 31, CHAS. In HH of Moses Levy m 45 taven keeper born SC.
PRESTON, WILLIAM C., 56, M, Pres. SC Coll., -, PA, 695, 714, RICH. President SC College.
PREVOST, MARY, 37, F, None listed, -, NY, 529, 488, CHAS+. In HH of Joseph Prevost m 45 born SC.
PRICE, ANNA, 5, F, None listed, -, NJ, 237, 242, RICH. In HH of Jeremiah C. Price m 35 born NJ.
PRICE, CATOOLA, 30, F, None listed, -, MD, 504, 470, CHAS*. In HH of Mary E. Price f 63 born SC.
PRICE, ELIZABETH, 7, F, None listed, -, NJ, 237, 242, RICH. In HH of Jeremiah C. Price m 35 born NJ.
PRICE, GEORGE D., 21, M, Gas fitter, -, NJ, 226, 212, CHAS-. In HH of William M. Dougherty m 45 born NY.
PRICE, JEREMIAH C., 35, M, Cabinetmaker, -, NJ, 237, 242, RICH.

PRICE, LINUS, 9, M, None listed, -, NJ, 237, 242, RICH. In HH of Jeremiah C. Price m 35 born NJ.
PRICE, LOUISA, 11, F, None listed, -, MD, 962, 939, CHAS%. Born : Baltimore {MD}. In HH of Mary Ann Price f 30 born Baltimore,{MD}.
PRICE, MARY ANN, 30, F, None listed, -, MD, 962, 939, CHAS%. Born : Baltimore {MD}.
PRICE, SARAH A., 32, F, None listed, -, NJ, 237, 242, RICH. In HH of Jeremiah C. Price m 35 born NJ.
PRINCE, JOHN, 40, M, Mariner, -, NY, 701, 659, CHAS+. In HH of Grace Alston f 26 mulatto born SC.
PRINGLE, W. ASHMEAD, 6, M, None listed, -, PA, 317, 317, GEOR*. In HH of St. J. Pringle m 32 born SC.
PRINGLE, CLARA A., 28, F, None listed, -, PA, 37, 37, CHAS*. In HH of Sarah M. Pringle f 45 born SC.
PRINGLE, E.H., 1, M, None listed, -, PA, 37, 37, CHAS*. In HH of Sarah M. Pringle f 45 born SC.
PRINGLE, JANE, 34, F, None listed, -, NY, 171, 171, GEOR*. In HH of J.J. Pringle m 43 born SC.
PRINGLE, MARY, 13, F, None listed, -,D.C., 171, 171, GEOR*. In HH of J.J. Pringle m 43 born SC. Mary Pringle born Dist. Columbia.
PRINGLE, R.J., 4, M, None listed, -, PA, 317, 317, GEOR*. In HH of St. J. Pringle m 32 born SC.

PRINGLE, SALIE, 26, F, None listed, -, PA, 317, 317, GEOR*. In HH of St. J. Pringle m 32 born SC.
PROTHER, JAS., 29, M, Clerk, -, NY, 836, 816, CHAS-. In Boarding House.
PRYOR, EMILY FRANCIS, 4, F, None listed, -, NY, 565, 523, CHAS+. In HH of John Pryor m 45 born Ireland.
PRYOR, GEORGE THOS., 8, M, None listed, -, NY, 565, 523, CHAS+. In HH of John Pryor m 45 born Ireland.
PRYOR, HARRIOT E., 10, F, None listed, -, NY, 565, 523, CHAS+. In HH of John Pryor m 45 born Ireland.
PRYOR, MARY R., 6, F, None listed, -, NY, 565, 523, CHAS+. In HH of John Pryor m 45 born Ireland.
PURCHASE, PETER, 56, M, Overseer, -, NY, 162, 162, BEAU+.
PURSE, J.S., 43, M, Upholsterer, -, MD, 726, 706, CHAS-.
PURYEAR, THOMAS, 36, M, None, -, MD, 470, 485, RICH. In Hotel

Q

QUACKENBUSH, T.L., 35, M, Grocer, -, NY, 259, 243, CHAS+.

R

RACHESTER, ROBERT, 32, M, Tanner, -,DE, 219, 224, PICK.
RADCLIFFE, VINCENT, 79, M, Farmer, -, MD, 995, 995, ABB.
RADEL, JOHN, 47, M, Ostler, -, NY, 2095, 2098, EDGE. In HH of

Elijah Radel 33 born SC.
RAHAN, BRIGET, 5, F, None listed, -, NY, 635, 593, CHAS+. In HH of John Moreen m 35 born Ireland.
RAMSAY, WILLIAM, 30, M, Music store, -, NY, 685, 665, CHAS-. In Victoria Hotel.
RAMSDEN, JOHN, 41, M, Master Mariner, -, NY, 247, 222, CHAS*. In HH of William Denny m 70 born Ireland.
RAMSHARDT, ELIZTH., 19, F, Milliner, -, PA, 852, 832, CHAS-. In HH of A.G. Parker f 38 born Germany.
RANDALLS, MARY ANN, 32, F, None listed, -, NY, 87, 79, CHAS+. In HH of Thos. Randalls m 40 born Ireland.
RANDOM, WILLIAM, 24, M, Harnessmaker, -, MD, 65, 66, ORNG+. In HH of James Harley at Hotel.
RANDOM, WILLIAM, 24, M, Harness maker, -, MD, 65, 66, ORNG+. In HH of James Harley - Hotel.
RANSOM, T.L., 42, M, Shoe/bootmaker, -, NY, 1014, 1014, EDGE.
RAWLES, RUDOLPH, 48, F, None listed, -, NY, 158, 149, CHAS+. In HH of Georgiana Rawles f 28 born SC.
RAY, JOHN, 24, M, Carriage maker, -, NY, 426, 427, ORNG+. In HH of Henry L. Smoke m 44 born SC.
RAY, JOHN, 24, M, Carriage maker, -, NY, 426, 427, ORNG+. In HH of Henry L. Smoke m 44 born SC.

RAYMOND, CHARLES, 5, M, None listed, -, NY, 1792, 1792, ABB. In HH of William P. Hill m 46, Baptist Clergyman born SC.
RAYMOND, SARAH A., 24, F, None listed, -, NY, 1792, 1792, ABB. In HH of William P. Hill m 46, Baptist Clergyman born SC.
READ, JAMES, 26, M, Seaman, -, NY, 326, 301, CHAS. On Steam Ship Southerner.
REDAH, ANDREW, 22, M, Labourer, -, MD, 1736, 1739, EDGE. In HH of Sarah Lockhart f 47 born SC.
REED, EDWARD, 35, M, Episl. Preacher, -, NY, 160, 160, EDGE. In HH of Nancy Blocker f 52 born SC.
REED, JOHN, 21, M, Clerk, -, NY, 472, 455, CHAS-. In HH of Mary Cooper f 50 born SC.
REED, WILLIAM R., 49, M, Farmer, -, NY, 387, 387, ABB.
REEDER, MARY, 22, F, None listed, -, NY, 321, 296, CHAS. In HH of Samuel Jones m 40 born SC.
REICKS, WILLIAM, 18, M, Merchant, -, MD, 75, 67, CHAS+. In HH of Gerhard Reicks m 44 born Germany.
RELYEA, C., 33, M, Mariner, -, NY, 532, 491, CHAS+.
RELYEA, CHARLES, 4, M, None listed, -, NY, 532, 491, CHAS+. In HH of C. Relyea m 33 born NY.
RELYEA, GEORGE, 2, M, None listed, -, NY, 532, 491, CHAS+. In HH of C. Relyea m 33 born NY.
RELYEA, HENRY, 6, M, None listed, -, NY, 532, 491, CHAS+. In

HH of C. Relyea m 33 born NY.
REYNOLDS, CATHARINE, 30, F, None listed, -, NY, 240, 240, BEAU*. In HH of J.W. Reynolds m 40 born NY.
REYNOLDS, J.W., 40, M, Mechanic, -, NY,240,240,BEAU*.
RHODES, JAMES, 36, M, Landlord, -, NJ, 3, 3, COLL.
RICARDS, C.W., 35, M, Clerk, -, MD, 469, 427, CHAS. In HH of Thomas Kinney m 74 born Ireland.
RICE, COSLANDO, 36, M, Music teacher, -, NY, 2107, 2107, ABB.
RICHARDS, BENJAMIN, 43, M, Principal, -, NY, 869, 879, RICH+. Principal Female Institute.
RICHARDS, MARY, 27, F, None listed, -, PA, 721, 701, CHAS-. In Boarding House.
RICHARDSON, JAMES, 28, M, Mariner, -, NJ, 356, 318, CHAS+.
RICHARDSON, JOHN K., 35, M, Engineer, -, NY, 267, 251, CHAS-.
RICHMOND, M., 26, F, None listed, -, NY, 1146, 1125, CHAS%. In HH of Harris Simons m 43 born Ireland.
RICLISBY, MARY, 50, F, None listed, -, NY, 7, 7, CHAS.
RIDGELY, EMMA, 20, F, None listed, -, MD, 198, 186, CHAS-. In HH of Emily Timbrook f 49 born PA.
RIGGS, JOHN S., 52, M, Sadler, -, MD, 854, 812, CHAS+.
RILEY, CHARLES, 14, M, None listed, -, PA, 187, 170, CHAS. In HH of Thomas Noland m 40 born Ireland.
RILEY, WILLIAM, 59, M,
Stationer, -, MD, 332, 306, CHAS.
RING, CONRAD, 50, M, Auctioneer, -, NY, 455, 422, CHAS*. In HH of David A. Ring m 60 born NY.
RING, DAVID A., 60, M, Auctioneer, -, NY, 455, 422, CHAS*.
RISING, WILLIAM C., 30, M, Clerk, -, MD, 882, 840, CHAS+. In HH of Thomas S. Nickerson m 36 born VA.
ROBERTS, ADOLPH, 35, M, Painter, -, NJ, 1089,1067,CHAS%.
ROBERTS, AMELIA, 12, F, None listed, -, NJ, 1089, 1067, CHAS%. In HH of Adolph Roberts m 35 born NJ.
ROBERTS, CAROLINE, 30, F, None listed, -, NJ, 1089, 1067, CHAS%. In HH of Adolph Roberts m 35 born NJ.
ROBERTS, CAROLINE, 19, F, None listed, -, PA, 855, 835, CHAS-. In HH of R.S. Oakley m 50 born PA.
ROBERTS, ELIZABETH, 23, F, None listed, -, PA, 855, 835, CHAS-. In HH of R.S. Oakley m 50 born PA.
ROBERTS, H.M., 30, M, Stage Driver, -, NY, 533, 537, AND. In Hotel.
ROBERTS, JAMES, 9, M, None listed, -, NJ, 1089, 1067, CHAS%. In HH of Adolph Roberts m 35 born NJ.
ROBERTS, PAMELIA A., 29, F, None listed, -, PA, 833, 813, CHAS-. In HH of James S. Roberts m 29 born SC.
ROBERTS, W.B., 25, M, Carpenter, -, NY, 346, 308,

CHAS+. In Boarding House.
ROBERTSON, JANE, 75, F, None listed, -, MD, 1053, 1053, UNION. In Poor House.
ROBINSON, E.G., 31, M, Accountant., -, NY, 33, 33, KERS. In boarding house.
ROBINSON, J.M., 16, M, Merchant, -, NY, 562, 562, CHES. In HH of John Dunnavant m 25 born SC.
ROCHESTER, ROBERT, 32, M, Tanner, -,DE, 219, 224, PICK.
RODES, O.E., 37, M, None listed, -, NY, 425, 425, LEX. In HH of William Hathwanger m 47 born SC.
ROGERS, CHARLOTTE, 42, F, None listed, -, PA, 1071, 1048, CHAS-. In HH of Silas Rogers m 50 born PA.
ROGERS, D.F., 23, M, Clerk, -, NY, 482, 439, CHAS. In Planters Hotel.
ROGERS, JAMES L., 26, M, Student, -, PA, 683, 702, RICH. Student at Theological Seminary.
ROGERS, JOHN F., 0, M, None listed, -, NY, 10,   9, CHAS$. In HH of Sidney Rogers m 25 born NY. John F. Rogers age 6/12 yr.
ROGERS, MARIA LOUISA, 50, F, None listed, M, MD, 301, 285, CHAS-.
ROGERS, SIDNEY, 25, M, Bar keeper, -, NY, 10,   9, CHAS$.
ROGERS, SILAS, 50, M, Jeweller, -, PA, 1071, 1048, CHAS-.
RONAN, WILLIAM, 42, M, Shop keeper, -, NY, 503, 496, CHAS%.

ROONEY, MARGARET, 7, F, None listed, -, NY, 309, 285, CHAS. In HH of Paul Rooney m 44 born Ireland.
ROONEY, SUSAN, 7, F, None listed, -, NY, 302, 278, CHAS+. In HH of Patrick Rooney m 57 born Ireland.
ROOSEVELT, H.L., 37, M, Merchant, -, NY, 851, 809, CHAS+.
ROPER, MARY, 72, F, None listed, -, MD, 457, 457, PICK+. In HH of Joshua Roper m 72 born NC.
ROSE, L.M., 25, M, Tinner, -, NY, 11, 11, EDGE. In HH of J.L. Doby m 32, landlord, born SC.
ROSS, CATHERINE, 80, F, None listed, -, PA, 973, 973, GREE. In HH of Mary Ponder f 60 born SC.
ROUMILLAS, A., 35, M, Confectioner, -, NY, 250, 227, CHAS.
ROUND, GEORGE H., 43, M, Met Clergyman, -, NY, 2125, 2135, ABB. George H. is a Methodist Clergyman and teacher.
ROUX, ELLEN, 20, F, Milliner, -, PA, 852, 832, CHAS-. In HH of A.G. Parker f 38 born Germany.
ROWAND, A.H., 30, M, Book binder, -, NJ, 2251, 2251, GREE.
ROWAND, CATHRINE, 25, F, None listed, -, PA, 2251, 2251, GREE. In HH of A.H. Rowand m 30 born NJ.
ROWARD, HESTER M., 30, F, None listed, -, NY, 87, 87, GEOR. In HH of R.T. Roward m 33 minister born SC.

ROWE, ELIZA, 51, F, Carpenter, -, NJ, 143, 143, GEOR*.
ROWLEY, C.M., 23, M, Teacher, -, NY, 293, 293, KERS. In HH of John Brown m 54 born SC.
ROWLY, ADDISON, 20, M, MD, -, NY, 358, 358, KERS. In HH of Lucian Dinkins m 29 born SC.
RUDDOCK, JOSEPH, 13, M, None listed, -, NY, 184, 168, CHAS*. In HH of Arthur Ruddock m 40 born Scotland.
RUNSFORD, JOSIAH, 12, F, None listed, -, PA, 1186, 1165, CHAS%. In HH of John Thorn m 40 black born SC.
RUNSFORD, MARGARET, 50, F, None listed, -, PA, 1186, 1165, CHAS%. In HH of John Thorn m 40 black born SC.
RUSSEL, SUSAN, 29, F, None listed, -, NY, 264, 247, CHAS+. In HH of John Russel m 31 born MA.
RUSSELL, JOB, 31, M, Chemist, -, PA, 149, 149, CHES.
RUTJES, THEONEA, 30, F, None listed, -, PA, 994, 973, CHAS-. In HH of J.A. Rutjes m 30 born Holland.
RYAN, JOHN, 28, M, Seaman, -, NY, 326, 301, CHAS. On Steam Ship Southerner.

S

SAFFLE, SARAH, 80, F, None listed, -, MD, 1596, 1596, ABB. In HH of Rebecca McKenzie f 50 born VA.
SALTAR, THOMAS R., 65, M, None listed, -, PA, 586, 578, CHAS%.

SARGANT, D.L., 27, M, Carpenter, -, NY, 1861, 1861, SUMT.
SASSARD, HARRIOT, 43, F, None listed, -,D.C., 593, 551, CHAS+. In HH of J. Sassard m 54 born France. Harriot born Washington, D.C..
SAUNDERS, GEORGE, 12, M, None listed, -, NY, 235, 213, CHAS. In HH of S. Saunders m 49 born Ireland.
SAVAGE, JOHN, 75, M, Planter, -, PA, 250, 250, UNN+.
SCHINE, MICHAEL, 6, M, None listed, -, NY, 189, 177, CHAS-. In HH of Ann Schine f 30 born Ireland.
SCHORB, GEORGE T., 3, M, None listed, -, NY, 491, 491, FAIR. In HH of J.R. Schorb m 31 born Germany.
SCHYLER, WM. M., 21, M, Teacher, -, PA, 226, 226, ORNG*. In HH of David Houser m 52, planter, born SC.
SCOFIELD, JOHN N., 35, M, Mechanic, -, NY, 630, 648, RICH.
SCOTT, G.T., 42, M, Post Master, -, MD, 17, 17, NEWB.
SCOTT, HENRY, 27, M, Seaman, -, NJ, 326, 301, CHAS. On Steam Ship Southerner.
SCOTT, MARY, 68, F, None listed, -, PA, 1284, 1284, UNION. In HH of James Scott m 65 born NC.
SCOTT, W., 25, M, Clerk, -, NY, 831, 811, CHAS-. In HH of J. Brawley m 30 born NY.
SCUYLER, WM. M., 21, M, Teacher, -, PA, 226, 226, ORNG*. In HH of David Houser m 52 born SC.

SEABROOK, GEORGE BUNKER, 22, M, Teacher, -, NY, 213, 213, BEAU+. In HH of Joseph B. Seabrook m 41 Episcopal Clergyman born SC.
SEBRING, EDWARD, 51, M, President State Bank, -, NY, 825, 808, CHAS%.
SELL, EDGAR E., 13, M, None listed, -, PA, 852, 832, CHAS-. In HH of A.G. Parker f 38 born Germany.
SELL, ELIZABETH, 30, F, Milliner, -, PA, 852, 832, CHAS-. In HH of A.G. Parker f 38 born Germany.
SEYLE, SAMUEL, 73, M, Master of Poor, -, MD, 237, 222, CHAS-.
SHACKELFORD, ELIZA B., 28, F, None listed, -, NY, 530, 489, CHAS+. In HH of F.R. Shackelford m 50 born SC.
SHARPE, CHARLES, 22, M, Carpenter, -, NY, 1025, 1002, CHAS-. In HH of Charles Seyle m 32 born SC.
SHAW, ANGELINE, 7, F, None listed, -, PA, 874, 851, CHAS%. In HH of Thomas Barnes m 40 born Ireland.
SHAW, RICHD. P., 15, M, None listed, -, PA, 351, 351, MARL. In HH of Wm. Moore m 42 born SC.
SHAW, SOPHY, 6, F, None listed, -, NY, 526, 476, CHAS. In HH of James Shaw m 40 born Ireland.
SHAW, THOMAS B., 13, M, None listed, -, PA, 351, 351, MARL. In HH of Wm. Moore m 42 born SC.

SHAW, WILLIAM, 27, M, Mariner, -, NY, 218, 196, CHAS. In HH of Chris. Nelson m 60 born Denmark.
SHAW, WM., 39, M, Laborer, -, DE, 381, 381, MARL.
SHEPARD, DANIEL, 58, M, Baptist Clergyman, -, NJ, 103, 103, CHAS^.
SHERDON, LEWIS, 37, M, Mariner, -, NY, 58, 52, CHAS+. In HH of Fetz Hallenback m 28 born Germany.
SHERMON, FRANCES, 26, F, None listed, -, NY, 1893, 1893, GREE. In HH of J.B. Shermon m 26 born NY.
SHERMON, J.B., 26, M, Manufacturer, -, NY, 1893, 1893, GREE.
SHIRER, JOHN, 3, M, None listed, -, NY, 565, 581, RICH. In HH of John Shirer m 28 born Germany.
SHOEMAKER, JAMES H., 35, M, Baker, -, NY, 40, 37, CHAS-. Listed as prisioner, date 1848.
SHOUSEN, HENRY, 21, M, Gardner, -, MD, 473, 470, CHAS%. In HH of Lambert Woorsen m 35 born Ireland.
SHUGART, REBECCA D., 71, F, None listed, -, PA, 1790, 1796, EDGE. In HH of John Shugart m 40 born VA.
SIMMONS, HENRY H., 35, M, Contractor of public works, -, MD, 1768, 1774, EDGE.
SIMONS, AFFEY, 50, F, None listed, M, NY, 199, 187, CHAS-.
SIMONS, ELIZABETH, 8, F, None listed, M, NY, 199, 187,

CHAS-. In HH of Affey Simons f 50 mulatto born NY.
SIMONS, JOHN C., 40, M, Painter, -, PA, 840, 820, CHAS-.
SIMONS, MARY, 22, F, None listed, M, NY, 475, 433, CHAS+. In HH of Sarah Drayton m 45 black born NY.
SIMONS, N.A., 30, M, Painter, -, PA, 840, 820, CHAS-. In HH of John C. Simons m 40 born PA.
SIMONS, W.F., 30, M, Painter, -, PA, 384, 348, CHAS.
SIMPSON, CAROLINE, 17, F, None listed, -, PA, 32, 29, CHAS-. In HH of Ellen Gillet f 60 born VA.
SIMPSON, E.A., 30, F, None listed, -, NY, 476, 434, CHAS. In HH of M.M. Stewart f 40, runs boarding house, born SC.
SINCLAIR, DANL., 26, M, Ice H. Keeper, -, NY, 22, 20, CHAS$.
SINGLEMAN, JOHN, 20, M, Cigar Manufacturer, -, MD, 454, 451, CHAS%. In HH of W.H. Boring m 28 born VA.
SINKLER, CHARLES, 32, M, Planter, -, PA, 1727, 1727, SUMT.
SISSFORD, WILLIAM K., 25, M, Bricklayer, -,D.C., 514, 429, RICH.
SKILMAN, ALPHENS, 23, M, Shoe maker, -, NJ, 520, 520, FAIR. In HH of David Cremer m 49 born NJ.
SLAMAN, JOSEPH, 5, M, None listed, -, NY, 1972, 1978, EDGE. In HH of George Slaman m 39 born Poland.
SLAWSON, LEVI, 31, M, Coach Maker, -, NY, 98, 98, NEWB.

SLOAN, SUSAN, 87, F, None listed, -, MD, 678, 683, AND.
SMART, LILDEN, 23, M, Planter, -, MD, 318, 318, FAIR. In HH of William Moore m 56 born SC.
SMITH, ANN C., 22, F, None listed, -, NY, 359, 359, KERS. In HH of Saml. Donnelly m 42 born NY.
SMITH, ELIZA L., 55, F, None listed, -, MD, 577, 535, CHAS+.
SMITH, F., 25, M, Carriage/ trimmer, -, NY, 8, 8, EDGE. In HH of H.R. Spann m 31 born SC.
SMITH, F.A., 17, F, None listed, -, NY, 46, 46, KERS. In HH of C.F. Carpenter f 47 born NY.
SMITH, H.S., 27, M, Painter, -, PA, 840, 820, CHAS-. In HH of John C. Simons m 40 born PA.
SMITH, HORACE W., 24, M, Servant, -, PA, 882, 840, CHAS+. In Charleston Hotel.
SMITH, J., 28, M, Carpenter, -, PA, 462, 445, CHAS-. In HH of William Patterson m 34 born MD.
SMITH, JOHN, 37, M, Engineer, -, PA, 491, 474, CHAS-.
SMITH, JOHN, 22, M, Stage driver, -, PA, 2245, 2245, GREE. In HH of J.L. Hemming m 27, landlord, born in SC.
SMITH, JOSEPH, 89, M, Farmer, -, MD, 936, 936, GREE.
SMITH, JOSHUA, 34, M, Engineer, -, PA, 439, 422, CHAS-. In HH of Truman Cook m 40 born NY.
SMITH, JULIA, 40, F, None listed, -, PA, 669, 669, DARL. In

HH of Frs. Smith m 21 born SC.
SMITH, JULIA ANN, 33, F, None listed, -, MD, 594, 552, CHAS+. In HH of William Smith m 29 born NY.
SMITH, MARGARET, 73, F, None listed, -, PA, 1274, 1274, YORK. In HH of Rhody Smith m 75 born VA.
SMITH, MARY, 23, F, None listed, -, PA, 840, 820, CHAS-. In HH of John C. Simons m 40 born PA.
SMITH, MARY JANE, 7, F, None listed, -, MD, 594, 552, CHAS+. In HH of William Smith m 29 born NY.
SMITH, R.A., 26, F, None listed, -, PA, 1003, 981, CHAS-. In HH of L. Watts f 32 born England.
SMITH, RACHEL, 75, F, None listed, -, PA, 936, 936, GREE. In HH of Joseph Smith m 89 born MD.
SMITH, RICHARD, 60, M, Messenger of Council, -, MD, 399, 382, CHAS-.
SMITH, SARAH, 19, F, None listed, -, PA, 208, 213, RICH. In HH of James W. Smith m 23 born SC.
SMITH, SARAH, 15, F, None listed, -, MD, 594, 552, CHAS+. In HH of William Smith m 29 born NY.
SMITH, WILLIAM, 29, M, Mariner, -, NY, 594, 552, CHAS+.
SMITH, WM. H., 58, M, Shoemaker, -, NY, 200, 200, SUMT.
SMOOT, DAVID, 61, M, Farmer, -, MD, 201, 201, DARL.
SNOOK, JAMES, 30, M, Carpenter, -, NY, 391, 355, CHAS. In HH of F.W. Theus m 28 born Germany.
SNOWDEN, FRANCES, 50, F, None listed, -, NJ, 369, 378, RICH. In HH of Gilbert T. Snowden m 56 born NJ.
SNOWDEN, GILBERT T., 56, M, Merchant, -, NJ, 369, 378, RICH.
SNYDER, ADAM, 62, M, Brick maker, -, PA, 1906, 1906, GREE.
SOHURS, FANNY, 17, F, None listed, -, NY, 587, 569, CHAS-. In HH of J.B. Davis m 43 born MA.
SOMMERS, LOUISA, 25, F, None listed, -, PA, 198, 186, CHAS-. In HH of Emily Timbrook f 49 born PA.
SONBEDA, FRANCIS, 17, M, None listed, -, NY, 193, 177, CHAS*. In HH of Peter Sonbeda m 44 born France.
SONBEDA, SARAH A., 50, F, None listed, -, NY, 193, 177, CHAS*. In HH of Peter Sonbeda m 44 born France.
SPARKS, JOSIAH, 86, M, Farmer, -, MD, 793, 793, UNION.
SPEAR, CAROLINE G., 12, F, None listed, -, NY, 1037, 1014, CHAS-. In HH of W.W. Spear m 38 born NY.
SPEAR, JAMES E., 31, M, Jeweller, -, NJ, 698, 678, CHAS-.
SPEAR, MARTHA J., 31, M, None listed, -, NY, 1037, 1014, CHAS-. In HH of W.W. Spear m 38 born NY.

SPEAR, W.W., 38, M, Jeweller, -, NY, 1037, 1014, CHAS-.
SPENCER, AMBROSE, 39, M, Teacher, -, NY, 909, 909, DARL.
SPENCER, THEODORE, 20, M, Bricklayer, -, NY, 959, 939, CHAS-. In HH of J.S. Riddell m 34 born MA.
SPURRIER, T.J., 47, M, Stone Cutter, -, MD, 526, 526, FAIR.
SQUIER, ABRAHAM C., 45, M, Merchant, -, NJ, 415, 426, RICH.
SQUIER, EMELINE, 35, F, None listed, -, NJ, 415, 426, RICH. In HH of Abraham C. Squier m 45 born NJ.
SQUIER, JONATHAN C., 3, M, None listed, -, NJ, 415, 426, RICH. In HH of Abraham C. Squier m 45 born NJ.
SQUIER, MARY E., 5, F, None listed, -, NJ, 415, 426, RICH. In HH of Abraham C. Squier m 45 born NJ.
ST.JOHNS, MARIA, 20, F, None listed, -, NJ, 32, 32, YORK+. In HH of Jearamiah Couster m 47 born NC.
STANELAKE, JOHN, 36, M, Clerk, -, NJ, 470, 485, RICH. In Hotel
STANSBURY, ABBY, 3, F, None listed, -, NJ, 472, 487, RICH. In HH of Henry Hawthorn m 29 born Canada.
STANSBURY, HARRIET, 16, F, None listed, -, NJ, 476, 491, RICH. In HH of Johnson Hunter m 24 born Ireland.
STANTON, MARY, 80, F, None listed, -, PA, 586, 586, ABB. In HH of Joseph Bridges m 54 born NC.

STARR, WILLIAM P., 26, M, None listed, -, NY, 11, 11, EDGE. In HH of J.L. Doby m 32, landlord, born SC.
STATE, FRANCES, 28, M, Seaman, -, NY, 326, 301, CHAS. In HH of William Rollins m 40 born {-}.
STAUNTON, ESTHER, 50, F, None listed, -, PA, 823, 833, Rich+. In HH of Joseph Staunton m 83 born PA.
STAUNTON, JOSEPH, 83, M, Planter, -, PA, 823, 833, Rich+.
STEELE, MARY, 71, F, None listed, -, PA, 72, 72, YORK+.
STEIN, JOHN F., JR., 18, M, Engineer, -, NY, 268, 236, CHAS. In HH of John F. Stein m 45 born Prussia.
STEIN, MARY ANN, 35, F, None listed, -, NY, 268, 236, CHAS. In HH of John F. Stein m 45 born Prussia.
STELLING, EMMA, 22, F, None listed, -, PA, 202, 189, CHAS-. In HH of Grace Piexolla f 30 born SC.
STERNES, ARBA, 36, M, Merchant, -, NY, 416, 427, RICH.
STEVENS, CATHERINE, 40, F, None listed, -, NY, 367, 340, CHAS*. In HH of Jose Stevens m 60 born Nassau N.P.
STEVENSON, JOEL, 51, M, Tailor, -, MD, 198, 202, RICH.
STEWART, JAMES, 29, M, Clerk, -, NY, 270, 254, CHAS-. In HH of Thomas E. Baker m 50 born VA.
STIEN, AMELIA, 10, F, None listed, -, NY, 386, 350, CHAS. In HH of Francis Stien m 45 born

Germany.
STIENBECK, ADAM, 22, M, Store keeper, -, PA, 368, 351, CHAS-. In HH of John Jeffords m 49 born SC.
STILLMAN, AMELIA, 21, F, None listed, -, NY, 310, 294, CHAS-. In HH of James Stillman m 50 born CT.
STILLMAN, RAYMOND, 4, M, None listed, -, NY, 310, 294, CHAS-. In HH of James Stillman m 50 born CT.
STOAKES, E.R., 38, M, Boot binder, -, NJ, 248, 226, CHAS.
STOCKTON, WILLIAM F., 35, M, Chief Eng. RR, -,DE, 470, 485, RICH. In Hotel
STODARD, LUCINDA, 28, F, None listed, -, NJ, 1069, 1047, CHAS%. In HH of William McIntoch m 65 born Scotland.
STODARD, WILLIAM, 30, M, Carpenter, -, NJ, 1069, 1047, CHAS%. In HH of William McIntoch m 65 born Scotland.
STODDARD, C., 54, M, Clerk, -, MD, 29, 29, CHAS*.
STODDARD, JOHN, 19, M, Clerk, -, MD, 29, 29, CHAS*. In HH of C. Stoddard m 54 born MD.
STODDARD, MARY ANN, 49, F, None listed, -, MD, 29, 29, CHAS*. In HH of C. Stoddard m 54 born MD.
STODDARD, MARY ANN, 17, F, None listed, -, MD, 29, 29, CHAS*. In HH of C. Stoddard m 54 born MD.
STOKES, JOHN J., 73, M, Farmer, -, MD, 1016, 1016, GREE.
STOKES, JOHNATHAN, 74, M, Farmer, -, MD, 1391, 1391, SPART.
STRANS, FRANCES, 14, M, None listed, -, PA, 147, 138, CHAS+. In HH of Margaraet Strans f 32 born Germany.
STRATTON, WILLIAM, 44, M, Baker, -, NY, 269, 253, CHAS-.
STREHER, RACHEL, 31, F, None listed, -, NJ, 15, 15, SPART. In HH of J.B. Streher m 28 born SC.
STRUM, A.P., 40, M, Teacher, -, PA, 2364, 2364, SPART. At Limestone High School.
STUBS, CINNIE, 36, F, None listed, -, NY, 1188, 1188, LEX. In HH of John Stubs m 43 born England.
STULTZ, NATHAN, 28, M, Labourer, -, NY, 1230, 1230, DARL.
STURGES, GEORGE, 69, M, Farmer, -, MD, 94, 94, YORK.
STURGINEGGER, MALVINA, 7, F, None listed, -, NY, 537, 537, FAIR. In HH of J.U. Zucker m 48 born Switzerland.
STYLER, BENJAMIN, 59, M, None listed, -, PA, 1416, 1416, YORK.
SULLIVAN, S.W., 24, M, Overseer, -, NJ, 584, 584, SUMT.
SUMTER, F., 37, M, Lawyer, -, PA, 1873, 1873, SUMT.
SUSDORFF, GUSTAVIS, 2, M, None listed, -, NY, 836, 816, CHAS-. In Boarding House.
SUTHERLAND, HENRETTA, 30, F, None listed, -, NY, 260, 260, KERS. In HH of J.F. Sutherland m 35 born NY.

SUTHERLAND, J.F., 35, M, Cabinet maker, -, NY, 260, 260, KERS.
SUTPHEN, JOHN C., 32, M, Saddler, -, NJ, 247, 252, RICH.
SUTPHEN, MARY, 25, F, None listed, -, NJ, 247, 252, RICH. In HH of John C. Sutphen m 32 born NJ.
SUTTON, THOMAS, 3, M, None listed, -, NY, 597, 555, CHAS+. In HH of Mary Sutton f 28 born Ireland.
SWADDELL, W., 28, M, Seaman, -, NY, 326, 301, CHAS. On Steam Ship Southerner.
SWAN, BENJAMIN, 63, M, Planter, -, MD, 222, 222, FAIR.
SWAN, JANE, 80, F, None listed, -, PA, 784, 785, FAIR.
SWARTWOUT, SAMUEL, 28, M, Seaman, -, NY, 326, 301, CHAS. On Steam Ship Southerner.
SWEENEY, CHARLES, 27, M, Merchant, -, NY, 391, 355, CHAS. In HH of F.W. Theus m 28 born Germany.
SWEENY, CHARLES, 35, M, Engineer, -, NY, 346, 308, CHAS+. In Boarding House.

T

TAFT, DAVID, 35, M, Merchant, -, NY, 382, 365, CHAS-.
TAILOR, MARY, 70, F, None listed, -, MD, 36, 36, GEOR. In HH of James Corson m 60 born PA.
TALBERT, LEWIS, 86, M, Laborer, -, MD, 732, 732, YORK. In HH of Reason Tobert m 42 born York Dist., SC.

TATE, CATHARINE, 81, F, None listed, -, PA, 433, 433, YORK*. In HH of Ruthas Tate m 33 born York Dist., SC.
TATE, MARY, 86, F, None listed, -, MD, 747, 747, UNION.
TAVEL, JOSEPHINE, 12, F, None listed, -, NY, 768, 748, CHAS-. In HH of Owen Campbell m 25 born Ireland.
TAYLOR, JAMES M., 28, M, Merchant, -, NY, 695, 675, CHAS-. In HH of J.S. Bird m 53 born England.
TAYLOR, MR., 73, M, Farmer, -, PA, 2608, 2608, SPART.
TAYLOR, O., 30, M, Merchant, -, NY, 721, 701, CHAS-. In Boarding House.
TAYLOR, THOMAS, 30, M, Seaman, -, NY, 326, 301, CHAS. In HH of William Rollins m 40 born {-}.
TAYLOR, W., 22, M, Clerk, -, NY, 692, 672, CHAS-. In HH of E.G. Brown m 41 born CT.
TEASDALE, JOHN H., 28, M, Clerk, -, NY, 326, 301, CHAS. On Steam Ship Southerner.
TENNANT, M.A., 25, F, None listed, -, PA, 533, 537, AND. In Hotel.
TERRY, L.C., 28, F, None listed, -, NY, 2364, 2364, SPART. At Limestone High School.
THARP, JOHN J., 32, M, Coach maker, -, NJ, 1795, 1795, ABB.
THAYER, CATHERINE B., 28, F, None listed, -, NY, 359, 332, CHAS*. In HH of T. Heyward Thayer m 45 born SC.

THOMAS, AMELIA, 5, F, None listed, -, NY, 631, 589, CHAS+. In HH of Jane Thomas f 34 born SC.
THOMAS, BRIDGET, 24, F, None listed, -, NY, 235, 210, CHAS*. In HH of William Thomas m 27 born England.
THOMAS, ELIZABETH, 28, F, None listed, -, NY, 335, 309, CHAS.
THOMAS, HESTER, 71, F, None listed, M, MD, 118, 118, KERS. In HH of Harriet Hammond f 20 black born SC.
THOMPSON, ALLEN W., 32, M, Shoemaker, -, NY, 954, 954, DARL.
THOMPSON, BENJ. A., 61, M, Accountant, -, PA, 424, 424, HORR. In HH of Henry Buck m 45 born Maine.
THOMPSON, HARRIET, 38, F, None listed, -, PA, 345, 345, MARL. In HH of Thos. J. Thompson m 29 born PA.
THOMPSON, MARY, 6, F, None listed, -, NY, 167, 158, CHAS+. In Boarding House.
THOMPSON, MARY ANN, 23, F, None listed, -, NY, 167, 158, CHAS+. In Boarding House.
THOMPSON, SUSAN, 23, F, None listed, -, PA, 473, 431, CHAS. In HH of George Allison m 32 born PA.
THOMPSON, THEODORE, 26, M, Boot maker, -,D.C., 473, 431, CHAS. {Born Washington, D.C.}. In HH of George Allison m 32 born PA.
THOMPSON, THOS. J., 29, M, Laborer, -, PA, 345, 345, MARL.
THOMPSON, W., 22, M, Clerk, -, NY, 721, 701, CHAS-. In Boarding House.
THORNE, MARY A.H., 26, F, None listed, -, PA, 467, 481, RICH. In HH of Micajah A. Thorne m 35 born VA.
THORNTON, EMMALINE, 39, F, None listed, -, NJ, 614, 632, RICH. In HH of John C. Thornton m 40 born SC.
THORPE, HARRIOT M., 22, F, None listed, -, NY, 202, 189, CHAS-. In HH of Grace Piexolla f 30 born SC.
THORTON, P., 70, M, None listed, -, NJ, 820, 820, KERS.
TILOTSON, DE WITT E., 43, M, Merchant, -, NY, 206, 206, ABB.
TIMBROOK, EMILY, 49, F, None listed, -, PA, 198, 186, CHAS-.
TINNERMAN, MARIAH, 59, F, None listed, -, NY, 240, 240, EDGE.
TOMLINSON, RUTH, 70, F, None listed, -, MD, 509, 509, YORK. In HH of William Tomlinson m 59 born York Dist., SC.
TORLAY, MARY, 34, F, None listed, -, NY, 68, 62, CHAS-.
TOWLEY?, M.M., 19, F, Teacher, -, NY, 84, 84, BARN. In HH of Wm. H. Peyton m 49 born SC.
TOWNS, RACHEL, 71, F, None listed, -, MD, 7, 7, GREE.
TOWNSEND, PRIMAS, 54, M, Shoemaker, B, NY, 349, 349, CHES.

TRAINER, H.B., 33, M, Engineer, -, PA, 513, 513, FAIR. In HH of J.M. Cranford m 27 born Ireland. At the Fairfield Hotel. H.B.Trainer born Philadelphia, PA.
TREKLEN, CHARLES, 33, M, Printer, -, MD, 237, 222, CHAS-. Poor House.
TRESONTHICK?, SAMUEL H., 9, M, None listed, -, PA, 1188, 1188, EDGE. In HH of George Fresonthick m 35 born England.
TRIMBO, C.C., 33, M, Builder, -, MD, 162, 149, CHAS*.
TROTTER, NANCY, 77, F, None listed, -, MD, 803, 803, PICK+.
TROY, JAMES, 36, M, Carpenter, -, NY, 607, 624, RICH.
TROY, MICHAEL, 65, M, None, -, NY, 607, 624, RICH. In HH of James Troy m 36 born NY.
TRUAX, J.H., 23, M, Printer, -, NY, 2251, 2251, GREE. In HH of A.H. Rowand m 30 born NJ.
TRUESDALE, D., 60, M, Tavern keeper, -, NY, 43, 39, CHAS$.
TRUESDELE, JANE, 53, F, None listed, -, NY, 417, 376, CHAS+. In HH of William Maiseman {sic} m 34 born Ireland.
TUCKERMAN, NATHANIEL, 60, M, Miller, -, PA, 234, 234, FAIR. In HH of George W. Hagain m 35 born NC.
TURNER, SAMUEL, 88, M, Farmer, -, MD, 252, 252, YORK*.
TUSTEN, JAMES H., 49, M, Carpenter, -, NY, 790, 790, ABB.
TUTTLE, CYRUS W., 6, M, None listed, -, NY, 779, 759,
CHAS-. In HH of John Ogeman m 26 born Germany.
TUTTLE, MOSES, 60, M, Farmer, -, NJ, 177, 177, GEOR*.
TYTUS, J.H., 58, M, Harness maker, -, NJ, 1797, 1803, EDGE.

U

UFFORD, EUGENE, 28, M, Saddler, -, NY, 474, 489, RICH.
UFFORD, EUGENE, 3, M, None listed, -, NJ, 474, 489, RICH. In HH of Eugene Ufford m 28 born NY.
UFFORD, MARY E., 27, F, None listed, -, NY, 474, 489, RICH. In HH of Eugene Ufford m 28 born NY.
URNER, ISAAC, 27, M, Teacher, -, PA, 1835, 1835, ABB. In HH of Henry H. Creswell m 38 born SC.

V

VALENTINE, HANNAH, 70, F, None listed, -, NY, 260, 260, KERS. In HH of J.F. Sutherland m 35 born NY.
VAN PATTON, M., 47, M, Manufacturing, -, NY, 3164, 3164, SPART.
VAN PETT, MARY E., 20, F, None listed, -,D.C., 216, 216, BEAU+. Born Washington, D.C. In HH of Mrs. Sarah Pope f 72 born SC.
VAN WART, REBECCA A., 22, F, None listed, -, NY, 608, 625, RICH. In HH of Walter Van Wart m 27 born NY.

VAN WART, WALTER, 27, M, Police Officer, -, NY, 608, 625, RICH.
VAN WINKLE, J., 45, M, Furnishing store, -, NY, 523, 506, CHAS-.
VAN WYCH, AUGUSTIN, 5, M, None listed, -, NY, 1007, 1008, AND*. In HH of Samuel Mavrick m 77 born SC.
VAN WYCH, DYDIA ANN, 1, F, None listed, -, NY, 1007, 1008, AND*. In HH of Samuel Mavrick m 77 born SC.
VAN WYCH, ROBERT, 3, M, None listed, -, NY, 1007, 1008, AND*. In HH of Samuel Mavrick m 77 born SC.
VAN WYCH, SAMUEL M., 15, M, None listed, -, NY, 1007, 1008, AND*. In HH of Samuel Mavrick m 77 born SC.
VAN WYCH, WILLIAM, 46, M, Lawyer, -, NY, 1007, 1008, AND*. In HH of Samuel Mavrick m 77 born SC.
VANHORN, JOHN G., 45, M, Farmer, -, NY, 1129, 1129, ABB.
VARNEY, MARY, 35, F, None listed, -, NY, 242, 227, CHAS-. In HH of Celisle Crawford f 30 mulatto born Cuba.
VINCENT, JAMES, 67, M, Planter, -, MD, 1069, 1069, UNION.
VOORHIES, CATHERINE A., 16, F, None listed, -, NJ, 168, 154, CHAS*. In HH of Maria C. Voorhies f 44 born NC.

W

WADDILL, MARY, 78, F, None listed, -, MD, 14, 14, GREE.
WAGNER, W., 25, M, Priv. U.S.A., -, PA, 47, 43, CHAS$. In HH of John Ewing m 50 born MA.
WAGSTAFF, SARAH, 6, F, None listed, -, PA, 683, 687, AND. In HH of William Wagstaff m 56 born England.
WAITE, THOMAS E., 26, M, Student, -, NY, 683, 702, RICH. Student at Theological Seminary.
WALDROM, HENRY, 84, M, Planter, -, MD, 101, 101, EDGE.
WALKER, J.T., 31, M, Dentist, -, PA, 563, 563, CHES.
WALKER, JOHN C., 36, M, Stationer, -, NY, 101, 93, CHAS+. In Boarding House.
WALKER, JOSEPH, 30, M, Stationer, -, NY, 515, 474, CHAS+.
WALKER, JOSEPH R., 54, M, Ep. Clergyman, -, MD, 151, 151, BEAU.
WALKER, MARY, 19, F, None listed, -, NY, 788, 746, CHAS+. In HH of William Norris m 28 born Ireland.
WALKER, REBECCA, 31, F, None listed, -, NJ, 370, 353, CHAS-. In HH of J.E. Walker m 42 born SC.
WALTER, JOHN J., 48, M, Tinner, -, PA, 243, 248, RICH.
WANEY, SAMUEL, 73, M, Farmer, -, PA, 434, 434, YORK*.
WARD, ADALINE, 40, F, None listed, -, NY, 1723, 1724, EDGE. In HH of Hiram Jordan m 36, landlord, born SC.

WARD, C., 16, F, None listed, -, NY, 1146, 1125, CHAS%. In HH of Harris Simons m 43 born Ireland. Marie Ramsay Simons age 8/12 yr.
WARD, G., 16, F, None listed, -, NY, 1146, 1125, CHAS%. In HH of Harris Simons m 43 born Ireland.
WARD, WILLIAM, 26, M, None listed, -, NY, 11, 11, EDGE. In HH of J.L. Doby m 32, landlord, born SC.
WARING, HENRIETTA, 48, F, None listed, -, MD, 527, 493, CHAS*. In HH of H.S. Waring m 60 born SC.
WARREN, ELIZABETH, 45, F, None listed, -, NJ, 153, 143, CHAS-.
WATERS, JOHN E., 55, M, Farmer, -, MD, 2191, 2191, ABB.
WATERS, WALTER E., 42, M, Farmer, -, MD, 1518, 1518, CHES.
WATERS, WILLIAM, 63, M, Clerk of market, -, MD, 374, 336, CHAS+.
WATSON, HELEN M., 51, F, None listed, -, MD, 260, 238, CHAS. In HH of Dunham Watson m 60 born MA.
WATSON, LEWIS, 50, M, Writing teacher, -, NY, 102, 102, FAIR. In HH of William F. Pearson m 66 born SC.
WEATHERLY, E. MRS., 70, F, None listed, -, MD, 562, 562, MARL. In HH of J.W. McLeod m 32 born NC.
WEBB, MARY ANN, 6, F, None listed, -, NY, 109, 104, CHAS*. In HH of Walter Webb m 50 born Ireland.
WEBER, ANDREW, 11, M, None listed, -, NY, 236, 214, CHAS. In HH of A.A. Weber m 52 born Germany.
WELCH, ELIZA, 30, F, None listed, -, PA, 138, 126, CHAS*.
WELCH, JESSE, 30, M, Engineer, -, NY, 346, 308, CHAS+. In Boarding House.
WELCH, MARY, 32, F, None listed, -, NY, 479, 437, CHAS+.
WELCH, MARY, 20, F, None listed, -, MD, 320, 304, CHAS-. In HH of L.E. Whilden f 47 born SC.
WELCH, ROBERT, 28, M, Store keeper, -, MD, 320, 304, CHAS-. In HH of L.E. Whilden f 47 born SC.
WELLE, ELENORA, 10, F, None listed, -, MD, 847, 827, CHAS-. In HH of Sophia Selle 34 born Germany.
WELLS, N.S., 35, M, Farmer, -, NY, 118, 120, AND.
WELSH, MART. A., 22, F, Milliner, -, PA, 852, 832, CHAS-. In HH of A.G. Parker f 38 born Germany.
WEST, MARGARET, 64, F, None listed, -, PA, 1186, 1165, CHAS%. In HH of John Thorn m 40 black born SC.
WESTERFIELDT, J., 25, M, Priv. U.S.A., -, NJ, 47, 43, CHAS$. In HH of John Ewing m 50 born MA.
WHALEY, EMILEE, 20, F, None listed, -, PA, 134, 134, CHAS^. In HH of James Whaley m 24 born SC.
WHALEY, JOHN, 3, M, None listed, -, PA, 134, 134, CHAS^. In

HH of James Whaley m 24 born SC.
WHALEY, MARY, 1, F, None listed, -, PA, 134, 134, CHAS^. In HH of James Whaley m 24 born SC.
WHALLEY, THOMAS, 26, M, Servant, -, NY, 882, 840, CHAS+. In Charleston Hotel.
WHEELER, JOSEPH, 41, M, Met. Clergyman, -, NJ, 2104, 2104, ABB.
WHEELER, THOMAS, 30, M, Harness maker, -, NY, 23, 23, NEWB. In HH of J. Wilson 33 m Hotel Keeper born SC.
WHILESIDES, MARGARET, 78, F, None listed, -, PA, 71, 71, YORK. In HH of James L. Jones born York Dist., SC.
WHITE, ALMIRA, 32, F, None listed, -, NY, 624, 605, CHAS-. In HH of Julia Jacobs f 45 born SC.
WHITE, HISTEN, 72, F, None listed, -, PA, 248, 250, AND. In HH of Isaac White m 61 born SC.
WHITE, JOHN, 25, M, Confectioner, -, PA, 786, 766, CHAS-. In HH of Joseph Whyte m 70 born Italy.
WHITE, JOSEPH JR., 28, M, Confectioner, -, PA, 786, 766, CHAS-. In HH of Joseph Whyte m 70 born Italy.
WHITE, W.F., 23, M, Confectioner, -, PA, 786, 766, CHAS-. In HH of Joseph Whyte m 70 born Italy.
WHITES, WILLIAM C., 3, M, None listed, -, PA, 793, 773, CHAS-. In HH of Robert White m 40 born Ireland.
WHITTRIDGE, JAMES, 19, M, Seaman, -, NY, 326, 301, CHAS. On Steam Ship Southerner.
WHYTE, ARCHIBALD, 50, M, None listed, -, NY, 1187, 1187, YORK.
WHYTE, MARGARET J., 17, F, None listed, -, MD, 1187, 1187, YORK. In HH of Archibalc Whyte m 50 born NY.
WICKIE, ELIZABETH, 2, F, None listed, -, NY, 25, 20, CHAS+. In HH of John Metzler m 34 born Germany.
WIDMER, JOHN, 22, M, Clerk, -, PA, 186, 190, RICH.
WIERFELDER, SARAH, 24, F, None listed, -, NY, 473, 439, CHAS*. In HH of S. Wierfelder m 30 born Germany.
WILKLES, JOHN, 60, M, Planter, -, NY, 525, 491, CHAS*.
WILLBERGER, JOHN R., 25, M, Druggist, -, PA, 612, 570, CHAS+.
WILLIAMS, ANDREW, 24, M, Seaman, -, NY, 326, 301, CHAS. On Steam Ship Southerner.
WILLIAMS, CATHERINE, 50, F, None listed, -, PA, 362, 345, CHAS-.
WILLIAMS, JAMES, 29, M, Clerk, -, NY, 923, 903, CHAS-.
WILLIAMS, JOHN, 43, M, Mariner, -, NY, 351, 324, CHAS. In Boarding House.
WILLIAMS, MARY, 56, F, None listed, -, PA, 202, 202, CHAS%. In HH of Thomas Swinton m 18 born SC.
WILLIAMS, REBECCA, 72, F, None listed, -, MD, 1104, 1104, PICK+. In HH of John Williams m 27 born SC.

WILLIAMS, SARAH J., 20, F, None listed, -, NY, 129, 121, CHAS*.
WILLIMAN, LIPEY, 70, F, None listed, M, MD, 971, 948, CHAS%. In HH of Alexander Norsett m 42 mulatto born SC.
WILLINGTON, MARIA, 20, F, None listed, -, NY, 198, 186, CHAS-. In HH of Emily Timbrook f 49 born PA.
WILLIS, MARIA, 30, F, None listed, -, MD, 814, 794, CHAS-. In HH of John G. Willis m 45 born NC.
WILLIS, ROGER, 70, M, None listed, -, MD, 1002, 1002, SUMT. In HH of Ezekiel Dixon m 52 born SC.
WILLSON, THOMAS, 30, M, Harness maker, -, PA, 2302, 2302, GREE. In Hotel.
WILSON, ANN, 31, F, None listed, -, NY, 690, 670, CHAS-. In HH of William Wilson m 35 born England.
WILSON, ANN, 26, F, None listed, -, NY, 198, 186, CHAS-. In HH of Emily Timbrook f 49 born PA.
WILSON, ANNA, 25, F, None listed, -, NY, 13, 16, CHAS.
WILSON, CURRY, 33, M, Stone quarrier, -, PA, 36, 36, FAIR. In HH of Benj. V. Lakin m 68 born VA.
WILSON, GERTRUDE, 6, F, None listed, -, NY, 690, 670, CHAS-. In HH of William Wilson m 35 born England.
WILSON, HENRY, 16, M, Tinner, -, NY, 361, 332, CHAS. In HH of N.A. Roye m 28 born SC.

WILSON, JANE M., 60, F, None listed, -, PA, 116, 116, BEAU. In HH of David Wilson m 58 born Scotland.
WILSON, JOHN, 38, M, Mason, -, NJ, 769, 752, CHAS%. In HH of Clemas Wilson f 40 born SC.
WILSON, JOHN, 21, M, Carpenter, -, NY, 118, 118, GEOR.
WILSON, LEWIS E., 60, M, Mechanic, -, PA, 1325, 1325, CHES.
WILSON, NELSON, 29, M, Seaman, -, NY, 326, 301, CHAS. On Steam Ship Southerner.
WILSON, PETER, 16, M, Mason, -, NJ, 769, 752, CHAS%. In HH of Clemas Wilson f 40 born SC.
WILSON, WILLIAM, 76, M, Farmer, -, MD, 762, 762, YORK.
WINPENNY, WILLIAM, 30, M, Servant, -, PA, 882, 840, CHAS+. In Charleston Hotel.
WITMIRE, HENRY, 80, M, Farmer, -, MD, 121, 126, PICK.
WITMIRE, NANCY, 74, F, None listed, -, MD, 121, 126, PICK. In HH of Henry Witmire m 80 born MD.
WITMIRE, NANCY, 30, F, None listed, -, MD, 121, 126, PICK. In HH of Henry Witmire m 80 born MD.
WOOD, ANN, 30, F, None listed, -, PA, 20, 16, CHAS+.
WOOD, EDWARD, 38, M, Master mariner, -, NY, 119, 133, CHAS.
WOOD, HANNAH E., 38, F, None listed, -, PA, 383, 393, RICH. In HH of William S. Wood

m 30 born SC.
WOODLY, JAMES, 41, M, Seaman, -, NY, 573, 565, CHAS%.
WOODRUFF, SAML, 51, M, House carpenter, -, PA, 518, 518, EDGE. Saml. Woodruff born Philadelphia, PA.
WOODWARD, A., 45, M, Epis. Clergyman, -, NY, 182, 182, BEAU+.
WOODWELL, WILLIAM, 20, M, Clerk, -, PA, 80, 74, CHAS-. In HH of Wm. Enston m 42 born England.
WOOLFE, AMELIA, 14, F, None listed, -, NY, 507, 473, CHAS*. In HH of Ann Woolfe f 37 born England.
WOOLFE, WINFIELD S., 9, M, None listed, -, NJ, 507, 473, CHAS*. In HH of Ann Woolfe f 37 born England.
WRIGHT, ANGELINA, 22, F, None listed, -, MD, 358, 341, CHAS-.
WRIGHT, CHARLES, 55, M, Ship mas{ter}, -, NY, 125, 125, GEOR.
WRIGHT, CHARLOTTE, 11, F, None listed, -, NY, 358, 367, RICH. In HH of George W. Wright m 43 born England.
WRIGHT, ELIZABETH, 15, F, None listed, -, NY, 358, 367, RICH. In HH of George W. Wright m 43 born England.
WRIGHT, HARRIOT, 18, F, None listed, -, NY, 996, 975, CHAS-. In HH of Harriot Wright f 60 born England.
WRIGHT, RUTH, 13, F, None listed, -, NY, 358, 367, RICH. In HH of George W. Wright m 43 born England.
WRIGHT, VIRGINIA, 23, F, None listed, -, MD, 358, 341, CHAS-. In HH of Angelina Wright f 22 born MD.
WRIGHT, WILLIAM, 25, M, Clerk, -, NY, 68, 66, CHAS*. In HH of Ann G. Ball f 40 born England.
WYLIE, A.S., 24, F, None listed, -, MD, 405, 405, CHES. In HH of Wm. Wylie m 30 born SC.

Y

YALLOWLEY, STEPHEN, 31, M, Cabinetmaker, -, NJ, 436, 447, RICH. In Boarding House.
YOUNG, ELIZH., 66, F, None listed, -, MD, 45, 45, KERS. In HH of Alexr. Young m 67 born Scotland. Elizh. Young born Baltimore, MD.
YOUNG, NAPOLEON B., 27, M, Trainer Race Ho, -, NJ, 202, 203, PICK+. Trainer Race Horses.
YOUNG, THOS., 18, M, Clerk, -, NY, 170, 153, CHAS. In HH of John Young m 23 born SC.
YOUNG, WILLIAM H., 23, M, Shoemaker, -, NJ, 599, 616, RICH. In HH of James J.W. Gaither m 29 born District of Columbia.

Z

ZIGLER, M.W., 28, M, Coach maker, -, PA, 134, 125, CHAS+. In HH of J.B. Nixon m 31 born NY.

Name Index

A

Abrahams, Aaron, 39
Aby, Peter, 39
Adams, Hiram, 1
Adams, Plecidia, 39
Adger, Robert, 63
Adkins, Thomas, 1
Alden, George, 39
Allison, George, 104
Alston, Grace, 93
Anderson, Robert C., 39
Anderson, Robt., 14, 51
Ansell, John, 40
Archer, Benjamin, 87
Ashby, Alice, 48, 64
Asher, Palmer, 25
Ashley, Jr. Moses, 40
Atherton, Thomas, 1, 40
Atkinson, Valentine, 83
Avants, N.B., 40

B

Baker, H.F., 84
Baker, Thomas E., 90, 101
Ball, Ann G., 110
Ballou, James, 7, 11, 12, 17, 18, 22, 33
Banskett, John, 41
Barnes, Thomas, 98
Bartliss, W.H., 41
Basset, Sarah, 2
Bates, Edwin, 2
Battles, Benj. P., 3, 90
Beasely, W.B., 4
Beatey, Thos. W., 27
Beaty, James, 12
Beck, Charles, 42
Beckman, George, 58
Behan, Thomas, 42
Belcher, Manning, 3
Bell, Samuel, 42
Bellair, William, 27
Benidick, J.H., 65
Bennett, William, 13, 26, 55, 58, 69
Bernard, S.B., 43, 56
Berry, John, 28
Bird, J.S., 103
Bird, Thomas B., 43
Blan, Geo., 44
Blanding, Shubel, 40
Blease, Oratio, 74
Blocker, Nancy, 94
Boesch, Nicholas, 63
Bolan, James, 44
Boozer, David, 44
Boring, W.M., 99
Bostwick, Amos, 40
Boswell, Thomas J., 44
Bours, J.B., 44
Bowie, James P., 45
Bradford, Jesse, 45
Bradshaw, Sarah, 65
Brady, Ellen, 45
Brandt, T.C., 46
Brannecker, Charles, 46
Brawley, J., 97
Breese, See Bruse, 5
Bregnan, H., 26, 87
Bridges, Joseph, 101
Bristol, Austides, 1
Bristol, T.M., 46
Brittingham, Joshua, 46
Bronson, Hiram. C., 46
Brown, Catherine, 47
Brown, E.G., 12, 26, 32, 42, 46, 91, 103
Brown, Isaac T., 5
Brown, Jas. M., 5
Brown, John, 88, 97
Brown, William K., 47
Bruce, Charles, 5
Bruse, See Breese, 5
Bruse, Wm. C., 5
Bryan, J.M., 5
Bryson, Josiah J., 72
Buck, Henry, 104

C

Caffrey, James, 48
Caks, T.M., 48
Calbert, Thomas H., 6
Caldwell, John, 48
Calhoun, Ephraim P., 34
Calhoun, Floreide, 48, 49
Campbell, Owen, 103
Campbell, Wm. B., 49, 91
Cannon, George, 25
Carpenter, William, 43
Carr, Glenn, 57
Carrington, William, 49
Carroll, William H., 49

Causse, Robert, 54
Cayass, Thomas, 50
Celler, Michael, 50
Champlin, Samuel, 39
Chandler, Mason, 50
Charlon, John, 51
Church, Francis, 51
Clarke, G.E., 7
Clarke, John M., 15
Clarke, Joseph, 7, 52
Clement, Isaac, 52
Clowing, William, 56
Cochran, James, 7, 8
Cohen, Thomas, 53
Cole, Geo. F., 82
Coleman, A. Walker, 54
Collins, Daniel, 53, 54
Collins, James, 53, 54
Collins. James N., 54
Collins, Richard M., 54
Connelly, Dennis, 58
Connelly, Patrick, 58
Connor, James, 54
Cook, Samuel, 69
Cook, Truman, 99
Cooper, Mary, 94
Cornish, A.H., 55
Corson, James, 103
Courtney, E.S., 55
Courtney, W.C., 8
Couster, Jeramiah, 55
Couster, Jeremiah, 101
Cox, Biddleton, 41
Cox, T.M., 55
Cramer, Geo. W., 55

Cranford, J.M., 104
Crawford, Celisle, 106
Crawford, James D., 3, 82
Cremer, David, 99
Creswell, Henry H., 105
Crogan, Peter, 56
Cromlay, Daniel, 56
Cropland, W.M., 9
Crosby, Stephen, 3
Crumpsty, William, 9
Cumpsty, William, 56
Curles, John, 56
Cuttine, Benson, 9

D

Dallison, Jos. B., 56, 91
Darby, Artemas F., 9
Darby, James, 57
Darnal, Thomas, 14
Davis, Cornelius, 57
Davis, J.B., 100
Davis, Martha, 29
Davison, Samuel, 57
Day, Fisher, 57
Delporte, Simon, 58
Denny, William, 94
Denton, Richard, 58
DeSanfure, Wilmont, 75
Dewley, John, 58
Dial, William H., 58
Dickson, Andrew, 58
Dinkins, Lucian, 97
Doby, J.L., 17, 46, 96, 101, 107
Dom, James, 25
Donnelly, Saml., 99

Dosenbery, G.W., 59
Dougherty William M., 92
Douglas, Joseph, 75
Douglass, John, 59
Doyle, Michael, 59
Dozier, Anthony W., 25
Drayton, Sarah, 99
Drummond, John, 81
Dubose, Theodore L., 3
Due, John S., 28
Dufort, A., 60
Dunham, C.T., 8, 11, 13, 80
Dunlap, James, 60
Dunnavant, John, 96
Dwing, John, 59
Dykes, Samuel, 60

E

Emanuel, Nathan, 61
Emanuelo, N., 61
English, Thos., 61
Enix, William, 61
Enston, Wm., 61, 110
Eretenden, John, 76
Erwin, William, 45
Ewart, John, 62
Ewing, John, 25, 34, 43, 45, 47, 58, 68, 69, 73, 79, 81, 106, 107

F

Fagan, Dennis, 62
Falls, Alexander, 77
Fancy, Margaret, 44
Farrar, Jno., 12

Favris, James, 62
Feckling, Eliza, 43
Fell, Elizabeth, 17
Felsh, Daniel, 18
Ferebee, John, 62
Ferguson, John, 62
Fielding, John, 46
Figerous, B., 84
Figeroux, B., 49, 69
Fischer, F., 63
Flagg, Patrick, 63
Flake, R.B., 49
Flordorer, John, 63
Fora, Lewis, 63
Forley, Joseph, 63
Fowler, William H., 29, 63, 64
Francis, John, 64
Fraser, R.E., 29
Frazer, Charles P., 13
Fresonthick, George, 105
Frilling, Edward, 64
Furguston, John, 41

G

Gable, R.W., 64
Gaillard, Theodore S., Dr., 13
Gannon, Roger, 64
Garrett, George, 25
Geiger, W.W., 13
Gevins, Samuel, 65
Gibson, Catherine, 63
Gibson, Elizabeth, 45
Giffer, Hans, 65
Gilchrist, R.B., Honorable, 53, 65
Gill, Mary, 82
Gillet, Ellen, 72, 73, 74, 99
Gilling, Mary Mrs., 9
Gladden, John, 65
Gleave, Thomas, 40
Glover, Charles J., 11, 21, 25
Glover, John, 66
Goldberg, Jacob, 66
Goodlite, R.P., 17
Goodman, W.W., 31, 66
Gordon, Catherine, 59
Gossett, Elijah, 66
Govereur, Peter, 66
Gower, E.M., 68
Gowing, Charles, 32, 66
Graham, John Q., 67
Graham, Richardson, 67
Gray, Chris, 67
Gray, Harriot, 13, 65
Gray, James W., 14
Gray, John B., 15
Green, John, 67
Greer, Wm., 67
Gregg, James, 15
Grice, Geo. D., 81
Griffin, David F., 92
Grimball, J.B., 67
Griner, Ann, 51
Groves, E., 12
Gunten, W.R., 91

H

Haberson, Lawrence, 50
Hagain, George W., 90
Hagnes, P., Major, 26, 47, 89
Haile, J.C., 31
Haley, John, 10
Hallenback, Fetz, 4, 98
Hamilton, Alexander, 68
Hamilton, Davis K., 68
Hamilton, D.H., Dr., 15
Hamilton, Jane, 15
Hamilton, John B., 68
Hammond, Harriet, 104
Haney, Stephen, 64
Hanlin, Eliza O., 73
Hanschild, Peter, 43
Harbert, Frederic, 68
Harkin, John, 68
Harley, James, 2, 12, 22, 94
Harris, Edward, 15, 60, 79
Harris, Sarah G., 68
Hart, John, 21
Hartz, F.P., 69
Hasell, Andrew, 15
Hasy?, William, 33
Hathwanger, William, 96
Hawthorn, Henry, 69, 101
Hayden, H.S., 26, 40, 92
Hayne, R.B., 69
Hazelius, E.L., 70, 85
Hazletons, A.L., 12
Heim, J.F., 33
Hemming, J.L., 6, 99
Henderson, Dr., E.R., 48

Henrick. W.F., 20
Henson, John, 70
Herbert, Michael, 70
Herndon, John J., 16
Herron, John, 62
Heyward, James J.B., 16
Higgins, Michael, 16
Higman, John W., 70
Hill, James, 70, 71
Hill, William P., 27, 58
HIll, William P., 94
Hobbs, William, 71
Hobson, James, 24
Hogan, Patrick, 50
Holland, Aaron, 61
Hollister, Howel W., 21, 71
Holmes, James G., 71
Holmes, Tho. H., 26
Hood, John P., 71
Hordan, Hiram, 106
Horsey, David, 72
Horton, William, 17
Houser, David, 97
Hubbard, William, 13, 65, 73
Hughes, John, 72
Hughes, John H., 53
Hunt, Alfred M., 72
Hunter, Alexander, 92
Hunter, Johnson, 72, 101
Hunter, Wm., 72
Hunter, Wm. R., 18
Hurlbut, M.A., 72
Hutchinson, Maxamilian, 62

J

Jackson, Samuel, 72
Jackson, Wm. H., 73
Jacobi, W.J., 73
Jacobs, Ferdind, 73
Jacobs, Jerdind, 18
Jacobs, Julia, 56
Jeffords, John, 20, 28, 102
Jenkins, Archibald, 73
Jennings, William, 73
Jervey, J.C., 11, 51
Jervey, Thomas D., 73
Johnson, Adna, 44
Johnson, Giles M., 19, 73, 74
Johnson, James, 74
Johnston, William B., 74
Jones, James, 74
Jones, James L., 108
Jones, Jane, 17
Jones, Samuel, 74
Jones, Thomas S., 19, 27
Jordan, Hiram, 1, 8, 21, 25, 30, 33, 74
Judd, D.C., 32
Just, George, 75

K

Kay, James J., 75
Keegan, Thomas, 42
Kennedy, G.F., 57
Kenny, Deas. H., 92
Kenny, James, 75
Kentock, Mary J., 67

Kerr, Daniel H., 20
Kimball, Benj., 7
King, James K., 75
King, N.S., 67
Kingsmore, Agness M., 55
Kinney, Thomas, 95
Kitcham, William, 20
Knepley, Solomon, 57
Know, William P., 76
Knowles, E., 59
Kurtz, John D., 76

L

LaCasto, Adolphus, 77
Laidler, Julius, 47
Lakin, Ben. V., 109
Lambert, Robert, 77
Land, H.A.W., 77
Lark, Charles, 77
Larkin, Catherine, 77
Larkin, Margaret, 80
LaRousselliere, T.H., 77
Latta, Robert, 77
Lawrence, Elizabeth, 83
Lawton, Hague, 20
Leaman, Jeannet, 77
Lee, John, 64
Legard, Susan, 77
Lenar, Joseph, 78
Lequere, Benjamin, 39
Lesly, David, 78
Levig, Abraam, 91
Levy, Moses, 46, 78, 92
Levy, Orlando, 78

Lieber, Francis, 20
Lightburn, William, 52, 53
Lindesay, John T., 21, 31
Lockhart, Sarah, 94
Lockwood, William, 78
Logan, Sarah, 66
Long, Andrew K., 79
Love, Charles, 32, 79
Lovett, William, 79
Lowland, Roger, 11
Lyman, Levi, 21
Lynap, B., 50
Lyons, Henry, 79

M

Mack, John, 87
Mackey, James J., 48
Maddox, Bassel, 49
Maguire, John, 80
Mahoney, Dennis, 80
Mahooney, Patrick, 80
Maiseman, William, 105
Mallery, Sarah, 62, 80, 87
Mallet, Frederick, 80
Mansield, Tarry, 80
Mapillon, Felice, 80
Margenhoff, E.H., 60
Marks, Elias, 22
Marquir, James, 22
Marsh, James, 73
Marsh, John, 21
Martin, Eliza, 81
Martin, W.E., 81
Mathieson, Elizabeth, 9
Matthews, Samuel, 81
Mauldin, Samuel, 21
Mavrick, Wamuel, 106
Maxcy, Hart, 22
Mazyck, Robert W., 21, 27
McAllister, John, 20
McBride, Nancy, 19
McCallister, Andrew, 82
McCants, James J., 82
McCaudles, L., 22
McCave, James, 82
McCormick, James, 75
McCoy, James, 81
McCully, John, 82
McCusker, E., 82
McDaniel, Andrew, 41
McDonald, C.A., 82
McDowell, Wm. D., 82
McGivley, Samuel, 82
McInnerny, Michael, 83
McIntoch, William, 102
McKensie, R.B., 83
McKenzie, John, 90
McKenzie, Margaret M., 17, 32
McKenzie, Rebecca, 97
McKeown, John, 81
McLeod, J.W., 107
McLure, Thomas, 83
McMahon, James, 83
McManus, Mary, 83
Mealey, John, 42, 84
Medlock, Henry, 66
Medon, Elizabeth, 88
Melton, C.D., 82
Memminger, C.G., 84
Merkherdt, M., 84
Metzler, John, 108
Meyer, Frederick C., 84
Middleton, N.R., 22
Middleton, Thomas, 84
Milan, John, 84
Miller, Harriet E., 2
Mitchell, Martha, 10, 79
Mobley, Biggers, 1
Monroe, Martin E., 8, 14, 15
Montgomery, Andrew, 85
Montgomery, William, 22
Moodie, A.H., 4
Moore, Elizabeth, 42
Moore, Samuel, 69
Moore, William, 99
Moore, Wm., 98
Moorhead, James, 75
Moorman, D.B.P., 52
Morcock, William A., 69, 78
Moreen, John, 94
Morgan, Benjamin, 86
Morgan, Benjn., 86
Morgan, Peter, 80
Morris, Ann, 9, 25
Morris, Samuel, 86
Morrow, D., 79
Moses, M., 86
Muir, Jane, 13
Muller, Lewis, 86, 87

Mulligan, A.B., 23
Mullikin, 87
Murdock, William, 23
Murrell, James H., 47
Murry, Thomas, 87
Myer, Nathan, 87

N

Nelson, Chris., 46, 87, 98
Nelson, Saml. A., 23, 25
Nettles, John Sr., 61
Newcomb, J.G., 59, 73
Newman, Jackson, 88
Newman, P., 6
Nichols, Horacea E., 88
Nickerson, Thomas S., 95
Nixen, Ann, 26
Nixon, J.B., 41, 110
Nochols, R.H., 91
Noland, Thomas, 95
Norman, Jane, 6
Norris, William, 88, 106
Norsett, Alexander, 109
Northrop, C.B., 88
Norwood, David, 24

O

Oakes, Z.B., 24
Oakley, R.S., 95
Oates, George, 17, 63, 89
O'Connel, John, 88
Ogeman, John, 32, 105
Oliver, Ann, 89
ONeell, J.F., 89
ORiley, James B., 25
Orr, William, 89
Osley, James, 1
O'Wen, Leslie, 27

P

Page, Elizabeth, 13
Page, William J., 90
Parker, A.G., 46, 71, 90, 94, 96, 98, 107
Parker, P.G., 90
Patterson, William, 49, 52, 99
Pearboon, Joseph, 26, 27
Peckerell, J.L., 26
Peers, Alice H., 47
Perry, Mary, 4
Perry, William, 89
Peterson, Christian, 91
Petit, James, 91
Peyton, Wm. H., 104
Pickerel, Jonathan, 26
Piexolla, Grace, 67, 101, 104
Plat, George, 26
Pluger, Henry, 47, 56
Plummer, Chs. W., 92
Pomeroy, Richard S., 82
Ponder, Mary, 96
Pope, Sarah Mrs., 105

Porcher, Peter, 92
Porter, W.D., 92
Powell, Thomas, 42, 92
Poyas, James Jr., 12
Pratt, Ellen, 26, 29, 90
Preston, James, 27
Prevost, Joseph, 92
Price, Jeremiah C., 93
Pringle, J.J., 93
Pringle, Sarah M., 93
Pringle, St. J., 93
Prior, Seth, 35
Pryor, John, 93

R

Radel, Elijah, 94
Rawles, Georgiana, 94
Redmond, George, 63
Reeder, Jane E., 73
Reicks, Gerhard, 94
Reynolds, J.W., 94
Reynolds, William L., 39, 91
Richards, Benjamin, 27
Richisby, Mary, 69
Riddell, J.S., 90, 101
Roberts, James S., 91, 95
Roddy, A.J., 58
Rogers, Sidney, 28
Rollins, William, 39, 41, 45, 52, 58, 60, 72, 83, 92, 101, 103
Rooney, Patrick, 96
Rooney, Paul, 96

Roper, Joshua, 96
Rottereau, Peter, 20
Roward, R.T., 96
Ruddock, Arthur, 97
Ruddock, Theodore D., 28
Russel, John, 97
Rutjes, J.A., 50, 97
Ryan, Mathew, 87

S

Saltus, F.W., 28
Sassard, J., 97
Saunders, S., 97
Savage, Sarah, 23
Schakelford, F.R., 98
Schine, Ann, 97
Schineder, N.R., 16, 68, 70
Scholtz, Henry, 3
Schorb, J.R., 28, 97
Scott, Alexander, 71
Scott, James, 97
Scott, Taba, 8, 15
Scott, William, 29
Scriven, R.B. Dr., 23, 29
Seabrook, Joseph B., 98
Selle, Sophia, 107
Selleman, Eliza, 43
Seward A., 11
Seyle, Charles, 98
Seymour, T.T., 55
Sharleyson, John, 60
Shaw, James, 98
Sheron, J.B., 98
Shirer, John, 98
Shugart, John, 98
Simmons, Sarh E., 29
Simmons, Thos. H., 27, 29
Simons, Harris, 88, 95, 107
Simons, John C., 99, 100
Skilton, Thomas, 86
Slaman, George, 99
Sloan, Thos. J., 33
Smith, Charles, 12
Smith, Elesinga W., 69
Smith, Eliza L., 30
Smith, Frs., 100
Smith, James W., 100
Smith, Joseph, 100
Smith, Rhody, 100
Smith, William M., 76
Smoke, Henry L., 53, 94
Smyth, John, 48
Snowden, Gilbert T., 76
Sonbeda, Peter, 100
Spann, H.R., 57, 78, 99
Spear, W.W., 100
Spencer, Maria, 78
Sperry, D.A., 12, 22, 32
Stams, Henry, 1
Steele, John, 22, 34
Stein, John F., 101
Stephenson, John, 44
Stevens, Jose, 43, 101
Stevenson, Joel, 92
Stewart, M.M., 56, 86, 99
Stewart, W.K., 10
Stien, Rosa, 84
Stillman, James, 102
Stokes, J.W., 31
Stoop, Hugh, 8, 53
Storr, John W., 17
Strans, Margaraet, 102
Street, Henry C., 24, 30
Streher, J.B., 102
Stroud, James, 41
Stubs, John, 102
Sutherland, J.F., 102, 105
Sutton, Mary, 103
Swinton, Thomas, 108

T

Tate, Ruthas, 103
Taylor, James, 54
Taylor, J.H., 1
Thayer, T. Heyward, 103
Theus, F.W., 48, 54, 100, 103
Thomas, Elizabeth, 21
Thomas, Jane, 104
Thomas, William, 104
Thompson, M., Gov., 29
Thomson, George, 72
Thorn, John, 97, 107
Thorne, Micajah A., 104
Thornton, John C., 104
Thorton, P., 31
Timbrook, Emily, 3, 50, 75, 76, 95, 100, 109

Tobert, Reason, 103
Tomlinson, William, 104
Townsend, B.D., 46
Trou, A.W., 31
Tunno, Rachael, 40
Tusten, James H., 92
Tyler, John S., 16

U

Uray, Elizabeth, 91

V

Van Wart, Walter, 75
Vandiver, Aaron, 2
Voorhies, Maria C., 106

W

Waddell, John, 32
Wagstaff, William, 106
Walker, J.E., 106
Walker, William W., 32
Walter, John J., 34
Ward, E.M., 10, 11
Ward, Mary, 33
Waring, H.S., 107
Watson, Dunham, 107
Watts, L., 100
Wear, John, 33
Weber, A.A., 107
Wetherspoon, Robert, 78
Whaley, James, 107
Whilden, L.E., 23, 107
White, Chs. C., 30

White, Edward B., 33
White, Isaac, 108
White, Robert, 108
Whyte, Joseph, 108
Wierfelder, S., 65, 108
Williams, James, 59
Williams, John, 108
Willis, John G., 109
Wilman, Augustus, 65
Wilmot, Saml., 19
Wilson, Clemas, 109
Wilson, David, 109
Wilson, Eliza, 87
Wilson, J., 57, 108
Wilson, John, 89
Wilson, Thos., 34
Wilson, William, 109
Winged, O.M., 40
Winkler, E.J., 34
Witmire, Henry, 62
Wood, Susan, 18
Wood, William S., 60, 109
Wooden, August, 34, 35
Wooley, Joseph, 85
Woolfe, Ann, 110
Woorsen, Lambert, 98
Wooton, Eber, 91
Wright, George W., 110
Wright, Harriot, 110
Wright, Jacob, 72
Wright, J.D., 24, 30, 35
Wyler, Vincent, 35

Y

Young, Alexr., 110
Young, John, 58, 110

Z

Zucker, J.U., 102

§§§

Place Index

B
Bermuda, 31, 55

C
Canada, 2, 69, 101
CT, 1, 2, 3, 4, 5, 6, 7, 8, 10, 11, 12, 13, 14, 15, 16, 17, 18, 19, 20, 21, 22, 23, 24, 25, 26, 27, 28, 29, 30, 31, 32, 33, 34, 35, 40, 44, 46, 57, 62, 65, 71, 76, 80, 87, 91, 92, 102
CT, Hartford, 6
CT, Middlesex, 5, 32
CT, New Haven, 2, 28
Cuba, 7, 106

D
D.C., Georgetown, 88
D.C. (See Washington, D.C.), 47, 64, 67, 70, 76, 77, 78, 88, 93, 99
DE, 58, 70, 73, 76, 86, 93, 98, 102
Denmark, 46, 65
District of Columbia, (See Washington, D.C.) 63, 86

E
England, 1, 9, 12, 15, 17, 20, 24, 29, 33, 35, 40, 47, 48, 56, 58, 60, 61, 62, 63, 64, 70, 71, 74, 77, 78, 81, 88, 89, 92, 100, 102, 104, 105, 106, 109, 110
Europe, 89

F
France, 43, 56, 58, 63, 66, 70, 80, 97, 100

G
GA, 5, 17, 34, 42
Germany, 1, 4, 16, 27, 28, 32, 33, 40, 43, 46, 47, 48, 49, 50, 54, 56, 58, 65, 66, 67, 68, 69, 70, 71, 74, 75, 77, 84, 86, 87, 92, 97, 98, 100, 102, 105, 107, 108

H
Holland, 49, 50

I
Ireland, 1, 8, 10, 16, 20, 26, 27, 28, 34, 42, 45, 46, 49, 50, 52, 53, 54, 56, 58, 59, 60, 62, 63, 64, 67, 68, 69, 72, 74, 75, 77, 80, 81, 82, 83, 84, 85, 87, 88, 93, 94, 95, 96, 97, 98, 103, 105, 106, 107, 108
Italy, 75, 78, 108

K
KY, 46

M
MA, 1, 2, 3, 4, 5, 6, 7, 8, 9, 10, 11, 12, 13, 14, 15, 16, 17, 18, 19, 20, 21, 22, 23, 24, 25, 26, 27, 28, 29, 30, 31, 32, 33, 34, 35, 40, 43, 45, 47, 55, 57, 58, 59, 66, 68, 69, 73, 79, 80, 81, 90, 97, 100, 101, 107
MA, Boston, 1, 3, 8, 10, 12, 20, 24, 28, 31, 33, 34
MA, Nantucket, 12
MA, Sommerset, 27
MA, Springfield, 25
MD, 29, 35, 39, 40, 41, 42, 43, 44, 45, 46, 47, 48, 49, 52, 53, 54, 56, 57, 58, 59, 60, 61, 62, 63,

64, 65, 66, 67,
68, 69, 70, 71,
72, 73, 74, 75,
77, 78, 80, 82,
83, 84, 85, 87,
88, 91, 92, 93,
94, 95, 96, 97,
98, 99, 100,
102, 103, 104,
106, 107, 109,
110
MD, Baltimore, 49,
50, 54, 68, 78,
93, 110
ME, 3, 4, 5, 6, 9, 10,
11, 12, 14, 15,
17, 18, 21, 22,
23, 24, 25, 27,
28, 32, 33, 35,
68, 104
ME, Freeport, 10
Minorca, 63

N

Nassau, N.P., 43, 101
NC, 1, 13, 42, 44, 52,
55, 59, 64, 65,
73, 79, 80, 82,
83, 90, 91, 97,
101, 105, 106,
107, 109
NH, 1, 3, 6, 7, 12, 13,
14, 16, 17, 18,
20, 23, 29, 31,
32, 34
NJ, 19, 20, 31, 39, 41,
43, 46, 47, 48,
51, 52, 54, 55,
56, 59, 60, 61,
62, 64, 66, 68,
69, 70, 72, 73,
74, 75, 76, 79,

81, 82, 85, 87,
90, 92, 93, 95,
96, 97, 101,
102, 103, 104,
105, 107, 109,
110
NJ, Burlington, 48
NJ, Newark, 51, 66
NJ, Patterson, 65
NY, 5, 13, 25, 26, 27,
39, 40, 41, 42,
43, 44, 45, 46,
47, 48, 49, 50,
51, 52, 53, 54,
55, 56, 57, 58,
59, 60, 61, 62,
63, 64, 65, 66,
67, 68, 69, 70,
71, 72, 73, 74,
75, 76, 77, 78,
79, 80, 81, 82,
83, 84, 85, 86,
87, 88, 89, 90,
91, 92, 93, 94,
95, 96, 97, 98,
99, 100, 101,
102, 103, 104,
105, 106, 107,
109, 110
NY, Troy, 43, 44

P

PA, 12, 19, 21, 39,
41, 42, 43, 44,
45, 46, 48, 49,
50, 53, 54, 55,
57, 58, 60, 61,
62, 63, 64, 65,
66, 67, 68, 69,
70, 71, 72, 73,
75, 76, 77, 78,
79, 80, 81, 82,

83, 84, 85, 86,
87, 89, 90, 91,
92, 93, 95, 96,
97, 98, 99,
100, 102, 103,
104, 105, 106,
107, 108, 109,
110
PA, Philadelphia, 47,
48, 55, 65, 79,
84, 105, 110
Poland, 39, 87, 91, 99
Prussia, 20, 49, 70,
85, 101

R

RI, 1, 2, 3, 4, 5, 6, 7,
8, 9, 11, 12,
14, 15, 17, 18,
20, 21, 22, 23,
25, 27, 29, 30,
32, 33, 43

S

SC, 1, 3, 4, 5, 6, 7, 8,
9, 10, 11, 12,
13, 14, 15, 16,
17, 18, 19, 20,
21, 22, 23, 25,
26, 27, 29, 30,
33, 34, 35, 39,
40, 41, 42, 43,
44, 45, 46, 47,
48, 51, 53, 54,
55, 56, 57, 58,
60, 61, 62, 63,
64, 66, 67, 68,
71, 72, 73, 74,
75, 76, 77, 78,
79, 81, 82, 83,
84, 86, 87, 88,

89, 91, 92, 93, 94, 95, 96, 97, 98, 99, 100, 102, 104, 105, 106, 107, 108, 109, 110
SC, Fairfield Dist., 65
SC, York Dist., 20, 22, 31, 62, 69, 74, 103, 104, 108
Scotland, 7, 15, 23, 42, 48, 52, 59, 78, 79, 81, 82, 83, 97, 102, 109
St. Domingo, 77
Sweden, 58, 63
Switzerland, 63, 102

Washington, D.C., 46, 59, 65, 82, 84, 92, 97, 104, 105
(See District of Columbia, D.C.)
West Indies, 48, 69, 84

§§§

T

TN, 53, 72
TN, Greenwood, 43

V

VA, 15, 16, 18, 48, 52, 57, 61, 70, 72, 73, 74, 75, 79, 80, 81, 89, 90, 92, 95, 97, 98, 99, 101, 104, 109
VA, Alexandria, 84
VT, 2, 4, 5, 6, 7, 9, 14, 15, 16, 18, 21, 22, 24, 26, 29, 32, 66, 88

W

Washington City, 57

Occupation Index

A

Accountant, 30, 40, 96, 104
Apothecary, 68
Artist, 28, 79
Attorney, 1, 4, 17, 58, 82
Auctioneer, 95

B

Baker, 4, 12, 32, 61, 65, 98
Bank Officer, 48, 77
Bar Keeper, 96
Blacksmith, 7, 10, 14, 22, 25, 27, 42, 49, 54, 59, 60, 61, 79, 84, 86, 91
Boarding house, 1, 2, 10, 17
Book keeper, 21
Bookbinder, 57, 74, 96, 102
Bookseller, 1, 16, 22
Boot frunder?, 48, 54
Bootmaker, 31, 32, 75, 94, 104
Bricklayer, 4, 7, 12, 17, 22, 39, 48, 57, 101
Brickmaker, 25, 100
Brickmason, 13, 18, 27, 57, 82
Broker, 24, 28, 34
Builder, 11, 105

C

Cabinet maker, 8, 20, 22, 31, 33, 43, 44, 46, 48, 78, 86, 90, 92, 103, 110
Canter, 70
Capt. Engineer, 45
Card repairer, 3
Carpenter, 4, 5, 6, 9, 10, 16, 17, 19, 20, 21, 24, 25, 26, 27, 41, 44, 47, 48, 49, 51, 52, 56, 57, 59, 63, 65, 70, 71, 72, 76, 81, 87, 88, 89, 90, 91, 92, 95, 97, 98, 100, 102, 105
Carriage builder, 70
Carriage dealer, 7
Carriage maker, 14, 27, 31, 49, 61, 82, 92, 94
Carriage trimmer, 99
Chancellor, 11, 60
Chemist, 97
Cigar manufacture, 4
City police, 30
Civil Engineer, 47
Clergyman, 8, 17, 33, 60
Clergyman, Baptist, 27, 98
Clergyman, Episcopal, 13, 26, 106, 110
Clergyman, Methodist, 2, 63, 96, 108
Clergyman, O.S.P., 91
Clergyman, P.E., 69
Clergyman, Protestant Episcopal, 8
Clerk, 1, 2, 3, 4, 5, 6, 7, 8, 9, 10, 11, 12, 14, 15, 17, 18, 19, 20, 21, 22, 23, 25, 26, 28, 29, 30, 31, 32, 34, 41, 42, 44, 49, 50, 51, 52, 56, 60, 61, 62, 63, 66, 67, 68, 69, 70, 74, 75, 76, 78, 79, 82, 85, 88, 90, 94, 95, 97, 101, 102, 103, 108, 110
Clerk Court Appeals, 70
Clerk of market, 107
Clockmaker, 14, 18
Cloth drippier, 4, 30
Coach maker, 6, 11, 14, 17, 30, 33, 49, 50, 55, 99, 103, 110
Coach painter, 16
Coach trimmer, 40,

122

57
Coalpasser, 60
Commander U.S.Arsenel, 67 (See U.S.A)
Commercial merchant, 17, 32
Commission merchant, 5
Confectioner, 27, 70, 73, 87, 96, 108
Contractor, 98
Corn merchant, 22, 48
Cotton Presser, 71
Courtney, W.C., 8
Croper, 59
Customs Inspector, 76, 91

D

Dagartype {sic}, 29
Daguereotypist {sic}, 91
Daguersian {sic} Artist, 14
Dentist, 3, 8, 25, 43, 90
Doctor, 43 (See Physician)
Driver, 95
Druggist, 9, 12, 52

E

Editor, 20, 27, 70
Engineer, 9, 14, 20, 22, 26, 32, 43, 53, 54, 57, 77, 80, 91, 95, 99, 101, 103, 105, 107
Engraver, 24

F

Farmer, 1, 2, 3, 6, 7, 8, 9, 10, 18, 19, 20, 21, 22, 23, 24, 26, 29, 30, 32, 33, 34, 39, 41, 42, 44, 47, 50, 53, 56, 57, 58, 60, 62, 63, 64, 65, 66, 67, 68, 71, 72, 75, 76, 77, 80, 82, 83, 85, 86, 87, 88, 90, 91, 94, 99, 100, 102, 103, 105, 106, 107, 109
First Mate, 52
Fisherman, 13
Furnishing store, 106
Furniture Store, 55

G

Gas fitter, 59, 78, 79, 92
Gilder, 59
Gin maker, 1
Grain merchant, 3
Grocer, 5, 10, 25, 66, 93
Gunsmith, 80

H

Harness maker, 17, 51, 94, 105, 108, 109
Hatter, 10, 64
Hireling, 40, 71
Hotel keeper, 6, 26, 43, 70
House carpenter, 110 (Also see carpenter)

I

Ice House Keeper, 99
Inspector, 30, 50

J

Jailor, 49
Jeweler, 16, 64, 96, 100, 101
Joiner, 69
Judge City Court, 83

L

Laborer, 1, 8, 10, 16, 24, 26, 33, 42, 47, 63, 66, 69, 74, 85, 91, 94, 98, 102, 103, 104
Landlord, 1, 21, 75, 95
Lawyer, 29, 83, 85,

86, 102, 106
Lieut. U.S.A., 34

M

Machinist, 1, 9, 12, 17, 18, 23
Mail Contractor, 63
Manager RR, 34
Manufacturer, 98, 105
Mariner, 1, 4, 12, 13, 24, 26, 27, 29, 32, 33, 34, 40, 45, 46, 55, 58, 69, 78, 80, 87, 93, 94, 95, 98, 100, 108
Marshall SC Collage, 79
Mason, 28, 32, 109
Master mariner, 11, 33, 43, 74, 94, 109
Master of Poor, 98
Mechanic, 1, 5, 6, 14, 17, 21, 23, 26, 27, 30, 32, 34, 39, 42, 50, 51, 57, 58, 60, 61, 91, 95, 97, 109
Merchant, 1, 2, 3, 4, 5, 6, 7, 8, 10, 11, 12, 13, 15, 16, 17, 18, 19, 21, 22, 23, 24, 25, 26, 28, 29, 30, 31, 32, 34, 39, 40, 42, 43, 44, 46, 49, 50, 51, 52, 54, 56, 61, 62, 63, 64, 65, 66, 67, 68, 70, 72, 73, 75, 76, 78, 79, 80, 81, 83, 84, 85, 86, 87, 89, 90, 91, 92, 94, 96, 100, 101, 103
Merchant tailor, 6, 11
Messenger of council, 100
Miller, 8, 25, 31, 75, 78, 105
Miller/sawmill, 29
Milliner, 32, 46, 71, 90, 94, 96, 98, 107
Millwright, 7, 20, 26, 41, 45, 46, 75
Miner, 20
Minister, 16, 26, 32, 56, 59
Minister, Episcopal, 23
Minister, Lutheran, 41
Minister, O.S., 58
Minister, Presbyterian, 86
Minister, Prot. Episcopal, 68
Minister, Unitarian, 14
Moulder, 45
Music Store, 53, 94
Music teacher, 39

N

Nautical store, 7
Notary public, 27

O

Ostler, 94
Oversee factory, 2
Overseer, 1, 90, 93, 102
Overseer/Mill, 8, 21, 30

P

Packer, 12, 80
Painter, 2, 6, 10, 12, 14, 24, 57, 70, 95, 99
Painter/Glazier, 15
Peddler, 22
Physician, (See Doctor) 3, 7, 26, 33, 40, 41, 45, 49, 52, 54, 65, 75, 76, 97
Planter, 1, 5, 8, 12, 13, 15, 23, 30, 33, 35, 41, 43, 44, 47, 53, 60, 68, 69, 71, 72, 73, 75, 76, 77, 88, 90, 99, 101,

103, 106
Planter/merchant, 18
Plasterer, 15
Plummer, 51, 79
Police Officer, 85, 106
Poor house, 2
Porter, 59
Post Master, 97
Postman, 83
Preacher, Episcopal, 28, 94
President S C College, 92
President State Bank, 98
Priest, DD, 9
Principal Female Institute, 95
Printer, 1, 10, 25, 49, 52, 53, 67, 74, 82, 88, 105
Professor of Music, 4, 28, 66
Professor of Theology, 20
Proprietor Stable, 71

R
RR Conductor, 10

S
Saddler, 7, 17, 18, 19, 21, 30, 39, 49, 52, 57, 68, 72, 73, 79, 83, 95, 103, 105
Sail maker, 85

Sash / Door manufacturer, 3
Sawmill (see Miller/Sawmill)
School mistress, 2
School teacher, 15, 29, 65, 67
Schoolmaster, 1, 6, 10, 15, 17, 92 (see Teacher)
Seaman, 2, 39, 41, 43, 45, 51, 54, 55, 56, 58, 60, 62, 67, 71, 74, 77, 81, 82, 89, 90, 92, 97, 101, 103, 108, 109
Seamstress, 74
Servant, 41, 61, 62, 70, 75, 108, 109
Ship (see Steam ship)
Ship carpenter, 44
Ship chandler, 33, 74
Ship master, 14, 55, 110
Ship wright, 81
Shipping master, 4
Shoe/bootmaker, 34
Shoe dealer, 2, 18, 19, 24, 31, 81
Shoe merchant, 4
Shoemaker, 1, 10, 14, 24, 25, 28, 29, 31, 49, 51, 56, 57, 60, 63, 81, 87, 94,

99, 104, 110
Shoestore, 33
Shop keeper, 19, 27, 34, 61, 64, 76, 96
Silversmith, 19, 34, 61
Slave trader, 1
Sodawater Mfg., 48
Stage driver, 99
Stationer, 17, 71, 95, 106
Steam Ship Isabel 60, 72
Steam Ship Southerner, 2, 41, 43, 44, 45, 51, 54, 55, 56, 66, 67, 71, 75, 77, 80, 81, 82, 89, 90,, 92, 04, 97, 103, 108, 109
Stevedore, 14
Steward, 92
Stone mason, 22, 24, 32, 44
Stone masonman, 15
Stone quarrier, 109
Stonecutter, 2, 7, 11, 12, 17, 18, 22, 33, 44, 73, 90, 101, 102
Store keeper, 5, 7, 9, 15, 26, 107
Stuardess, 83
Student, 90
Student, Theological Seminary, 96, 106
Sugarmaker, 77
Superintendent driping room,

5 Superintending Spinning, 79
Surgeon dentist, 4, 40

T

Tailor, 4, 13, 25, 40, 42, 49, 55, 59, 62, 63, 78, 79, 87, 90, 92, 101
Tailor/tayor {sic}, 4
Tanner, 7, 13, 23, 34, 72, 93, 96
Tavern keeper, 19, 23, 55, 59, 62
Teacher, 1, 13, 20, 25, 29, 30, 33, 44, 47, 53, 58, 66, 75, 81, 97, 98, 101, 102, 104, 107
Teacher of writing, 107
(See School teacher)
Telegraph operator, 11
Tinner, 11, 13, 20, 25, 28, 33, 42, 77, 96, 106, 109
Tinplate maker, 4
Tinplate worker, 4, 22
Tinsmith, 61
Tobbacconist, 62
Trainer race horses, 110
Trimmer, 7, 8, 29

Tuner, 4
Tutosek?, 10

U

Upholsterer, 93
U.S.A., Capt., 79
U.S.A., Pvt., 3, 58, 73, 106, 107

W

Wagon maker, 42, 68, 69
Waiter, 72, 80
Watchmaker, 3, 55, 67, 85
Watchmaker and jewler, 17
Watchman, 26
Weaver, 7
Wharfinger, 1, 46, 65
Wheelwright, 3
Windowshade maker, 20

§§§

126

www.ingramcontent.com/pod-product-compliance
Lightning Source LLC
Chambersburg PA
CBHW072155160426
43197CB00012B/2401